Contemporary Mexican Women Writers

Texas Pan American Series

Contemporary Mexican Women Writers
Five Voices

 Gabriella de Beer

University of Texas Press, Austin

Requests for permission to reproduce material from this work should be sent to
Permissions, University of Texas Press, P.O. Box 7819, Austin, TX 78713-7819.

♾ The paper used in this publication meets the minimum requirements of
American National Standard for Information Sciences—Permanence of Paper
for Printed Library Materials, ANSI Z39.48-1984.

Library of Congress Cataloging-in-Publication Data

de Beer, Gabriella.
    Contemporary Mexican women writers : five voices / Gabriella de Beer.
       p.   cm. — (Texas Pan American series)
    Includes bibliographical references.
    ISBN 0-292-71585-4 (alk. paper). — ISBN 0-292-71586-2 (pbk. : alk.
paper)
      1. Mexican literature—Women authors—History and criticism.
    2. Mexican literature—20th century—History and criticism. I. Title.
II. Series.
PQ7133.D4 1996
860.9'9287'0972—dc20   96-1302

To Lou,
who shares my love of Mexican literature and art

Contents

Acknowledgments

Many people were instrumental and indispensable in making this book possible; however, my warmest expression of gratitude goes to Raquel Chang-Rodríguez, who, as guest editor of an issue of *Review: Latin American Literature and Arts* devoted to women writers and artists, planted the seed for this project when she asked me to contribute an article on contemporary Mexican women writers. Having already been attracted to a number of women writers as a result of my conversations with Carolyn and John Brushwood during my frequent trips to Mexico, I drew up a list of writers who I felt were representative of the surge in women's writing. As I began meeting with the writers I had selected and reading their work, it occurred to me that a combination of essay, interview, and translation would form a cohesive and interesting unit, and I decided to expand what had begun as a limited project into a full-length book. Therefore, it is with great pleasure that I thank Raquel Chang-Rodríguez, loyal friend and colleague of many years, for her unflagging enthusiasm and help with many aspects of this book. To John Brushwood, whose gentle advice is always timely, I express my respect and gratitude.

No words are adequate to describe the debt I owe María Luisa Puga, Silvia Molina, Brianda Domecq, Carmen Boullosa, and Angeles Mastretta, who, without hesitation, responded to my requests to meet and interview them and were totally receptive to my project. Each one accommodated me into her schedule for the interviews, discussions, and selections of pieces for translation. To them I extend my gratitude and affection for their courtesies, graciousness, and cooperation that allowed this book to materialize.

Theresa J. May, assistant director and executive editor of the University of Texas Press, has been, from my very first conversation with her suggesting this book, a strong and enthusiastic supporter. To her I am most grateful.

To the staff of the University of Texas Press I owe my thanks for their meticulous attention to every aspect of the publication of this book. I am especially pleased to thank the manuscript editor Leslie Tingle and the copy editor Nancy Warrington for their care with my manuscript, and Zora Molitor for her assistance in obtaining permissions from the Mexican publishers.

The research for this project was supported in part by a grant from The City University of New York PSC-CUNY Research Award Program, which I acknowledge with thanks. Additionally, I am grateful to the Simon H. Rifkind Center for the Humanities of The City College of New York for awarding me the Rifkind Center Fellowship for the fall of 1994, which granted me the time to write a large part of this book. I am especially indebted to the former dean of Humanities, Paul Sherwin, and the current dean, Martin Tamny, for their enthusiastic support of this project.

I acknowledge with thanks the permission to publish material granted by:

Authors: María Luisa Puga, for the unpublished story "Los invitados;" Silvia Molina, for "La casa nueva" (pp. 13–15) and "¿Qué hubieras hecho?" (pp. 61–70) from *Dicen que me case yo* and "El problema" (pp. 11–17) from *Imagen de Héctor;* Carmen Boullosa, for "Propusieron a María" (pp. 83–101) from *Teatro herético;* and Angeles Mastretta for "Tía Clemencia Ortega" (pp. 77–81) and "Tía Cristina Martínez" (pp. 25–28) from *Mujeres de ojos grandes* and "Memoria y acantilado" (pp. 171–176) from *Puerto libre.*

Publishers: Editorial Grijalbo, for María Luisa Puga's "Lucrecia" (pp. 27–35) from *Intentos* and "Uno" (pp. 15–18) from *Las razones del lago;* Fondo de Cultura Económica, for Brianda Domecq's "Balzac" (pp. 19–22), "In memoriam" (pp. 70–75), and "Galatea" (pp. 55–59) from *Bestiario doméstico;* and Editorial Vuelta, for Carmen Boullosa's "III" (pp. 27–34) from *Antes.*

Photographers: Miguel Bracho, photo of María Luisa Puga; Barry Domínguez, photo of Silvia Molina; León Rafael, photos of Brianda Domecq and Carmen Boullosa; and Guillermo Kahlo, photo of Angeles Mastretta.

Journals: An abbreviated version in Spanish of the interview with Angeles Mastretta appeared as "Entre la aventura y el litigio: Una entrevista con Angeles Mastretta" in *Nexos* 16, no. 184 (April 1993). An abbreviated version of the interview with Angeles Mastretta was published in *Review: Latin American Literature and Arts* 48 (Spring 1994) as "Interview with Angeles Mastretta," along with the translation of "Tía Clemencia Ortega" by Angeles Mastretta and the translation of "III" from *Antes* by Carmen Boullosa.

Contemporary Mexican Women Writers

Introduction

The literature of Mexico, rich and varied as it has been all through the twentieth century, is of increasing appeal both within and beyond that country's borders. The very nature of our time—with its growth of the communications media, the ability to travel from one end of the globe to the other, the proliferation of newspapers and magazines, and the rapid translation of books into other languages—has transformed literature from a local, limited, and sometimes exotic phenomenon to one that is broad-based and international. Writers, willingly or not, have assumed a more public role, coming into our homes via television, into our schools and workshops as teachers and mentors, into our casual reading material as contributors to newspapers and magazines, and onto our bookshelves as writers of novels, short stories, poetry, and essays. No longer distant and faceless, today's writers have a real presence in our lives, and our curiosity about them often matches our interest in their work.

An integral part of this literary activity in Mexico is the presence of a significant number of women writers. Although striking, it is not an isolated phenomenon. The twentieth century has opened to women many fields of endeavor and numerous professions that were once almost solely occupied by men. Consequently, it should not be surprising that Mexican women have taken up the pen to write as they have also entered other professions in ever-increasing numbers. Although one can view this as a natural outgrowth of changing customs, technological advances, and greater opportunities for higher education and advanced training, the large number of women writing professionally today is indeed impressive.

Among the writers that illustrate the range of contemporary Mexican women's writing are María Luisa Puga, Silvia Molina, Brianda Domecq, Carmen Boullosa, and Angeles Mastretta. They were born in the 1940s and 1950s and began to publish in the late seventies and eighties. They share some characteristics and differ in many others, thus making them representative of the spectrum of today's writers. Each one has published a significant number of works, and each continues to write and participate in numerous literary activities. As their work has evolved, so have the tendencies, techniques, themes, settings, and uses of language that place these five writers in the mainstream of

Mexican literature of the last two decades. More important, they all have a desire to be known and judged on their merits as writers and to be included in Mexican literature without reference to their gender.

This book approaches each of these five writers through (1) an essay focusing on what made her pursue a career as a writer, and a discussion of her major works; (2) an interview that touches on her background, writing, view of herself and others; and (3) selections of her work not previously translated and published in English. Each approach is wholly independent, but their combination offers the experience of being with the writer and sharing her work, hearing her voice telling about and evaluating herself, and reading her words, allowing one's own judgment to come into play. For each of the five writers there is a bibliographical listing of her publications and of the published English translations. A critical bibliography with emphasis on studies and reviews in English will be found after the Conclusion.

In dealing with contemporary writers it is not possible to be completely current. Each writer was interviewed at length in August 1992, followed by a shorter interview in January 1994 to bring things up-to-date. However, publications that came out in late 1994 or afterward could not be discussed in the essays and are mentioned as works in progress. They are cited in the bibliography. All the interviews were conducted in Spanish, and the translations are mine as are all the translations of the selections chosen to represent each writer.

Although the interviews with the five writers require no interpretation, one question and its responses should be singled out. The question about notable women writers who preceded them elicited strong and passionate responses. Clearly, each of these contemporary writers recognized the ground-breaking importance of the women whose work was innovative, whose perspective was different, and who brought voices and themes to literature that had not been heard before. The five writers acknowledged the debt they owed their predecessors, who, in overcoming obstacles and establishing themselves as serious practitioners of their craft, made their own acceptance by the literary world easier. From the names that were mentioned in the interviews, four stand out for their unique contributions: Nellie Campobello (1909–?), Elena Garro (1920), Rosario Castellanos (1925–1974), and Elena Poniatowska (1933). No discussion of contemporary women writers would be complete without giving these pioneering authors the recognition they have earned.

One of the major currents of twentieth-century Mexican literature that has endured long past the event that gave rise to it is the "novel of the Mexican Revolution." Considered a subgenre of the novel, it describes, criticizes, and questions the Revolution's leaders and goals and has inspired many leading Mexican writers of the century. Among them is Nellie Campobello, the only woman of her generation recognized as having made a contribution to the genre. Her *Cartucho: Relatos de la lucha en el norte* (1931; *Cartucho: Tales of the Struggle in Northern Mexico*, 1988) belongs to the corpus of early writing on the Revolution produced by its participants and observers. Composed of short sketches recreating images of the author's childhood in northern Mexico, *Cartucho* presents sometimes poignant, always graphic, impressions of the absurdity and cruelty of the civil war she witnessed as well as heard about from her mother. Campobello's work passes before the eyes of the reader like rapid fire from a machine gun, her prose unadorned, her images stark, her message clear. *Las manos de Mamá* (1938; *My Mother's Hands*, 1988) is also composed of short prose pieces that form a lyrical elegy to Campobello's mother, a woman who struggled to raise her family during the Revolution. She describes her with tenderness and love, giving us a moving and poetic portrait of a mother-daughter relationship. Campobello was also devoted to dance, working as a choreographer, teacher, and collector of indigenous dances.

Elena Garro—playwright, short story writer, and novelist—uses the Revolution as a theme in her acclaimed novel *Los recuerdos del porvenir* (1963; *Recollections of Things to Come*, 1969). However, this work—a novel set in the twenties during the Cristero rebellion against the forces of the secular government that closed churches, forbade masses, and expelled priests—is among those that examine the aftermath of the Revolution. In this dense and complex work, Garro, using lyrical prose and weaving in a complicated love story, describes a small town occupied by the victorious army of the government under the command of a brutal general. Through the use of realistic descriptions, magic realism, cyclical time, and other narrative techniques, Garro created one of the most original novels of the sixties. She has been totally involved with her writing, producing filmscripts, plays, novels, and short stories.

Rosario Castellanos in her short life made significant contributions to Mexican literature and had far-reaching influence on women writers. The central theme of her work was her condition of being a Mexican and a woman, and all of her writing, to a greater or lesser degree, reflects her inquiry into women's place in culture. Like no woman before her, Castellanos wrote about gender, sexuality, and language.

Using poetry, drama, essay, and fiction, she reversed the myths and stereotypes of women in Mexican society and rejected linguistic conventions that limited women's use of language. Her fiction, the novels *Balún-Canán* (1957; *The Nine Guardians*, 1958) and *Oficio de tinieblas* (Office of Tenebrae; 1962) and the short story collection *Ciudad Real* (1960), focuses on the racial and cultural oppression of the indigenous peoples of Chiapas and the position of women in urban and provincial Mexico. Her poetry, collected in *Poesía no eres tú* (Poetry You're Not; 1972), and her several collections of essays in which she takes up feminist issues have become "classic texts" that are studied, quoted, and translated with increasing frequency. Castellanos's life as a professional woman—journalist, teacher, writer, and diplomat—has served as a model to those who followed her.

The very active contemporary writer Elena Poniatowska, who started publishing in the fifties, has become a mentor to her peers as well as to younger women writers. Her guidance and help in writing workshops as a reader of other writers' manuscripts, and her generosity with her time in addition to the corpus of her writing, have made her the prototype of today's women writers. Accomplished, well-established in Mexico and abroad, translated into numerous languages, Poniatowska is almost a legendary figure. She is much admired for having taken up the issues of gender, class, and ethnicity and for becoming an advocate for the poor and repressed. Starting as a journalist, she has refined the art of interviewing and investigative journalism to produce several testimonial works, both novels and essays. Poniatowska is particularly concerned with real events, often uncommon, and real people, sometimes marginal and nameless. Her *Hasta no verte Jesús mío* (Until We Meet Again, Dear Jesus; 1969), a novel that reproduces and recreates the tape-recorded testimony of a *soldadera* (camp follower) during the Revolution, is both a very original work and evidence of the viability of the Mexican Revolution as a theme in literature. The massacre of student demonstrators in October 1968 was captured by Poniatowska in a work that is simultaneously creative and documentary. *La noche de Tlatelolco* (1971; *Massacre in Mexico*, 1975)—a collage of short texts, official statements, graffiti, taped accounts by victims, and photographs—bears witness to this tragedy. *Nada, nadie: Las voces del temblor* (1988; *Nobody, Nothing*, 1995) is a work that records through image and text the 1985 earthquake that devastated large areas of Mexico City. Poniatowska's recent novel, *Tinísima* (1992), about the Italian photographer Tina Modotti (1896–1942), portrays the political and artistic life of the world of the twenties and thirties through the tragic life of this unusual woman. Elena Poniatowska is the author of numerous other works and participates actively in a myriad of literary and cultural events.

These four writers represent four crests in a long and unending wave of women writers of this century. Many others could be mentioned whose voices brought something new or different to literature. However, Campobello, Garro, Castellanos, and Poniatowska, each in her own way, frame the work of women writers and mark significant high points of this phenomenon. They were and are the ground-breakers, leaders, and teachers of the craft that so many women are now practicing. The fact that these accomplished writers made a name for themselves as writers and used the lens of their gender to bring their point of view to their writing eased the way for other women to follow their example and pursue writing professionally. María Luisa Puga, Silvia Molina, Brianda Domecq, Carmen Boullosa, and Angeles Mastretta, as their words and works will show, have taken this legacy seriously. With this in mind, one may predict that the momentum of Mexican literature written by women will be maintained and will extend into the next century to produce a continuum of new writers.

Selected Bibliography

Nellie Campobello

Publications

Cartucho: Relatos de la lucha en el norte de México. Xalapa: Ediciones Integrales, 1931.
Las manos de Mamá. Mexico City: Ed. Juventudes de Izquierda, 1938.
Apuntes sobre la vida militar de Francisco Villa. Mexico City: EDIAPSA, 1940.
Mis libros. Mexico City: Compañía General de Ediciones, 1960.

Translation

Cartucho and My Mother's Hands. Trans. Doris Meyer and Irene Matthews. Austin: University of Texas Press, 1988.

Elena Garro

Publications

Un hogar sólido. Xalapa: Universidad Veracruzana, 1958.
Los recuerdos del porvenir. Mexico City: Joaquín Mortiz, 1963.
La semana de colores. Xalapa: Universidad Veracruzana, 1964.
Felipe Ángeles. Mexico City: UNAM, 1979.
Andamos huyendo Lola. Mexico City: Joaquín Mortiz, 1980.
Testimonios sobre Mariana. Mexico City: Grijalbo, 1981.
La casa junto al río. Mexico City: Grijalbo, 1983.
Y Matarazo no llamó. Mexico City: Grijalbo, 1991.

Translation

Recollections of Things to Come. Trans. Ruth L. C. Simms. Austin: University of Texas Press, 1969.

Rosario Castellanos

Publications

Balún-Canán. Mexico City: Fondo de Cultura Económica, 1957.
Ciudad Real. Xalapa: Universidad Veracruzana, 1960.
Oficio de tinieblas. Mexico City: Joaquín Mortiz, 1962.

Juicios sumarios. Xalapa: Universidad Veracruzana, 1966.
Mujer que sabe latín. . . . Mexico City: Secretaría de Educación Pública, 1973.
El eterno femenino: Farsa. Mexico City: Fondo de Cultura Económica, 1975.
Poesía no eres tú: Obra poética: 1948–1971. Mexico City: Fondo de Cultura Económica, 1972; 2d ed., 1975.

Translations

The Nine Guardians. Trans. Irene Nicholson. London: Faber & Faber, 1958.
A Rosario Castellanos Reader. Ed. Maureen Ahern. Austin: University of Texas Press, 1988.
Meditation on the Threshold. Trans. Julian Palley. Tempe: Bilingual Press/Editorial Bilingüe, 1988.
Another Way to Be. Trans. Myralyn F. Allgood. Athens: University of Georgia Press, 1990.

Elena Poniatowska

Publications

Lilus Kikus. Mexico City: Col. Los Presentes, 1954.
Hasta no verte Jesús mío. Mexico City: Era, 1969.
La noche de Tlatelolco. Mexico City: Era, 1971.
Querido Diego, te abraza Quiela. Mexico City: Era, 1978.
La "Flor de Lis". Mexico City: Era, 1988.
¡Ay vida, no me mereces! Mexico City: Joaquín Mortiz, 1985.
Nada, nadie: Las voces del temblor. Mexico City: Era, 1988.
Tinísima. Mexico City: Era, 1992.

Translations

Massacre in Mexico. Trans. Helen R. Lane. New York: Viking, 1975.
Dear Diego. Trans. Katherine Silver. New York: Pantheon Books, 1986.
Nobody, Nothing. Trans. Aurora Camacho de Schmidt and Arthur Schmidt. Philadelphia: Temple University Press, 1995.

María Luisa Puga

María Luisa Puga (1944)

About the Author and Her Writing

María Luisa Puga is the consummate writer, completely immersed in her craft. When one speaks with her and reads her work, it becomes clear that her entire life, consciously and unconsciously, has been devoted to being a writer. There were no sudden revelations or discoveries of talent. Simply put, she always wrote and knew that writing was to be her life. But it is a life that she has created in an unorthodox way, without the traditional background in literature and without university degrees. María Luisa Puga is self-taught. Reading is her lifeline, and the writers can be Mexican, Latin American, British, French, Russian, or North American. Time and again she goes back to known writers for sustenance and tackles new writers with relish. Both in person and through her books she gives off a sense of order and self-confidence; she chooses her words with care and is not prone to excesses. Like the ceramicist described in one of her books, *La cerámica de Hugo X. Velásquez: Cuando rinde el horno* (The Ceramics of Hugo X. Velásquez: When the Oven Produces; 1983), she has designed, shaped, molded, fired, and polished her life to make it fit into and complement her profession. Writing is her life, and all of life's necessities and demands are merely things that are met in order to allow her to write.

María Luisa Puga is very much part of the contemporary literary scene, despite her deliberate efforts to disengage herself and find that space where she can work in privacy and without distractions. She participates in symposia, teaches, and writes regularly for the newspaper *El Economista*. Her own life and experiences have provided her with themes and material for her work. However, the autobiographical elements of her books only form the basis from which she builds the fiction of her stories and novels. Puga is particularly concerned with the act of writing, and many of her works are metafictional in that the writer describes her own act of creation. But what characterizes Puga's fiction is her ability to penetrate her characters and let them express their innermost thoughts, feelings, and conflicts. Often there are pages with little action, where the anecdote doesn't move forward but the character's deepest thoughts are laid out, dissected, and expressed in words and tones that completely absorb the reader to the point where s/he enters the character's psyche. Many of her characters are so memorable that one believes one has always known and lived with them.

María Luisa Puga works at being a writer by constant reading and writing, by teaching writing, and by reviewing books. Her career since the publication in 1978 of her first novel, *Las posibilidades del odio* (The Possibilities of Hatred), has been successful because of her rare ability to draw her readers into her texts and to create a bridge between the writer and the reader. She explains that connection in her introductory essay to *Lo que le pasa al lector* (What Happens to the Reader; 1991), a volume of brief reviews of Spanish American, European, and North American novels. For her, a novel doesn't exist until it meets a reader, for whom the efforts of the writer are intended. However, the reader is no longer like a passenger on a moving train who views the text like a passing landscape. The reader stops, maneuvers, determines the rhythm, and participates.

In her short autobiographical book, *MLP/De cuerpo entero* (MLP/In Full View; 1990), significantly subtitled "El espacio de la escritura" (The Space of Writing), Puga tells of her life from childhood to 1978. Although it provides some details about her early years, the book is more of an essay on her development as a writer, her search for space, her need for distance from which to view the world, and her obsession with words. As she does with her fictional characters, María Luisa

Puga bares her own soul and allows us to feel what it is to be a writer.

Born in Mexico City, Puga went with her family to live in Acapulco. There, sharing a room with two brothers and a sister, the beach served as her first "room" from which to spy on the world. The death of her mother occasioned a move to her grandmother's house, where she shared a room with her sister. Later, after her father's remarriage, she shared another space with her sister in their new home in Mazatlán. There she wrote a "novel" with ideas supplied by her sister. After a few years, Puga, now twenty years old, and her sister moved back to Mexico City, taking their own apartment where Puga could write in the privacy of the bathroom. Another larger apartment finally provided a study for writing, but it all seemed like a game. Not having any formal background in literature, she believed that one imitated novels. Therefore, influenced by Virginia Woolf's *A Room of One's Own* (1929), she separated herself from her sister and, for the first time in her life, had her own bedroom. She knew she wanted to write, but didn't know how or where to begin. At that time she tells us that she heard "the silence of writing before hearing its voice" (*MLP/DCE*, 17). She describes the pain associated with writing, a kind of madness or emptiness because something of yours has transferred its existence to something else. During all those years she always kept a journal, a *cuaderno*, or notebook.

In 1968, Puga left Mexico planning to spend a year in England. However, it wasn't until ten years later that she returned, having acquired on her own the background that she had lacked. In London she worked on a novel (that was never published), writing everywhere, and keeping a journal that served as her tape recorder, camera, and conscience. Language became her room, an island of her own, and she began to read the Mexicans Carlos Fuentes (1928), Carlos Monsiváis (1938), Elena Poniatowska (1933), and Octavio Paz (1914). There were periods of time spent in Paris, Rome, Madrid, and on a Greek island. She had a number of boyfriends, became involved with different politically oriented groups, and returned briefly to Mexico in 1973 to participate in an agrarian project. While working on another novel, Puga decided to join her Hungarian companion who had accepted a United Nations position in Kenya to work on a magazine dealing with economic development and the environment.

Kenya became a turning point in Puga's life; it was a country not so different from Mexico, and for the first time, she was able to see her own country clearly. She understood that her novel could take place in

Kenya, a country that had much in common with Mexico—colonialism, racism, poverty, corruption, tourism. And in Kenya she wrote her African novel, *Las posibilidades del odio*, seeing her own reality through her writing. From Africa she went to Oxford and returned to Mexico in 1978.

María Luisa Puga's return to Mexico after a ten-year absence was a return that marked both an end and a beginning. It was not the same Mexico she had left, nor was she the same writer who had gone to London. Mexico would now become the stuff of her writing, a Mexico seen from new windows and different perspectives. But the most significant change was Puga's realization that the writer was an outsider, probing from another plane, a kind of voyeur. But after her absence she also found a stronger link to the reality in which she was born, to familiar sounds, smells, and tastes. Here her writing would have direction, purpose, maturity. And so, after ten years of searching, Puga found "the space of writing" in herself and in her Mexico.

In 1985 Puga distanced herself from Mexico City once again by moving to Zirahuén in the state of Michoacán, where she currently resides. There she found the ideal place to write, far from the demands of the big city. Like her other experiences, this move renewed her perspective as an outsider, as a voyeur. Of equal importance is the opportunity to participate in writing workshops for children, adults, and teachers, which permits her to share her talents with others.

María Luisa Puga has been writing as long as she can remember and publishing steadily since 1978. Her work can be classified as fiction and essay. As a writer of fiction, Puga has published seven novels—*Las posibilidades del odio* (The Possibilities of Hatred; 1978); *Cuando el aire es azul* (When the Air Is Blue; 1980); *Pánico o peligro* (Panic or Danger; 1983), awarded the Xavier Villaurrutia Prize; *La forma del silencio* (The Shape of Silence; 1987); *Antonia* (1989); *Las razones del lago* (The Reasons of the Lake; 1992); and *La viuda* (The Widow; 1994)—and three collections of short stories—*Inmóvil sol secreto* (Secret, Immobile Sun; 1979); *Accidentes* (Accidents; 1981); and *Intentos* (Attempts; 1987). Her nonfiction writing includes *La cerámica de Hugo X. Velásquez: Cuando rinde el horno* (The Ceramics of Hugo X. Velásquez: When the Oven Produces; 1983); *Itinerario de palabras* (Itinerary of Words; 1987), co-authored with Mónica Mansour; *MLP/De cuerpo entero: El espacio de la escritura* (MLP/In Full View: The Space of Writing; 1990); and *Lo que le pasa al lector* (What Happens to the Reader; 1991). Although this large body of writing is varied, there are a number of threads that tie it together. Puga's fiction reflects a wide range of social concerns. She views Mexican society with a wide-angle lens and captures its problems in muted tones. Whether it be poverty, corruption, the conflict between generations or between men and women, or the struggle for self-realization, the writer gets to the core of the issue through her fictional characters. Some works seem to have an autobiographical cast, but more often than not Puga's own life and experiences only form a framework for her creativity. Some of her works are metafictional, employing self-conscious narrative techniques that reflect on the writing itself. For her, writing allows one to affirm one's identity, to step aside from one's reality and view the world from different perspectives.

Las posibilidades del odio is composed of six novellas that can be read independently or together. Each is preceded by a timetable listing events in the history of Kenya from 1888 to 1973. The events do not correspond to the narrations, but lend them a sense of authenticity. The untitled narrations all deal with Kenya, a third-world country whose problems can be extended to other countries. There the whites constitute a minority, the "others" set up as models of colonialization and viewed as enemies. The first narrator, a white Kenyan tourist guide, relates his story to a European visitor in a bar. His family, having lived in Africa for two generations, wouldn't consider life anywhere else. After all, blacks have always lived with whites and understand their own need for the assistance of Europeans. The "problem" lies with the Asians, who stick together, dominate business, and exploit the blacks. The narrator, despite his protestations to the contrary, shows the prejudices of one who considers himself superior. He can't accept the fact that, despite his European professional training as an engineer, he is only the manager of a tourist bureau that organizes excursions to wildlife preserves.

The story that is most disturbing—because of its stark depiction of poverty and misery—is that of a beggar, a wretched soul who is as familiar on the streets of Nairobi as in Mexico City or any big city. This is a depiction of the invisible Africa not included in tours to the exotic and picturesque. The beggar, a young man of twenty-six, learns the rules of the street after being released from a hospital as an amputee, but without a crutch. He manages to drag himself around and establish his "turf"; he lives with hunger as his only companion and has no desire other than food for survival. He tells the sad story of his early years as an orphan living in a village with an uncle who despised him. Although hard-working, he was viewed as a pariah and feared by the townspeople. A hut he built for himself in order to marry is burned down, and he is jailed and later run out of town. Now all that is a distant memory, and his life is reduced to protecting his plastic and cardboard as he struggles to survive among competing beggars. After much dragging himself around on the stump of his amputated leg, an Asian man gives him an old but usable crutch, allowing him to see the world from an upright position.

The longest and most fully developed novella is the last one about Nyambura, a young African woman now studying in Rome. She describes her childhood and simultaneously her growing awareness of the social and political realities of Africa. The only daughter of a black middle-class family, she is sent to a local Catholic school by her father. There, where her father wants her to acquire a Christian education, she learns firsthand the truths of racism. The white sisters did the teaching, and the black sisters the domestic chores. The girls themselves, mean and arrogant, divided themselves along tribal lines. The sisters considered Nyambura proud and not sufficiently obedient. They were disturbed that her father, by dint of his own efforts, was advancing too rapidly. Through her brother Ngongo, Nyambura becomes involved in politics and begins to read seriously. Back at the Catholic school she realizes how God is invoked to cover up facts and realities, how Africa is but a small detail in the teaching of British history, and she begins to ask questions. Expelled for writing a letter critical of the sisters and the school, Nyambura attends the university as an auditor. There she meets a Mexican woman, a writer, who wants to write a book about Africa and doesn't want to be viewed as one of the "others," part of the white minority. But for Nyambura this Mexican woman is not part of her world and is just another white face. Here Puga plays with the concept of "otherness" by inverting the perception, which is always relative. The writer does so a second time when in Rome Nyambura is viewed as the "other," a minority in a European setting. Although Nyambura seems to forget her "otherness" among the foreign students who befriend her, her underlying hatred of whites is more powerful than her love for her boyfriend. She returns to Kenya without him, determined to reaffirm her identity, realizing that it is only in Africa that she can be herself. The happiness she enjoyed in Europe was but an accidental stage in her life, a life too short to be happy.

Pánico o peligro is most likely Puga's densest novel, one that illustrates the writer's preoccupation with writing and, at the same time, presents a complex protagonist who struggles to achieve her independence and self-determination. The work is so intense and absorbing that one is drawn in as a participant rather than an observer. In this novel, Puga draws on her knowledge of Mexico City to capture its pace, immensity, and capacity to swallow its inhabitants.

Pánico o peligro is the story of and by Susana, who is the subject and object of her discourse. Divided into twelve chapters of unequal length, each of which corresponds to a *cuaderno*, a notebook or journal she is writing, the novel traces Susana's life as she changes from an insecure, dependent, and bewildered young girl into a mature, independent, and satisfied young woman. The path that Susana follows, the people she meets, and the experiences she undergoes to become the new Susana make up the story she relates to an anonymous listener or reader. For Susana, the act of writing and hearing her own story is her way of finding and affirming herself. By creating an image of herself outside of the reality in which others see her, she is able to coexist and reconcile with herself and the world around her. She is able to shed the otherness that defines her and live on her own terms.

Susana takes us back to her childhood as the only child of a modest, hard-working family. She and three other neighborhood girls have been together all through school and maintain their friendship over the years. One of the girls, Lourdes, is outspoken, self-confident, and curious. She too keeps a diary. Lourdes is critical of Susana and always trying to educate her, telling her to read and to wake up to the world around her. However, Susana functions at her own pace, keeps to herself at home and at her job, and doesn't really comprehend all that her friend is trying to tell her. Lourdes's maternalistic attitude frightens her as does her constant insistence on telling her that she is *pasmada* (bewildered) and passive. After the death of Susana's parents, she and Lourdes share a succession of apartments where friends and boyfriends come and go. Susana, seeking her private space, arranges a small corner in front of a window. From that space she sees Mexico with her own eyes and captures her own vision, not the one others want her to see. Several men pass through her life, but they too want her to see the world as they see it, convinced they are free to assign her a role in it.

As her story progresses through many anecdotes, characters who come and go, and descriptions of trivial situations that are part of living, Susana talks to the person she is writing to and makes him a character in her fiction. She doesn't want him to change her; she wants to continue writing because she senses in the rhythm of her writing a movement toward something. The feeling of movement or displacement as Susana gradually grows into her own person is made manifest by the parallel movement along Insurgentes Avenue, one of Mexico City's main arteries. We observe Susana and her friends as they change apartments and as she moves from job to job. To get from home to work Susana traverses the avenue on foot, by bus, or by *pesero* (a communal taxi that moves along a fixed route). There, too, she absorbs sensations and perceptions that she can't handle, realities that both bewilder and frighten her. Like the rhetoric she hears from her friends, who are superficially involved in political and social activities, these realities are too abstract for her to deal with. She cannot recognize herself.

As the narration progresses so does Susana's consciousness of her life and her acceptance of that which constitutes her as a person. Life, she realizes, is a constant struggle to give sense to her acts. Through a brief relationship with Ramiro, a character from an earlier story of Puga's ("Ramiro," *Accidentes;* 1981), Susana begins to see herself as an individual outside of her relationship to her best friends. She seems happy, wants to live alone and work where she pleases, and feels free of the need to understand or even care about what others are saying. No longer *pasmada*, she is at peace with herself and strong enough to face whatever realities or dangers life may hold.

Pánico o peligro is very much María Luisa Puga's novel, not because of any autobiographical elements—of which there are some—but because more than any other single work it illustrates her concerns and style. Susana's preoccupation with writing in order to see and hear herself, and her need to write in order to affirm her identity, have been Puga's concerns all her life. The protagonist's search for a space from which to view the world from her own perspective mirrors Puga's need for space. The slow pace of the novel, the lack of emphasis on external details, the concentration on thoughts, feelings, and the interaction of characters—all are hallmarks of the novelist's narrative style. She reaches into Susana and some of the other characters and exposes their innermost feelings through a prose style, conversational in tone, composed of dialogue, narration, and rhetorical questions. Susana has learned that she must express her own feelings in order to exist, that others cannot educate or dominate her, and that she will find happiness in doing what pleases her and not by assuming roles that others want to impose.

Antonia (1989) is another novel that deals with strong women characters. Here the writer, after some twenty years, recalls her life in London at the end of the 1960s. Some of the details are autobiographical, but the protagonist, Antonia, is a fictional character. In this novel Puga is again concerned with writing and, in her first-person narration, speaks of the *cuadernos* she writes.

The story revolves around two young Mexican women who meet by chance on the plane to London and decide to live together. Antonia, the daughter of a well-to-do family from Mazatlán, has lived and studied in the United States and has come to England to study theatre. The author/narrator is from Mexico City and has traveled to England to write and to trace the steps of Virginia Woolf. Antonia is completely absorbed by the theatre and when, six months later, she is diagnosed with a malignant breast tumor, she shrugs it off as insignificant. Nothing, not even cancer, is going to distract her from her aim in life. It is the narrator who suffers and who lives with the specter of death as a constant presence in her life. With their respective boyfriends—Jean Paul, a Frenchman also involved in theatre, and Enrique, a Colombian journalist who works at the same magazine as the author/narrator— they form a happy "family" sharing each other's joys and problems.

Antonia, undergoing therapy, acts unperturbed and insists on keeping her deteriorating condition from her family. She conducts herself as if everything were normal, continues her relationship with her boyfriend, and travels to Italy and Paris. Acting in a play that Jean Paul is directing becomes her only purpose in life. Those around her suffer terribly as they helplessly watch the life of a young woman extinguishing itself. Antonia cannot be reasoned with, even by her own brother, a physician who comes to visit and favors more aggressive treatment. She will decide what she will do and when to tell her parents of her illness. It is her life and she wants to live it on her terms. Whether she is as strong as she seems, or whether her acting background allows her to become another character, is never clear. Her friends, young and inexperienced, live and feel the pain Antonia so carefully hides. When, after a two-year battle, the doctors declare her condition hopeless, Antonia agrees to join her brother and parents to return to Mazatlán. The author/narrator is left with her friend's *mochila* (backpack), a bag with many little compartments to hold all sorts of things, which Antonia so casually used to sling over her shoulder.

Antonia is a less intense work than *Pánico o peligro*. Whereas Susana's narration was composed of twelve long chapters with paragraphs that often occupied several pages, this novel is made up of fifty brief chapters. The descriptions are less detailed, and the dialogue moves more freely. The author/narrator tells us in the novel that she didn't consult her *cuadernos* but relied on her memory to write her novel. For her, living with Antonia and watching her use her acting to become someone else in order to be and affirm her identity made her see her writing in a similar light. Antonia, much like Susana, decided how she would live and refused to allow the advice and even the goodwill of others to determine her fate.

Las razones del lago (1992) is a novel that reflects a different stage of María Luisa Puga's life. Having left Mexico City in 1985 to live in Zirahuén and enjoy the peace of a small town, she uses this event in her life to offer a different vision of Mexico. This novel, composed of forty short chapters, is narrated in the first person plural by two street dogs who see, hear, and know all that goes on in the town. The dogs, who only wish to survive, are personified and act as the conscience of the town. They are almost invisible and no one really cares about them. From their vantage point they describe the town as a typical rural town, ugly except for a beautiful lake, and inhabited by people who are sad and bored. The men drink and the women seem to live in a perpetual state of waiting—for the meals to cook, for the husbands to come home, for the children to fall asleep, for death. Only weekends bring people from the outside to enjoy the lake.

One weekend some "tourists" come to look at land on which to build a house. They want to leave Mexico City and live in Zirahuén to work and write. The dogs accompany them on a small boat to a restaurant across the lake. There they see the town and lake from a different perspective and begin to ascribe human qualities to the lake. The dogs feel warmly toward Sabina, a woman who runs a corner general store that also sells liquor. She is like the dogs in observing all that is happening in the town. Unlike the other women, who are afraid of life and hesitant to express their feelings, Sabina is outspoken and says precisely what she thinks. Her nephew Damián becomes the focus of the story as he, against his father's wishes, goes to work for the *fuereños* (outsiders) who have bought property and are building a house. The young man, restless and uncommunicative, wants to leave the town but really does not know what he wants to do. The dogs accompany him to the construction site, where the couple try to engage him in conversation. His story and that of his family appear in italics narrated in the third person in several chapters of the novel.

The dogs share the life of the humans, feel their sadness and despair, and see hunger as their greatest problem. However, contrary to the humans who want to conquer nature, the animals try to understand

and live with it. They observe the lake when it "cries" during the rain, when in the afternoon "it sits and begins to chat with the sun," and when at night it becomes "invisible" (*LRL*, 55).

On Sundays the town takes on some life, especially when there are fiestas with dancing and drinking. On Mondays it suffers from a hangover, with a feeling of defeat permeating the air. Damián continues to work for the *fuereños* and, in his own way, enjoys the camaraderie of eating and talking with the couple. At an annual fiesta he sees Yadira, a young woman from a neighboring town, and decides she will be his wife. However, another young man, a friend of Damián's, goes off with her, leaving Damián even more depressed than usual.

When the couple from Mexico City inform Damián that they will halt construction, and invite him to spend two months with them in the city to learn plumbing, he agrees to accompany them. The woman insists on taking the dogs, now named "Novela" (Novel) and "Relato" (Story), to Mexico City. There the couple and Damián encounter a strange existence—a house with a permanent roof over their heads, a room of their own, regular meals, noises that are difficult to become accustomed to, and where even the rain is not the same. The dogs miss the lake, and Damián feels even more insecure than at home. When asked about his plans for the future, he cannot reply. He spends all his free time watching the news on television, fascinated by the faces and gestures of a world he doesn't know. A young man he meets shows him around the city, and one day he suffers a beating outside a dance hall.

After a two-month stay in the city, they all return to Zirahuén, where the dogs are happy to see their beloved lake. Damián is a changed man—determined, resolute, and mature. He decides to seek out Yadira and ask for her hand in marriage, despite her having "disgraced" herself with a friend of his, and to build a place for himself on the construction site and live away from the center of town. Notwithstanding his father's shouts and his mother's tears, Damián holds his ground and carries out his resolve. The *fuereños* accept him and his bride without conditions, whereas the entire town is gossiping and classifies Damián as a *fuereño*. He asks the couple why they want to live in a small town, and they explain to him that not only did they choose to leave the big city but they chose to live differently. Then Damián declares that he doesn't ever want to leave the town, that he wants to live and have a family there, and that it was his experience in Mexico City that made him decide. In Mexico City he couldn't recognize himself. The novel ends with the wedding and the legend of the lake—the princess Zirahuén lies at the bottom, smiling enigmatically, hiding, sleeping, most beautiful when unaware she is being observed. "She probably has her reasons" (*LRL*, 180).

Las razones del lago is Puga's most innovative novel. Here she uses an event in her life—her move from Mexico City to Zirahuén—to portray the life of a small town. The dogs she significantly calls "Novela" and "Relato" narrate the novel by telling us what they see, hear, and know about the town and its inhabitants. They are given human attributes and, when comparing their lives to those they describe, they seem to be the happier. The town is a sad place, punctuated by moments of joy at fiestas and *borracheras* (drinking sprees). Everyone follows the same routine, which is handed down like a legacy from parents to children. To be different is to fall under a cloud of suspicion, and *fuereños* are viewed with fear and distrust. The main human characters are Damián and his aunt Sabina. Withdrawn, hermetic, uncommunicative, but determined not to work with his father tending cattle, Damián becomes his own person and will live his life on his own terms. Having had a taste of the big city and having felt the outside world through his contact with the *fuereños*, he realizes that his future is in the town, but away from his family and the other townspeople who feel free to tell him how to live his life. He will marry the woman he chooses, live where he pleases, and work at what he wants to do. Damián is still developing his self-determination, but one senses that he, now considered an outsider, will not be like everyone else in town. Sabina, perched at her corner store, like the two dogs is aware of all that goes on. However, she does not share the life of the other women, those who wash clothes in the lake as if it were a ritual and talk about irrelevant things. The dogs describe them as "ensconced in their fear of life and all they do is feel their way along the walls of their prisons" (*LRL*, 23). Sabina learned early on to be strong when her father abandoned her mother and she chose to leave school at the age of eight. Although fun-loving and popular, she never married so as not to be stuck in the role of all the women in town, and instead devoted herself to her store and to her brother Fermín's children. Her closest companion is the lake, which speaks to her. Damián is particularly close to Sabina, and for him she represents both mother and father. Her innate common sense and strength of character make her an independent and memorable woman.

The question of the *fuereño* is one that preoccupies Puga. She knows that in Zirahuén she is not accepted and is not part of the town. Thus she writes about that world from the perspective of the outsider. In *Las razones del lago* the theme is handled by the dogs and by Damián, who becomes an outsider in his own town. That, too, is a feeling that Puga comprehends because in Mexico City she is considered something of an outsider for having abandoned it.

María Luisa Puga's three volumes of short stories deal with a broad range of themes. There are stories of love affairs, of family crises, of children and their relationships to one another. In addition, a number of the stories touch upon characters and events depicted in the novels, and some have autobiographical elements. In "Inmóvil sol secreto" (Secret, Immobile Sun), a young woman relates her trip to a Greek island with her boyfriend Enrique. There they want to live together and write. However, the relationship is strained because Enrique is very jealous because the young woman has had an affair with another man, and she is possessed by feelings of guilt. Puga describes the woman's innermost feelings as she tries to rebuild a relationship that has been shattered. When a postcard arrives from the lover, the fragile bonds are broken forever.

From the collection *Accidentes*, "Difícil situación" (Difficult Situation) is an absorbing story of a young woman who enters a camera store in Oxford, England, to have a roll of film developed. There she becomes involved in an interchange with the shopkeeper that evolves into a threat and escalates into a confrontation. The man is frightened, and she all the more confident as she argues with him and digs in her heels. She is annoyed by his very self-satisfied and condescending attitude and by his insistence on closing the shop to have his afternoon tea. When he threatens to call the police because she refuses to leave, for reasons that escape even her, she tells him that she is holding a bomb in an envelope. The situation, now out of hand, comes to an end when she leaves the store.

"Joven madre" (Young Mother) is about a woman who has just given birth to a baby girl. She tells of her pregnancy when she felt possessed by another being, not the child, as if she were two people trapped in a vault. After the birth of the child, she falls into a depression and jumps from a window with her baby to their deaths. As she falls, she feels that the vault is shattered and she is no longer trapped inside.

"Helmut y Florian" (Helmut and Florian) is a strange, gripping tale about two German men who run a beachfront hotel in Mexico. Exquisite in every detail, the hotel is administered by Helmut, who sees to it that everything is done with good taste and perfection. No one knows anything about the two Germans; it seems as if they have always been there. The only other character is José Luis, a young man in charge of the beach and water skiing. One morning Helmut and Florian are found dead, the victims of poison. The German consulate has no record of them, and the hotel is closed. José Luis is later seen working as a stevedore in Acapulco.

"Ramiro," the longest story in the collection, concerns a young man, the son of a hardware store owner who has worked hard to achieve economic security. Although Ramiro is lazy, spoiled, and of average ability, his father dotes on him and thinks he is wonderful. By chance, the father meets a British couple in Mexico, befriends them, and arranges to send his son Ramiro to England to live with them and perfect his English. Ramiro is lost in England; he feels isolated and bored and is unable to make friends. He suffers terribly until he meets a young woman from Spain and begins to feel more secure. One day he is beaten up in the metro by a group of young toughs who take him for an Asian. When his parents come to take him back to Mexico, he decides to stay in London. It is as if the physical beating has awakened the determination in him. This is the same Ramiro who appears in the novel *Pánico o peligro* and tells Susana of his experience in London.

Whereas the stories of *Accidentes* seem to hinge on an unexpected event, a mishap, or an accident, the scope of *Intentos* is broader. Two stories, "Una, dos, tres por mí" (One, Two, Three for Me) and "Nuevos caminos" (New Paths), are sensitive portrayals of children. The first tells of a family—mother, father, and three boys—who go to spend a few days with relatives in Querétaro. The oldest brother feels very important and considers his younger brothers dumb kids. The visit is wonderful in every respect—beautiful weather, many other children, warm family dinners, new friendships, and finally the leave-taking. During the drive home a heavy rain and hailstorm pelts the car. The family decides to wait out the storm under a bridge, feeling warm and safe in a heated car with the windows shut. They all fall asleep and die of toxic fumes.

The second story, "Nuevos caminos," is about a child who has lost his sight after the removal of a tumor. There are three parts to the story and three narrators. The mother speaks first, having just come home from the hospital with her six-year-old child. She explains where everything is located, how many steps to take to go from here to there, how to feel things in order to identify them. Acting and speaking as if the child had just returned from a vacation, she tries through her tears to make a heart-breaking situation seem normal. The second part is narrated by the nine-year-old brother who feels rejected and is jealous of all the attention his younger brother is receiving. If that weren't enough, he now has to give up his room that faces the street so that the blind child can hear the traffic and the noise. In the last part we hear the voice of the child. He is cheerful, happy to be able to do things with his brother, and inquisitive about what he hears. He explains simply that not seeing is like being able to look inside of things and see them closely, even hear them, and when touching them they talk to you.

There are stories that touch on the theme of petty corruption and how it permeates different facets of life in Mexico. "Una mañana en la playa" (A Morning at the Beach) describes two worlds on the beach in Acapulco. There is the world of the young and beautiful, stretched out in the sun looking like models of fitness and good health. Then, separated by a rope from the bathers, there is the world of the local vendors who offer their wares and can, with a quick glance, calculate who will be their potential customers. Manuel Enrique and his girlfriend are on the beach one morning. They are young, good-looking, and tan. He decides to go into the water and, although an experienced swimmer, is overcome by the force of the waves. Shouting for help, he is relieved to see two fellows with an air mattress who tell him to grab hold of it. When the three are floating, Manuel Enrique asks them if they are going to get him out of the ocean. Smiling, they announce that it will cost him five thousand pesos, and Manuel Enrique agrees to pay. Struggling against the current, they finally come out of the water. Manuel Enrique, feeling embarrassed and angry, asks the men if they always charge like that. They reply: "Or more, it depends on the ocean. You don't really think we'd risk our lives for a tourist?" (I, 58). Meanwhile a crowd has gathered, and Manuel Enrique goes off by himself. When he returns to the beach, his girlfriend tells him that she has paid the money because the men were making a scene. Manuel Enrique sits on the beach unable to speak, watching the beautiful people. Without saying good-bye, he returns to Mexico City.

Puga depicts a different form of corruption or dishonesty in "Lucrecia," a story based on a recollection of an event that had occurred some twenty years earlier. The author/narrator, reliving that incident in her life, makes it graphically real by telling it in nine pages, all in one para-graph without interruptions. She recalls how, when working as a book-keeper in a downtown Mexico City office, she was astounded to learn that a check had bounced because of insufficient funds. Although the owner of the business seems unperturbed, she is devastated because she knows that she is exceptionally careful with checks, deposits, and withdrawals. Lucrecia, the young girl who works as a clerk and messenger, confesses that she has stolen a check for 25,000 pesos but that she no longer has the money. When Lucrecia doesn't appear at the office and a call to her home establishes that she is at the beauty parlor having her hair done, the narrator is beside herself with anger and anxiety. Mr. King, the boss, is calm, and the cashier, as always, is filing her nails. The narrator goes to Lucrecia's house, located in a poor section on the outskirts of the city, and speaks with the girl's mother. The woman knows nothing and seems to be overburdened with the daily chores. Back at the office, Lucrecia, the police, and Mr. King are trying to resolve the situation when Lucrecia confesses that she had to give the money to the cashier. Mr. King, the epitome of tranquillity, fires the cashier, declares that Lucrecia will no longer be sent to the bank, and that the matter is now closed. It is the narrator who is left with the gnawing question of why Lucrecia went to the beauty parlor.

The story, on the surface an ordinary incident in the workings of any office, touches on pervasive problems of a big city: the poverty of families, the despair in which they live, and the temptation of money to be spent on the most frivolous things. Lucrecia, symbolizing a woman who lives in this situation, is dazzled by money and what it can buy. The narrator, on the other hand, is hard-working, conscious of her efforts to better herself, and is both shocked at Lucrecia's action and sympathetic to her plight. Here Puga, in a few tightly woven pages, presents a thought-provoking and profound dilemma.

Two stories that are fictionalized accounts of the author/narrator's love affairs are "Recuerdos oblicuos" (Oblique Memories) and "La naturalidad" (The Natural Thing to Do). The first takes us back to Puga's time in Europe and is an account of a three-month affair in Rome with a married Austrian diplomat. This affair, although clear from the outset to both participants that it would be no more than an interlude, is what broke up the relationship with Enrique, the boyfriend in "Inmóvil sol secreto." In "Recuerdos oblicuos" the author/narrator, living in a rundown old palace in Rome with her lover, recalls how Rome prompted her to think about Mexico—"that

Mexico from which I was escaping in order to return to it and no longer view it from the window" (*I*, 52). Memories of her childhood in Acapulco, her life in Mexico City, and the life she was living in Rome all came together and with them, her acceptance of Mexico and the realization that she would return. Even the three-month affair, a game with rules, was a space where she learned to be, to discover her world.

In "La naturalidad" Puga describes a brief affair with a man who is separated from his wife and is the father of a young child. Focusing on the modern *pareja* (couple) in Mexico, she depicts a complicated relationship that leads nowhere. The narrator, a divorcee, and the man begin a relationship that includes the child on weekends. However, things take a strange turn when the man's mother arrives from Argentina to meet her grandson, and the man's wife and her boyfriend are included in their outings. Although things go very naturally for a while, the narrator realizes that she is out of place and breaks off the relationship.

María Luisa Puga's life and works are one and the same. Ever since early childhood, she has struggled to find her space from which to view the world. Now, many years after the publication of her first novel (1978) and with a steady output of other publications, Puga has settled into her ideal space. In Zirahuén, Michoacán, completely isolated from her neighbors and the literary world, she feels at ease and able to write without the demands and interruptions of city life.

As a writer of fiction, Puga is a keen observer of human relations, of our inner conflicts, and of life with all its routine events and unexpected turns. Whether, as in *Las posibilidades del odio*, she concentrates on relations between blacks and whites or among blacks of different classes, or, as in *Pánico o peligro* and *Antonia*, she focuses on a young woman and her personal struggle to be herself among those who want her to conform to their ideas, Puga delves deeply into her characters and gives her readers a profound understanding of them. The autobiographical presence that permeates her work allows her voice to be taken over by other voices and her pen to write the books of others. Her reflections on writing itself are an underlying theme that manifests itself in her self-conscious narrative techniques.

Puga's short fiction also illustrates her capacity to capture a moment, a feeling, a conflict in a world where things happen that are unexpected, unplanned, and inexplicable. Her prose style in both her novels and her short fiction is slow-paced, deliberate, with few external details and greater emphasis on thoughts and feelings, often like a confession. That is why, despite their setting, her works transcend national boundaries and speak to all of us.

Puga is now at the high point of her career, and one can expect that her forthcoming works will add to her stature. Her life away from the big city promises to provide the distance and space she requires for her craft.

NOTE: Quotations or direct translations from María Luisa Puga's works are cited using the following abbreviations: *I* (*Intentos*); *LRL* (*Las razones del lago*); *MLP/DCE* (*MLP/De cuerpo entero*).

Conversations with the Writer
AUGUST 11, 1992; JANUARY 11, 1994

How and when did you begin to write?

I began writing as a young girl, keeping a kind of diary, a notebook of adventures, in which my sister and I were the characters. And my only reader was my sister. But already at that age I told myself I would be a writer. Then, more or less since I was nine, I constantly kept a kind of notebook, not strictly a diary, more of an attempt at writing stories or a novel.

When and how did you begin to publish?

Well, as I've told you, I was convinced that I was going to be a writer. And at school if there was a student newspaper, I wrote little plays. But it never occurred to me to try to publish anything. In 1968 I left Mexico. My plan was to go to England for a year. I was certain that during that year I was going to write a novel and that I would return with it and offer it to a publisher. The fact is that I stayed ten years, and it wasn't until about the seventh year that I began to write a novel, *Las posibilidades del odio*, although I already had four manuscripts put away, finished. An Argentine friend of mine, who was going to Mexico to publish a book on sociology, read my novel and insisted on taking it with him and presenting it to a publisher. I accepted his offer, and the novel was published in 1978. That was my first novel.

And what did you do with the finished manuscripts?
Are they still unpublished?

I entered one of them in a contest but it didn't win, and the others are still put away. I don't think they are publishable.

Are they short stories?

No, they're novels.

And you're not planning to rework them?

No, I think what happened was that many of the ideas in those novels have come out in other publications of mine. That's why I haven't revised them, but I have a very strong feeling that they are not publishable.

As part of your literary training, what writers did you read?

I didn't study literature formally. I took courses. I left school after high school. I took literature courses on my own, and the first ones were on English literature. I think the writer that impressed me most was Virginia Woolf [1882–1941] and, in general, the English writers of that period. At the same time I discovered the South American writers and those of the "Boom." I also read Austrian writers such as [Robert] Musil [1880–1942] and [Heimito] von Doderer [1896–1966], Italian writers, but unlike my Mexican contemporaries, I read very little of North American and French writers, which are precisely those that I read most now.

You mentioned Austrian and Italian writers. At that time did you read German and Italian or did you read translations?

I read English translations.

Had you studied English in school?

In the literature courses I took here in Mexico, I more or less knew English as practically every Mexican knows English. But in studying literature, I learned English in a more comprehensive way. I studied at the British Institute, and my literary studies sparked in me a greater curiosity about the language, not just to speak it but to read it. In those courses I began to read a great deal in English. By the time I arrived in England I knew English perfectly. French and Italian I learned in Paris.

What writers influenced your prose?

I would like to think Virginia Woolf and Musil, but Latin American writers, I believe many. Several of the Argentines, such as Roberto Arlt [1900–1942]; the Uruguayan Felisberto Hernández [1902–1964]; and the more modern ones—[Julio] Cortázar [1914–1984], [Carlos] Fuentes [1928]. I think they were always present in my readings. I go back to them all the time.

We may already have touched upon this, but do you prefer European, Spanish American, or North American writers?

No, I think mine are cyclical curiosities. Suddenly I feel a great need to go back to the Russians, especially to [Fyodor Mikhailovich] Dostoyevsky [1821–1881]. And just as suddenly I go back to Virginia

Woolf, and, in fact, I give courses on her. But as I was saying, I am reading the French writers for the first time, and I am dazzled by them, by Stendhal [1783–1842], [Honoré de] Balzac [1799–1850], [Gustave] Flaubert [1821–1880]. And the North Americans surprise and fascinate me, the modern ones. I read a great deal. There is one I like very much called Don DeLillo [1936]. I read many new things, writers who are not very well known, because I have North American friends who live in Michoacán and who travel to the United States frequently, especially to New Mexico. They bring me the latest things. The one writer I have followed ever since I read his first book is Don DeLillo. I am drawn to contemporary narrative in general, not so much to specific writers.

What is your opinion of the women writers of your generation?

I think I have been able to see very clearly how they have developed and how they have become solid, strong writers of fiction. I suppose I was present at the birth of women writers, first, of those with a feminist identity and later of those with a well-defined literary identity. At the beginning we saw isolated women writers like Rosario Castellanos [1925–1974], Elena Garro [1920], Inés Arredondo [1928–1989], and since then, Elena Poniatowska [1933]. Then suddenly one would see at a meeting of writers that there were seven men and five women. Now it is likely that at a conference of writers there are eight women and four men. It is very obvious to me that at the beginning the range of topics of women writers was feminism, the rebellion of women, women's liberation, but little by little they began expanding their literary themes. They often used women's identity as one of their themes, but no longer in defense of women but rather to deal with themes that hadn't been explored in literature. I believe that even young writers are now tackling those themes: certain aspects of women's lives, certain aspects of women's identity. I think that although the successful women writers have caused many women who write to imitate certain themes and to produce literature that is more imitative than original, they have managed to incorporate women into literature. They have opened pathways for the understanding of human nature viewed from a woman's perspective, and not only the understanding of women.

Can you mention a writer who exemplifies your ideas?

Angeles Mastretta [1949] impresses me a great deal, especially her first book, *Arráncame la vida* [1985; *Mexican Bolero*, 1989]. It is not only a novel that is pleasurable to read, but I think it has many profound things in it. It has a handling of the world of women, a very strong and interesting handling of morality and sexuality, and it has a literary brazenness that I like a lot. This novel gives rise to a very new voice in literature—not only in literature written by women, but in Mexican literature—that is very daring, very bold. There are other women writers who interest me a great deal, but these are more like intellectual kinships. The prose of Esther Seligson [1941], which is exceptionally strange and awesome, is deeply appealing to me. There are probings of writers like Jennie Ostrosky [1955] that have a lot to do with the theme of motherhood. It is not isolated books that make an impression on me but rather these probings. And many of these writers have their origin in feminist groups that have become somewhat the literary avant-garde. Without casting aside the banner of feminism, these writers are moving into new literary terrain.

Is there a Mexican literature "written by women"?

I would like to clarify what "feminine" means. Feminine literature clearly discernible from masculine literature? No, I don't think so. I think there are many more women who write and who write well. There are probably more women than men writers at this time.

Do you think there is a feminine way of writing that is different from a masculine way of writing?

No, I don't think so. I haven't been able to see it. I do believe that there is a difference of attitude toward writing as there is a difference of attitude toward life, and here we can speak of masculine and feminine attitudes. Perhaps it is reflected in the writing of women, but I haven't been able to detect it in Mexico or in any other country. As I mentioned before, I believe women have abandoned the feminist debate in order to broaden their literary world and, in doing so, they have revealed to the reader of either sex a series of themes that hadn't been dealt with before by literature. These themes deal with women, but that doesn't mean that their treatment is feminine. One would really have to talk about effective and ineffective treatments of themes, and these have no gender.

Is there a relationship between your journalism and your literary creativity?

The journalism that I practice is a kind of very personal chronicle. My book reviews are like that as well. Rather than an evaluation, they are more like a narration of what happens when reading the text. And above all, they are conversations between the reader and me, something which surely stems from the writing workshops I coordinate. My journalism has a lot to do with my writing because it too is writing, because it too is literature, and I think it is inseparable from what happens in my novels. What I mean is that my journalism is another way of experiencing writing and the understanding of things, and I do believe that it is reflected in what I write.

Do you still write for newspapers?

Yes, I write regularly for the cultural section of *El Economista*. And one might almost say that the articles are not journalistic, they are more like the reviews that were compiled for my book *Lo que le pasa al lector*. They have a great deal to do with my having left the big city and distanced myself from the literary world. For me, the reader became a friend to whom I tell what happens when one leaves the big city, when one leaves the urban setting, when one becomes an outsider. And in fact, one of the most frequent themes in these articles that I send to *El Economista* is about outsiders, the state of being an outsider, how the world feels from the perspective of one who has left the big city but still doesn't become part of the town where one went to live and remains a permanent outsider. And an outsider also in the big city, because the city ejects, if you leave, the city drives you out. It takes you out of its routine.

Why did you decide to leave the city?

In part because when I met my husband his dream was not to live in the city. I had a vague plan of going to live in Acapulco where I had spent my childhood and a great desire to create a cultural activity that would offset the tourism of the port. But it was a long-range plan: one of these days I am going to leave here. Actually, I was quite happy in Mexico City. My life wasn't very chaotic, I was well organized at my place of work, in my home, and all that. But my companion did have that dream of leaving. So I went to get to know the place, Zirahuén, and I accepted the possibility of living there. But simultaneously the literary world was becoming oppressive. Literary life has little to do with writing. It demands a great deal of the writer and often demands writing which is not literary, which is not aimed at the literary world. I liked the idea of isolating myself, of disconnecting myself.

Are there any autobiographical elements in your narrative work?

There are many, but they are all confused. There is no chronological order. And none of my books has aimed to be exclusively autobiographical. I have made use of many personal episodes as a basis for a story which is not necessarily my story, as, for example, in the novel *Antonia*, in which I use in a very autobiographical way my years in London to relate the story of a fictitious character, Antonia.

Are you working on something new?

There are two books that are finished and whose publication has been delayed, in large measure, because of the economic situation. *La viuda* [The Widow] is a novel, and the other is a book for adolescents that I did for the Fondo de Cultura Económica called *La ceremonia de iniciación* [The Initiation Ceremony]. The second book is for a collection dealing with history. The publisher put the project's participants in contact with a researcher, gave us a specific historical context, and from this we had to create a fictional work. I was asked to write the story of an Angolan at the time of the arrival of the Portuguese. And the historical moment is the Christianization of the Angolan king. Since it is a novel for young people, I chose as my protagonist the best friend of the king's son. I wrote something akin to a novel of adventures in which there is slavery, rebellion, pirates, and so on.

And this book is part of a series?

It is part of a collection. I think Carmen Boullosa [1954] is also participating in this project, as well as several other writers. The collection is entitled *Travesías* [Voyages]. I imagine that the books will be coming out this year. They are meant for high school or preparatory school readers. I believe that my novel is a book that a ten-year-old can read and, without being patronizing, so can any adult. What might be particularly attractive for a young person is that the action moves very rapidly and the protagonist is an adolescent.

And the other book in press, La viuda, *what is it about?*

It is the story of a woman who becomes a widow at about seventy and suddenly, several months after the death of her husband, at a family gathering in her house, she realizes how tired she is of being the matriarch of the family and decides to begin a new life in another city with a girlhood friend of hers. She then settles into a house by herself in the new city and comes to the realization that she can pick up the life she left pending when she got married. She then develops an identity that is a continuation of that young girl she ceased to be in order to become a wife and mother.

Is this woman based on a real person or is she fictitious?

The story is fictitious, but the woman has the personality of a real person.

Besides these two books that are in press, are you working on something new?

I am working on a novel that will be called *Inventar ciudades* [Inventing Cities], and my aim in this book is to explore new ways of structuring one's daily life. My leaving the city to live in a place as isolated as Zirahuén has a lot to do with it. It has forced me to reinvent my time, my activities, my way of doing things. But the fiction of the novel concerns a child who loses both parents almost simultaneously and then goes to live with an older couple. I am attempting to reinvent emotions, sensitivities, ways of speaking to a child. I am probing a great deal into the nature of women, of men, of children. My exploratory lenses are three senses: hearing, feeling, and looking.

Does your character have any relationship to the young man, Damián, in
Las razones del lago?

No, the only similarity is the reality of the town. The child is a city child, from a comfortable middle-class family, who had never been out of the city. The girl goes to the town school and gets to know the people of the town. The novel is not set in a place with lakes but with a forest.

In Mexico there has been a generation of notable women writers before yours. Which of them do you admire and why? Do you think that the presence of this group of writers has helped those who followed them?

Here I have to mention the two that matter most to me—although I know one well and the other I never met—Elena Poniatowska and Rosario Castellanos. I consider Elena more important because she is closer to me, she is more like me in her choice of themes, in her approach, and because she helped me a lot as a writer. I believe she was among the first women writers who spoke of my books as serious work. But what impresses me most about Elena is her tenacity, not a stubborn tenacity but a very vital one that does not permit her to become discouraged for any reason at all. It is as if she were always working on her first book. Her enthusiasm is incredibly intense.

And Castellanos?

I know Castellanos only as a reader of her books. I must have been fifteen when I read *Balún-Canán*. And I came out of that experience saying that I wanted to be a writer and that I didn't want to devote myself to anything else. Reading *Balún-Canán* was an eye-opener: "But, of course, that's how it should be."

And what other writers do you admire?

I have very much enjoyed sharing the profession of writing with my contemporaries. I enjoy being a colleague of Silvia Molina [1946], of David Martín del Campo [1952], of Carmen Boullosa, of Mónica Mansour [1946], because when we were getting started we were very close. There was a pleasant atmosphere in the literary world, a spirit of camaraderie that was perhaps due to the personality of José Agustín [1944]. Actually I am José Agustín's age, but since I spent time in Europe, I began to publish with a group somewhat younger than I am. When I returned to Mexico from Europe, which was when my first book came out, Silvia Molina was publishing her first book, as were many of the people of the group that interests you and that we have been talking about. The publishing industry began to group writers not by similarities or common interests, but simply by presenting the reader with the mosaic of what was happening in contemporary Mexican literature. We realized that it wasn't a matter of being a generation with common interests, but that there was an unquestionable diversity of interests that did not prevent us from being unified. There was no need to compete; there was no need to create cliques as had been the case in previous generations, or as is happening right now.

We had a meeting a short time ago that was a kind of anniversary. There were twenty writers, ten women and ten men, and each of us had published more or less the same number of books. We had all gotten older. We were all still writing. It was a nice get-together. Undeniably, each one of us was convinced that he or she was better than the others. One couldn't keep on writing if it weren't that way. Without question, some had a greater liking for some texts than for others, but it didn't matter. Our elders, on the other hand, keep on fighting, keep on arguing, and keep on forming little groups. I believe that what we discovered was that diversity is healthy.

At a conference that we attended in Germany, several of us decided to make up a name and call ourselves "the generation at the crossroads." It was something of a game, but at the same time, we began to find a meaning in it. At our start as writers—and currently as we continue to produce, as we struggle for better conditions for writers, as we struggle so that people read more of Mexican writers—we never had to argue among ourselves. It was never necessary to form groups or cliques.

When do you write, and how do you relate your writing to your other responsibilities—domestic, professional, family?

Here I must point out that our life in Zirahuén is made for writing. My husband was married before and has two adult children. We live alone. Our house was designed by us so that we each have the space we need—we each have a computer, we each have our music, our own entrance and exit. We permit the domestic areas to be joined when we both require them: we may eat together or not, we may or may not sleep together.

I write early in the morning because I always had to work in some office. I wanted to use the best hours to write. I could never manage to write when I came back from the office, nor am I like some writers who write at all hours of the night, because I fall asleep, I get tired. On the other hand, I am perfectly capable of getting up at three in the morning.

In a place as isolated as Zirahuén (and my house is in the middle of the woods a mile from town), the domestic part of one's life is a constant and very pleasant occupation. It is ideal for those moments when one has writer's block. I get up, cook, make the bed, clean, and then return to my writing. One's daily chores are very much intertwined with reading and writing.

My solution for economic survival has been the literary workshops that I give, thanks to a friend who outfitted a large house in order to be able to accept children from the entire country, especially from urban areas. During the school year they come with their classes, and in the summer as individual campers. We try to give them the opportunity to experience rural life, a life of craftsmanship. This place, called "El Molino," is in Erongarícuaro, very close to where I live. The town is filled with all kinds of artisans. The children learn to work with clay, to work with wood, to make traditional sweets; they learn ecology, veterinary science, painting, embroidery, music, and I teach them the short story.

And they live in that house?

Yes.

How long do they stay in the summer?

In the summer we have four camp sessions of eleven days each.

*I assume there are other people who are in charge of
different aspects of this camp.*

Yes, there are young assistants to take care of the children, adult assistants to attend to the adolescents, and specialized teachers and psychologists.

And you go there every day to give your short-story class?

Practically every day because we don't have workshops just for children. Sometimes we arrange workshops for teachers or for adults who also come from all over the country. We organize them when there are long holiday weekends or when there is a vacation period. The workshops last four or five days, but the adults also live, eat, and sleep there. This activity has permitted me to organize my economic life, and at the same time it is work that is a perfect complement to my writing. It is very enjoyable work.

*But you began this way of life in 1985 when you moved to Michoacán.
Prior to that, when you lived in Mexico City, did you also write
early in the morning?*

Yes, by the time I got to my office I had already written for some three hours. I have never had the experience of writing a book in two weeks, in a month. My method is to write daily and probably to finish a novel in a year and a half to two years. But yes, I definitely write every day.

*Is there anything else you wish to add about your own work or about
contemporary literature written by women?*

I see a very clear progression in the books that I have written. It is very clear to me because ever since I can remember I have been writing, and writing for me has been inseparable from living. I have made basic decisions because of this. For example, I didn't have children. I didn't even have a traditional marriage. My writing always took precedence. I believe that my writing did undergo a change when I left the city. I don't know whether the change was good or bad, I only know that something changed. Probably what happened was that people began to be of greater importance. By people I mean not only as characters in my novel. The voices of people prevailed over the voices of literature.

What do you mean by "voice"?

The voice of reality; reality is use of language, but it is also the people who have no literary space for a variety of reasons, and not only because they are not interested in reading. I believe that another one of the consequences of my having left the city was discovering that education interested me a great deal. The literary workshops that I direct at "El Molino" can be considered workshops for middle-class children. During my early years in Zirahuén, I directed the workshops in the town's high school, and I realized that the effects were identical. If these children were given the natural space to read and write, they would be reading and writing just like we do. But the object "book" does not fit into the reality of Zirahuén. Children, when they leave school, become the little "slaves" of their families. But when you give them the space and the time to make up and write a story, they are as creative as anyone else.

The same can be said for the women. During the first year that I lived in Michoacán, I directed workshops subsidized by an agency of the government. There the participants were women, ordinary house-wives who had fulfilled their obligations. Their children were grown, their homes functioned on their own, and they suddenly had time on their hands and didn't know what to do with it. In the workshops they wrote really marvelous things that they themselves could hardly believe. They were more amazed than was I, who read their texts.

These housewives attending the workshops, did they begin to read as well?

Yes, part of the aim of the workshop was to make them read. I began by coordinating workshops at the National University of Mexico. The participants were university students in a variety of disciplines, but all had a very specific interest in writing. When I left the city, I began to coordinate workshops with groups from other social classes and to organize them differently because they were no longer permanent workshops. The children's workshops lasted five or ten days. It was then that I realized that they really weren't workshops to teach writ-ing, but they were spaces to practice the use of language and develop a taste for reading.

Your work reminds me of the cultural campaign of José Vasconcelos
[1882–1959] in the 1920s, when teachers like Gabriela Mistral
[1889–1957] traveled through the country to teach reading and to share
their knowledge with the people. Didn't you ever want to be a teacher or
university instructor?

No, I wouldn't know how, I couldn't do it. In the workshops I can do well because I don't feel that I am in a position of authority from which I am going to teach something. The table at which we sit in the workshop is a space on which the central focus of attention is everyone's text. I am there so that the participants don't become distracted from the text, and to prevent anyone from setting him- or herself up as the boss. There all that counts, all that speaks, all that says something is the text and the opinions of the others about the text. We all help build the text. All of us are concerned that the text be a good one. All of us help the text to take shape and stand on its own.

How many are there in the children's workshops?

The workshops generally have a maximum of twelve. Sometimes when we organize workshops for adults, I get to work with twenty-five or thirty, but with so many participants the quality of the workshop suffers. Nevertheless, it can be useful in making the participants shed their fear. The larger the group, the more apt the members are to speak because they feel a little more anonymous. And perhaps as a first experience in a workshop, it is not such a bad idea that it be a big one. For the adult workshops we invite other writers. Since I live nearby, usually when the participants arrive I give the first workshop, and that's why I have large groups. Afterward, when the other writers arrive, the group is broken up and each writer takes his or her students. The ideal number is ten.

Do you think you have had any influence on younger writers?

Probably on some and not only on women writers. But I think what may have had a greater influence are the workshops that I coordinate and in which I work with young people. Some of those who are publishing now have been in my workshops—Pablo Soler Frost [1965], Ana Clavel [1961], and others. In Morelia there are many who were in my workshops and who now make up the dominant literary scene.

How would you summarize your contribution to contemporary Mexican literature?

At the risk of sounding presumptuous, I do believe that I brought to literature a voice of the independent woman, an "I" who knows she is a woman and does not restrict herself to what is feminine to explore the world and who, at the same time, constitutes the perspective of a woman.

Representative Selections

One

["Uno," from *Las razones del lago*]

We don't like the lake. All the others do. But that doesn't mean anything; we don't like it because there is no reason to. No one cares.
Nevertheless, here we are; they don't realize it but here we are. We'll
always be here, whether it rains, or is cold, or there's a drought, or
arguments among the townspeople. They can die or go to school or
get married or cross over to the other side. Here we are observing it
all. And no one cares whether we do or not. No one cares if we like the
lake or not.

Unlike the town, which is horrible, the lake is dazzling at any time
of the day. They say only men drown in it. Probably because they're
drunk. Those who get closest to it are the women, who go there to
wash clothes and bathe their children. Since the men are always drinking in the street, there is always someone who loses his way and lands
in the lake and drowns. That's how easy it is.

There is nothing in this town, except liquor. You can always get
liquor, at any time on any day. Only a few places sell it, but those three
or four are more than enough.

On weekends many people come from elsewhere. They come in
small boats and go to the restaurant on the opposite side of the lake
which is famous. But there are also those who camp on the shore of
the lake, those who stay in cabins, those who invariably buy beer from
Sabina. They bring their radios and make a lot of noise. We don't
know what the lake does to people to make them yell so loud. Perhaps
it's seeing the water. Because around here the people are quiet,
gloomy, calm. They go about their business along the cobblestone
streets, and one would think that it was very difficult for them to leave
their houses. They greet each other without joy. They go off, and then
we realize that they live by turning their backs on one another. They
hate each other.

That is probably how all the small towns of this country are. With
the church always bigger than any other building. The ugly cement
plaza. The miserable businesses for poor people. And the radios blar-
ing constantly, the public loudspeakers, someone's cassette player

going somewhere. That's how it is if there isn't a wedding or a baptism or a fifteenth birthday party or a funeral, because then there is a band and a lot of drinking among the guests. After a couple of drinks, everyone feels like the bride or groom, or even like the deceased, like whoever is the guest of honor.

Our life is not easy, as you can probably tell from the large number of dead dogs all over, especially on the highway. One might say they like to run us over. Perhaps among the drivers it's a great sport. So many dogs are flung from here to Pátzcuaro or to Uruapan. And our bodies remain there rotting like carrion for buzzards. We are so many, and that's why no one even notices when one of us disappears. We move in a pack and try not to make noise so as not to be noticed. Children and adults have fun kicking us, throwing stones at us, or whatever. We grow up with these people, but they don't see us. They don't even realize that we are alive and, like them, feel pain and hunger. But the important thing is that they don't realize that we notice everything about them. We go everywhere and really know everything.

What good is it if we don't live better because of that? That's what we live for and that's not unimportant. At any rate, the meaning of a dog's life is different from a man's and one shouldn't make the comparison. Instead we have learned to make comparisons among their lives. And we've done that without even trying because it's really none of our business. It is just that always being here, almost invisible, has allowed us to understand some things.

We often wonder whether life is like that everywhere. Is life that dreadful and violent in other small towns? We would like to know. What would life be like without a lake that is so beautiful all the time that it becomes annoying because it seems to be making fun of us? Of everyone, men, women, and dogs. It would seem that it is making fun of life itself, of the things that happen to us.

Anywhere you go you can always see it giving off those sharp, violent reflections. As if it were watching over us. Peaceful there, always the same, always surprising. And the tourists arrive and say: How beautiful! They don't know what they're saying. But that is normal. Then they get into their cars and leave.

They say there was once a great indigenous culture here in Michoacán . . . can you believe it. Something should have remained, even if it were just a blurred memory. The fact is that the people here live as if in a state of voluntary oblivion. They don't want to know about anything. The women hide under their shawls and there they stay. The men under their broad-brimmed hats don't want to look you in the face either.

This is a sad town, stuck in a rut. One can tell at different times of the day, but maybe the worst is at dusk. That's when we breathe in the dissatisfaction, the restlessness of adults and children. It is when the day has already ended, and they have all done what they had to, and they have some free time. We imagine that is when they wonder what the purpose of it all is. Why another night, another ritual. The town is filled with the sound of music, of radios and phonographs. None of it has any joy. One feels more of a quiet desperation, closed in and tense. The people disguise themselves as always. They look at one another less than ever. And that is when they harass us most. Especially the children, who don't know what to do with their energy, their anxiety. The women water their plants, with a devotion which is somewhat frightening. Almost angrily they give them life, hoping to see them bloom. It is as if, not being able to do so with their own lives, they console themselves with that. The vibrant and colorful flowers never cease to contrast with the ragged and filthy look of the children.

The men form sullen little groups on the corners. They speak, spitting out tense monosyllables. We understand only too well that anything at all is enough to unleash their violence. Somewhere in the town, someone is always getting drunk. Something like bubbles take form in the air, and the others look at them with frightened nostalgia. The drunkards are surrounded by a dense silence everyone flees from. We sometimes hang around there, nearby, staring at them, more invisible than ever. We hear them whimpering and see them doubling over little by little until they fall to the ground like sacks of potatoes. We stay close to them, very quietly, and even take care of them, although no one does them any harm. They don't even come near.

That is the most distressing time of the day, but another terrible time is noon. It is when the lake makes the most fun of us and the sun helps it along. Only we are on the street at that time.

Lucrecia

["Lucrecia," from *Intentos*]

What I just cannot understand is when she took the check from me. And the check was already signed, because she simply couldn't have forged the signature... if she hardly knew how to write. This was her first job. She had only recently gotten out of high school. She had been working in the office longer than I and seemed to be quite familiar with it. She was clever... but I can't believe she would spy. That she would intend to steal and would have been planning it. More likely the cashier... she was a little older and they were friends. Lucrecia used to tell me that the cashier took her to parties and made her drink rum-and-cokes. And I would ask her: And your mother lets you? She looked at me with surprise: And why not? I am an adult. I work and give her money. I do what I want. That was another thing: she told me every-thing... although now that I think about it, perhaps not everything; perhaps not even the half of it. But one thing that I never saw in her was viciousness. Like the viciousness of the cashier, for example, that one could sense in the entire office. It was a very tense office. When Mr. King was there no one said a word. It's just that he was very quiet. Very cold. We sold dental equipment, but he lent money besides. He was a Russian Jew from New York. I never understood why he hired me as a bookkeeper when I told him I knew absolutely nothing about numbers. I don't want to discuss it, he said, I am sure you'll do the work very well. Perhaps that was the time we spoke the most. After-ward, only for things relating to the office. When he arrived, he greeted everyone very properly, and then in the room an icy silence set in. Except for the cashier, who was always chewing gum and suddenly it sounded as though she were sighing ostentatiously. The office was one large room. My desk was right next to Mr. King's, and both of us were quite a distance from the cashier and from Lucrecia's small table at the door. There were some armchairs for the people who came. Many people came, all the time. And there were some enormous windows that looked out on Madero Street. One could hear the traffic a lot, although not like now. All this happened about twenty years ago. The stolen 25,000 pesos would now be a quarter of a million or more. That's why I don't understand. Lucrecia couldn't possibly have con-ceived of it. I don't believe she could even have imagined what 25,000 pesos were. She used to make the deposits and cash the checks, but I handed her the bank slips. If Mr. King had only known how difficult it was for me to learn all of that... to keep the checkbook in order. I spent an entire morning studying it. I had never concerned myself with numbers. Before that I had worked for a movie company doing things completely different from bookkeeping. I was a student of anthropology. Numbers frightened me, especially when they had to do with money. And I had to calculate the interest; to apply the rule of three. My hands trembled out of nervousness. The fear of making a mistake... that's why I was so sure, when they informed us that a check of ours had bounced, that it couldn't be an error of mine. I used to check a thousand times before issuing a check. If it had been the economist who was here before me, the one who had trained me, most likely it would have been his error, because since he felt so knowledgeable about everything, he was careless. He wasn't afraid of errors because he understood them. But I was living in hell. I almost envied the cashier when I saw her filing her nails while listening to the radio (when Mr. King wasn't there). Lucrecia came and went about doing the many errands that had to be done. I liked her a lot. She was a very pretty girl, very cheerful. She always seemed bewildered; she had a certain carefree air about her. I pictured her skipping along the street, her eyes shiny, looking at everything with the curiosity of a child. She liked me because she realized how my work made me suffer. When Mr. King wasn't there, her laugh could be heard everywhere. The office seemed to be sunnier and more spacious. Of course, that was when the cashier turned on the radio and I, who wanted to study, couldn't, but at least the atmosphere became more relaxed. I heard their voices, the cashier's and Lucrecia's, in an endless whispering sprinkled at times with laughter. I stayed at my desk next to Mr. King's because I was never completely certain that I had done the calculations properly. Time and again I checked them, and the day the client returned with the bounced check I, with all my insecurity, said: It is just not possible that there aren't any funds. They must have made a mistake. Why don't you go to the bank yourself? suggested Mr. King, without being particularly concerned (he had already lent the money, since I had assured him that there were funds. That's why he had gone on to do other things). Yes, I'd go to the bank, but even though I was sure that it couldn't have been an error of mine, I was so insecure about everything: about hearing myself say that it couldn't have been an error of mine. And when I saw how everyone accepted my statement as if it were the most natural thing in the world (that's how it must have been with the economist who preceded me, and he *did* make mistakes), my insecurity increased. Therefore, before going to the bank, I sat and went over the checkbook one more time. I think I was perspiring, that one could see my hands trembling. The client had left after having been assured that he could cash the check the next day. I think I was pale. Mr. King took his leave as always: Don't forget to go to the bank, he said so confident, so sure of me. So without knowing me. And when there was no choice but to go to the bank because, if not, they'd be closed, Lucrecia came over to me and said: I took a check for 25,000 pesos. I thought it was a joke, that the fun was beginning because Mr. King had already gone. What surprised me was not hearing the radio accompanying those words. I took it about two weeks ago, she told me, and there I was, unable to connect Lucrecia to the check. I don't know why I looked in the direction of the cashier, who had her back to me, and then at Lucrecia. She seemed frightened: But I no longer have it, she said. I remembered that the previous day, or two days before, I'm not sure, Lucrecia had arrived with a carton of coca-colas as a treat for the entire office. Lucrecia's treat, I said to Mr. King, when I offered him one instead of coffee, and he barely forced a smile. He accepted it as the most natural thing ever. Only when I associated Lucrecia's face with the coca-colas and, looking at her out of the corner of my eye, with the check, I almost cried. Was it possible that her idea of squandering a fortune was limited to a carton of coca-colas? I had a fleeting image of many, of thousands of cartons of coca-colas and I wanted to laugh; and I would have had it not been for the amount of the check: a quarter of a million pesos or more (now), and which had to be deposited in the bank. I no longer have the money, Lucrecia repeated, her voice trembling, and I remembered the day she had come dressed in a sheer thing, like tulle, or organdy, more for a fifteenth birthday party than for an office. The girl seemed all innocence in her naive attempt at elegance. It's my new dress, she explained to me. Mama made it for me. And that evening she was going to a party and wouldn't have time to go home and change. I realize now that in the midst of her amazement, there deep inside, there was something that was beginning to change. I am not imagining it. When I would lift my eyes from my book, or from the paper on which I would be doing my calculations, the freshness of Lucrecia always surprised me, but that day, the day of the dress, very deep inside, very suddenly, there was an almost scared expression much like the one she had now. What do you mean you no longer have the money? I asked her, alarmed. No,

I no longer have it. And what are we going to do? We have to speak to Mr. King. Yes, she said immediately, almost relieved that someone was making decisions. Well, tomorrow, you come very early, I said to her, and you speak to him. Before the banks open. Yes, yes, she agreed to everything. And I didn't sleep that night, as if it had been my error, my fault. Over and over I tried to imagine what Mr. King would say, what he would do. All I saw was his cold face. I couldn't picture anything else. And the following day, it was ten o'clock, and neither Mr. King nor Lucrecia had arrived. The cashier was in her place as always; I didn't even want to look at her. I was listening for every sound out of my eagerness that Lucrecia get here, that Lucrecia arrive, but it was Mr. King who arrived first and who, upon seeing me, stopped cold: But what's going on? What's the matter with you? I must have had some face. And I didn't want to say anything to him without Lucrecia, but he, surprisingly alarmed, insisted: What's the matter with you? That problem of the check yesterday is because Lucrecia took 25,000 pesos. And he, laughing: What a scare you gave me. Is that all it is? Why are you acting like that? But the thing is that she says she no longer has the money and... OK, OK, calm down, we'll see, just calm down for the moment. Go to the bank to make a deposit and then we'll talk. I felt bewildered. I think I had expected him to have a nervous breakdown. A kind of icy, iridescent anger that would cut through the air. I walked to the bank searching for Lucrecia among all the people. As I was approaching the office on the way back, I felt that something was tensing up in me: the moment I opened the door something would come out and undo all the anguish. I would hear Lucrecia's laughter and see the cashier filing her nails. Mr. King, as always, studying his papers. My little adding machine (with a lever. They came with levers in those days), and I would only feel the strangeness of Mr. King's smile, and of course, when I opened the door everything was exactly like that, except that Lucrecia wasn't there. Frightened, I went over to Mr. King, who again was startled: What's the matter now? She hasn't come, I said. Who? Lucrecia, Lucrecia hasn't arrived, and she promised me that she would come early. Mr. King looked at me dismayed: But calm down, call her at home. It seemed incredible to me, but the cashier knew where to call her, at a little store nearby, and she gave me the phone number. Also the name of the mother, who answered after a long while during which I imagined a million things. She told me that Lucrecia had gone to have her hair done and that from there she would come to the office. Everything sounded so normal. The cashier seemed to be dozing. Mr. King had gone back to his papers. And I was burdened with all the horror: Who was Lucrecia? How was it possible that she had gone to have her hair done? I returned to my desk and, shaken, I announced to Mr. King: I am going to her house. Again I saw him become startled: To whose house? What's the matter with you today? Mr. King, I said on the verge of tears, Lucrecia stole 25,000 pesos (a quarter of a million or more today), she hasn't come to work, and apparently she is having her hair done in a beauty parlor at this very moment. I am going to her house to speak to her mother. You are still upset by that? Just stop worrying, the girl will come, and if she doesn't we'll send the police for her. But it's not that, I became exasperated, the police will ask her for the money and she doesn't have it. I don't even think she is fully aware of what is happening... she went to have her hair done! (Why had she gone to have her hair done?) I don't understand why you are so concerned, said Mr. King, shrugging his shoulders, if there is nothing that you can do, since the girl must have already spent the money. I wanted to explain to him that no, it wasn't so simple, but I was keenly aware of the fact that time was running out and that I had to hurry. But besides, I had such an enormous feeling of uneasiness: on the one hand, the office with its everyday atmosphere, which I believe the cashier accentuated. She seemed more detached, more passive and indifferent than ever. And on the other hand, the unexpected attitude of Mr. King, who didn't seem to be the least upset by the theft. I felt that he was urging me to be just like always, that I shouldn't allow myself to be distracted. I almost felt that he was asking me not to leave him alone, which surprised me because I had gotten used to his coldness, to his distance. I always thought the only thing that mattered to him was his work. His money. And there he was facing me, somewhat defenseless, looking at me from behind his desk in complete awe with his little blue eyes, while I was gathering up my bag and tidying up my desk somewhat. But, are you really going to go? I could never have stayed there as if nothing were happening, just mulling the matter over in my head. Of course I am going, and if she gets here before I return, please don't say anything to her. Let her speak. And if she doesn't, wait for me. I hadn't the faintest idea of where I was going. The cashier had jotted down the address and phone number for me on a scrap of paper. A street, a neighborhood unfamiliar to me, and I just read it off to the taxi driver. I don't know where it is, I said. He didn't answer. He took off, and with the movement of the car I calmed down somewhat. Through the window I saw the city go by. I saw how we were leaving behind the downtown area, a small residential area, and then the world was taking shape with concrete and rods, unfinished houses like broken dreams. I tried to picture Lucrecia living there every day and suddenly, one fine morning, with 25,000 pesos in her bag in the face of that despair of the semiurban landscape, with its patches of plain squalor, or its sometimes surprising little corners of optimism, where the people prevailed over the city, where the tin cans painted with lively colors and filled with enormous plants gave off a broad smile. I searched for Lucrecia in each face, in each ragged little girl running down the street. It filled me with terror because I realized that I really didn't know her, and suddenly we were in front of a rickety old door of what looked like an auto mechanic's shop, and the driver said to me: Here it is, should I wait for you? Yes, and I got out quickly and went into a dirty and narrow courtyard with doors on the sides, a railing, a second floor, women washing, a wild sound of music of many radios playing at the same time, a face that looked at me questioningly and showed me which was Lucrecia's house, but said that she wasn't home. Her mother was, she was that woman in the blue dress, that one, the one hanging out clothes. Sarita, someone's here asking for you! And a round face that didn't in any way remind me of Lucrecia, looked at me in amazement. I am from Lucrecia's office. I am the one who called before. The woman dried her hands on her dress. Come in, come in, the stairway is over there, and then she led me through hanging clothes, flowerpots, and garbage cans to an open door, behind which was a darkened room with stagnant air, and indicated to me that this was her house. But the woman opened a window, showed me a table covered with a flowered plastic cloth, and invited me to sit down. With great dismay I discovered a new bed, its mattress still wrapped in plastic, leaning against the wall. It looked like it hadn't been used yet. I became distracted and unable to concentrate on the moment, that moment when I would have to tell this proud-looking woman with reddened hands and a questionably clean dress that her daughter had stolen. How much! she exclaimed in disbelief. And I repeated: 25,000 pesos. And she didn't give me anything! she protested, and I, unwittingly, looked toward the bed. That we got on credit, she replied skeptically, and I understood the unreality of it all, because the entire neighborhood could have been demolished for less than that amount (now a quarter of a million or more), but also the terrible reality: The fact is that Lucrecia says she no longer has that money, I said, and she looked at me sarcastically.

And you are not really going to believe her? Once again I had before my eyes the image that I had formed of Lucrecia after six months, that way one has of perceiving people, their look. Yes, I said, I think she's telling the truth. And you have no idea to whom she may have given the money? Oh, Miss, she whimpered, I don't know what she does any more. The only thing that consoles me is that she comes home to sleep every night, but beyond that... And you, you? You, I wanted to ask her, what have you done to contribute to that look of bewilderment in Lucrecia's eyes, that fragile innocence, that moral awareness that is so dormant. Had she done something or was she just an older and more worn-out Lucrecia? I took my leave amiably, assuring her that most likely everything would be cleared up, although I don't know why it didn't seem to matter to her, or rather it was as though she didn't comprehend; from the balcony she said good-bye to me and saw the taxi driver, who had gotten out of his car and was waiting for me, leaning against the doorway, looking sleepily at the courtyard. And now? he asked me. Back to the place where I got in. And the way back was even more silent, even more graphic, I suppose, because now it wasn't the streets that I was seeing, but different stages of Lucrecia's life that had little by little led into the office without anything piecing them together, and suddenly everything was there. And I thought about the check again. When could she have taken it? Could she have been spying? Why that one and not a bigger or smaller one? Trying to make sense of the matter, I figured out there was something accidental, involuntary or unconscious, which I knew when I saw the bank's armored car in front of the door of the office, so very normal at any other time, for any other person, but not for me, that I ran up the stairs and the moment I opened the door I saw how Lucrecia rushed to throw herself weeping into my arms: Tell them that I no longer have the money! The policemen from the bank (two), Mr. King, and there in the back, the cashier, everyone was looking at her, then at me, until Mr. King said: A deposit has already been made, you can go quietly. We will settle this. Lucrecia was crying, and in a low voice, choking with emotion, she whispered into my ear: I had to give it to the cashier, she knew from the very beginning, but don't say anything to her because she will go and tell my mother. I don't know why the only thing I noticed was the odor of hair-spray on her. She had really gone to have her hair done. Mr. King seemed uncomfortable: I think it will be best to get back to work. Lucrecia won't go to the bank anymore. That's all he said, and he went back to his desk like someone who has finally reached dry land. Why, on the one hand, did he have that help-less look and, on the other, did he want the whole matter forgotten? I calmed Lucrecia down and asked her to do some filing. Then I approached Mr. King and told him about the cashier. In a single ges-ture, having heard me and understood, he lifted his hand, called her, and in a dry, distant, brief tone, said: You're fired. You can go immedi-ately and don't even think of talking about severance pay. She didn't say a word, but swallowed hard, kept on chewing her gum slowly, made a half turn, took her bag, and left. Lucrecia didn't see her. All right, Mr. King asked me, now are you calm? Can we work now? Lucrecia was running to answer the phone, I was standing in front of Mr. King's desk, profoundly, completely bewildered. And without knowing anything about bookkeeping, besides. I wanted to ask a ques-tion, two, a hundred, but the man had already pushed back his glasses and was checking his papers... and I, what I still don't understand even now, is why Lucrecia went to have her hair done that morning . . . well, one of so many things that I don't understand.

The Guests

["Los invitados," Unpublished Story]

We have a room for guests. We made it very self-contained so that they will feel comfortable. So that they won't feel obligated to act like guests or we like hosts. It is an entire wing of the house. It has a small living room, a terrace, a bathroom, its own access to the kitchen... We can picture the guests settling in (a little like they were coming to live here for good). Living in the country does that to you: one's social life is different. No telephone to speak to this or that one whom one hasn't seen for ages. We invite people and know they'll come and settle themselves in the midst of our lives. That's why we built this special little corner for them. The one we call the guest room.

The idea is a little like pretending they live here just as we do. Like neighbors. That they do things on their own time, their activities, their daily routine. That one day perhaps they'll invite us over for dinner.

When we know they are coming, we are full of enthusiasm. We check the room thoroughly. Make sure there are ashtrays, many of them. Reading lamps. Blankets. I think what we like most is to visualize them. How they are going to move about among the furniture. At what time they'll turn off the light. How it will feel to see the lake from their perspective.

Almost all our guests come from the city and arrive with their eyes clouded over from all that bustle. Invariably they stand on the terrace and look at the lake as if they were mesmerized. They always say: How beautiful! And then they look all around: the wooden roofs, the adobe walls, and again the lake: But how beautiful! And they don't know what else to do.

We are eager for them to go into their room and get to know it. To see where they are going to live. To see the place that will be theirs, but it is sort of like getting tangled up with each other on the terrace and a little like taking the subway: some go one way and others another, and then we run into each other.

Finally we get them to go in and settle down and we go to our studies meanwhile. From there we spy on them: *there are guests* in the room. The house feels very strange. As if a piece of it had collapsed. There are noises, footsteps that aren't ours. We don't dare look openly in that direction, lest we catch them doing something intimate.

Guests are very strange. That has always surprised us: how unusual they all are. They give the impression that instead of going into the room, they are trying it on and it fits too tightly. From all sides, arms, legs, exclamations come out. Perhaps they bump into each other frequently. Or maybe it has to do with the fact that they come from the city, from living in tall buildings, from walking on pavement. Because they come out on the terrace and walk off to the side as if they were dodging the crowds, ignoring the space around them. Once again they look at the lake and exclaim: How beautiful! When looking at it they are very still. They are very odd.

Afterward they seek us out. We are hiding. Not out of maliciousness, but so that they learn to move about by themselves. So that they begin their daily routine, but it is as if they are unaware. The look for us because they want to sit down with us and look right at us. And if after a while we get up and go to do something, they follow us, very closely. Then what we do is guide them little by little to their place and when we manage to get them to go in, we go off quickly.

Sometimes we hide a long time in the forest and listen to them. We hear them calling us and resigning themselves to our not being there. They begin to talk among themselves like people in a waiting room. From time to time they look at the lake and say: How beautiful! Or they ask each other: Do you think there are rattlesnakes around here?

And that's how it is until nightfall.

We serve them a light supper and begin to look at them sternly so that they will go off to sleep. Finally they take their leave and that is when the mysterious part begins.

All guests are alike. Perhaps the reason is the room, or the night in Zirahuén. The presence of the lake becomes a space that threatens them. Or maybe it is the cold that forces us all to close the doors, to cover ourselves, to quiet down.

The fact is that the same thing happens with all of them: they put up a wall of silence between their part of the house and ours, and slowly that wing becomes distant for us, unknown, impregnable.

We would like to be able to hear something, to picture something at least. But no. The night swallows them, it carries them away as if they were its guests. Often we have been tempted to knock on the door in the early morning; we wanted to burst in abruptly (with flashlights, so that it would be more striking). At times, we planned that one of us would remain hidden inside. It has even occurred to us to plant a concealed tape recorder.

We don't understand why, if we prepare the room with such attention to detail, and we know it so well with all its possibilities, it slips out of our hands like that. And the guests, those who repeat with such persistence: How beautiful!, those who during the day walk like invalids, how is it possible that they all become so hermetic, almost antagonistic?

Can it be that something in the forest causes them to organize evil nocturnal ceremonies, which they didn't consider themselves capable of? Or can it be that they fall into a trancelike state that they can't remember the next day? Sometimes too much oxygen has that effect.

The thing is that when they get up for breakfast the next day you can't notice anything about them (what an incredible ability to pretend they all have).

They eat breakfast hungrily. They rub their hands and say: "How cold it is."

They are very strange.

Bibliography

Publications

Las posibilidades del odio. Mexico City: Siglo XXI, 1978.
Inmóvil sol secreto. Mexico City: La Máquina de Escribir, 1979.
Cuando el aire es azul. Mexico City: Siglo XXI, 1980.
Accidentes. Mexico City: Martín Casillas, 1981.
La cerámica de Hugo X. Velásquez: Cuando rinde el horno. Mexico City: Martín Casillas, 1983.
Pánico o peligro. Mexico City: Siglo XXI, 1983.
La forma del silencio. Mexico City: Siglo XXI, 1987.
Intentos. Mexico City: Grijalbo, 1987.
Itinerario de palabras (with Mónica Mansour). Mexico City: Folios, 1987.
Antonia. Mexico City: Grijalbo, 1989.
MLP/De cuerpo entero: El espacio de la escritura. Mexico City: UNAM/Corunda, 1990.
Lo que le pasa al lector. Mexico City: Grijalbo, 1991.
Las razones del lago. Mexico City: Grijalbo, 1992.
La ceremonia de iniciación. Mexico City: Fondo de Cultura Económica, 1994.
La viuda. Mexico City: Grijalbo, 1994.
Crónicas de una oriunda del kilómetro X en Michoacán. Mexico City: Consejo Nacional para la Cultura y las Artes, 1995.
La reina. Mexico City: Seix Barral, 1995.

Translations

"Helmut and Florian." Trans. Leland H. Chambers. *Mississippi Review* 16, no. 1 (1987): 66–70.
"The Trip." Trans. Nick Caistor. *The Faber Book of Contemporary Latin American Short Stories,* 86–91. London & Boston: Faber & Faber, 1989.
"The Hidden Language of Reality." Trans. Leland H. Chambers. *Rolling Stock* 17/18 (1990): 28.
"You Take Off for the Beach." Trans. Leland H. Chambers. *Rolling Stock* 17/18 (1990): 29.
"Butterflies." Trans. Alfred Mac Adam. *Review: Latin American Literature and Arts* 44 (January–June 1991): 17–38.
"Memories on the Oblique." Trans. Leland H. Chambers. *Scents of Wood and Silence: Short Stories by Latin American Women Writers.* Special issue of *Latin American Literary Review* 19, no. 37 (January–June 1991): 165–171.

"A Difficult Situation." Trans. Leland H. Chambers. *Latin American Literary Review* 20, no. 39 (January–June 1992): 58–61.

"The Hidden Language." Trans. Annette Cowart and Reginald Gibbons. *New Writing from Mexico*. Special issue of *TriQuarterly* 85 (Fall 1992): 317–335.

"The Natural Thing to Do." Trans. Judith de Mesa. *New Writing from Mexico*. Special issue of *TriQuarterly* 85 (Fall 1992): 219–225.

"New Paths." Trans. Elizabeth Gamble Miller. *Manoa: A Pacific Journal of International Writing* 4, no. 2 (Fall 1992): 17–20.

"The Trip." Trans. Nick Caistor. *Pyramids of Glass: Short Fiction from Modern Mexico*, 157–163. San Antonio: Corona, 1994.

Silvia Molina

Silvia Molina (1946)

About the Author and Her Writing

Conversations with the Writer

Representative Selections

The New House ["La casa nueva,"
from *Dicen que me case yo*]

What Would You Have Done? ["¿Qué hubieras hecho?,"
from *Dicen que me case yo*]

The Problem ["El problema," from *Imagen de Héctor*]

Bibliography

About the Author and Her Writing

Silvia Molina is serious, straightforward, and unassuming. She impresses one as a private person who has decided how to divide her professional life into its various interrelated components. In speaking with her, one notes that she chooses her words with care and comes across as well-bred, modest, and pensive. Whether explaining her own background and work or commenting on other writers, Molina strives to express herself with clarity and precision. Although more than busy with her many-faceted career and her family life, she finds time to attend to all of her responsibilities and to do so with an enviable level of equanimity. Molina gives off a sense of order and deliberation, qualities that are reflected in her writing as well. Her prose is simple and unadorned so as not to overshadow the characterizations or images that she is creating. She is variously amusing, serious, or erudite; she appropriates history, anthropology, and literature to lend authenticity to her fiction. Her novels give the impression that they are autobiographical when they are not. Silvia Molina plays at inventing herself in her work because, for her, writing is a game with its own rules. She so engrosses us, the readers, in her game of creation that we believe we recognize and can identify the author in her female protagonists. But all of this is what makes Molina the creative writer she is: a blend of her background, history, readings, and invention.

Silvia Molina, as one might expect, does not reveal much about her early years. One can glean some details from her fiction, but these are clearly questionable because the writer deliberately invents and reinvents herself and her family. Perhaps for Molina the early years were not particularly significant in her development as a writer. Born in Mexico City, the daughter of María Celis and Héctor Pérez Martínez, Molina is very much the product of the metropolis. Although she had been writing ever since she was a young girl, she never entertained the idea of becoming a professional writer. As an adolescent in preparatory school, she wrote her first (unpublished) novel, spilling out all that she wanted to tell in two months of frantic activity. Somehow, the Mexican writer José Agustín (1944) awoke in her an interest in literature, and for the first time, she viewed it as something personal and intimate. At that time, Molina believed that one wrote as one spoke, and only much later did she comprehend the craft of the writer. She came to be a reader of literature relatively late, something she attributes to the educational system that did more to distance her from reading than draw her to it.

Molina first studied anthropology at the Escuela Nacional de Antropología e Historia (National School of Anthropology and History), and this interest is present in her fiction, essays, and children's books. A number of years later, in 1976, she joined a writing workshop directed by Elena Poniatowska (1933) and Hugo Hiriart (1942), and it was there that she learned what it meant to be a writer. Almost by chance she produced her first novel, *La mañana debe seguir gris* (1977; *Gray Skies Tomorrow*, 1993), when, as part of the program, she began working on a short story with the aim of entering it into a contest. The story developed into a novel, was accepted by a publisher, and was awarded the Xavier Villaurrutia Prize.

The unexpected success of this first real effort made her lack of background in literature all the more patent to Silvia Molina. Now she realized that she wanted to be a writer, and that desire perforce required discipline and background. She was particularly concerned about her limited reading experience. To acquire this knowledge in a structured setting, she entered the National University in 1977, a decision that would lead to her active career as a writer, teacher, and editor. In 1979, she was awarded a scholarship at the Centro Mexicano de Escritores (Mexican Writers' Center).

Silvia Molina's literary output has been varied and constant since the 1977 publication of *La mañana debe seguir gris*, a novel about a young woman who leaves Mexico at the end of the 1960s, breaks with her family, and takes up with a lover. Three more novels have followed: *Ascensión Tun* (1981), concerning the ethnic struggles of the mid-nineteenth century in Yucatán and the miraculous ascent of a Mayan orphan; *La familia vino del norte* (The Family Came from the North; 1987), about a young woman's search for herself and the secrets of her grandfather, a general of the Revolution; and *Imagen de Héctor* (Image of Héctor; 1990), about the author's research to learn who her late father was. In addition, Molina has published three volumes of short stories: *Lides de estaño* (Tin Fights; 1984), *Dicen que me case yo* (They're Telling Me to Get Married; 1989), and *Un hombre cerca* (A Man Nearby; 1992). Her bibliography includes a one-act play, *Circuito cerrado* (Closed Circuit; 1995), and two volumes of essays—*Leyendo en la tortuga* (Reading About the Turtle; 1981) and *Campeche: Punta del ala del país* (Campeche: Wingtip of the Country; 1991), a book that traces the history of letters of the state of Campeche from pre-Columbian times to the present. It is noteworthy that in this work, which includes a brief anthology and bibliography, Molina writes about her father, Héctor Pérez Martínez, who was a writer, and includes a selection of his work.

Silvia Molina has also made a significant contribution to children's literature. She has written several books, some based on early Mexican legends, that make reading and learning about one's history attractive to young readers. Most likely her own early experience with reading has prompted her to produce books that will draw children to the printed page. Her efforts were rewarded in 1992 with the Premio Nacional de Literatura Infantil Juan de la Cabada (Juan de la Cabada National Prize for Children's Literature). Other facets of Molina's professional life involve teaching pre-Columbian literature at the National University, participating in writing workshops, and directing a small publishing company, Ediciones Corunda.

If one were to identify one thread that connects most of Molina's writing it would be her use of Mexican history to explore one's existence. To a greater or lesser degree, her four novels appropriate history to lend authenticity to her narration, bring a past event into the present, and show how reality can be seen from multiple points of view.

For this writer, using something real as a point of departure for her fiction is a necessity. From there, firmly anchored in a historical event or character, she begins her "game" of creation or recreation. It is game without an end or a solution, for it is the reader who must decide which version is real.

La mañana debe seguir gris, Molina's first novel, sets the tone and style for her later works of fiction. It begins with two preliminary chapters, each composed of brief diary-like entries by date. The entries chronicle the protagonist's relationship with the Mexican poet, José Carlos Becerra (1937–1970), and, as a counterpoint, report a contemporary world event. Consequently, in this chronology that runs from November 10, 1969, to May 27, 1970, the author has already told her entire story. But then the story is retold in twenty-three chapters, each preceded by Becerra's verses. The narrator/protagonist, a young woman whose name is never given, tells of her stay in London where she had gone to learn English. Shortly after her arrival, she meets the poet, and the attraction is mutual. Becerra and the new environment spark a feeling of independence in her. She begins to question who she is and strives to be free of the burden of her family. Contrary to what is expected of an upper-middle-class Mexican woman, she enters into an amorous relationship with Becerra, takes "the pill," looks for a job, and arranges to leave the home of her domineering aunt and share a flat with two other women. Just as things are falling into place and she has the money to join Becerra, who is traveling in Italy, she receives word that he has been killed in an automobile accident.

In this novel, which Molina insists is not autobiographical despite certain facts that coincide with her own experiences, the author presents a theme that will appear again and again in her later novels: the search for identity and self-realization which characterizes many of her female protagonists. In *La mañana debe seguir gris*, the unnamed narrator/protagonist is somewhat daring for her time and social position. Molina, using her sparse, rhythmical, and graceful prose, combines the public and the private by creating a story with real events and characters—Becerra, the Mexican poet, *was* killed in an automobile accident in Italy—and invented ones. Thus she lends authenticity to her work of fiction and makes it believable.

Ascensión Tun has a more complex structure. Here Molina makes use of her background in anthropology and history to create a novel that brings to life a historical period, the time of the caste wars in mid-nineteenth-century Yucatán. The work is situated between a preliminary chapter, "El mito" (The Myth), and a historical chronology and list of characters at the end. Thus the narration is propped up by documentary evidence to make it believable, even though some of the characters and events may be fictional. The myth is what the first-person narrator, an anthropologist, is investigating during a visit to the former poorhouse of Campeche. Little is known about the supposed miraculous ascent of a young Mayan orphan, Ascensión Tun, who lived there. The anthropologist, wanting to learn and document the facts, also consults the archives and a manuscript left by the former director of the poorhouse. From this research, a much larger and sadder picture emerges, constituting the bulk of the novel narrated in the third person. We are introduced to the poorhouse and its cast of characters, each with a personal story to tell. Ascensión Tun is orphaned through a disastrous flood and taken to live in the poorhouse. There he feels completely uprooted in an alien environment until he befriends an old Mayan healer, Juan Bautista Puc. This man, who had fought against the Mexican army in defense of Campeche, tells the child of their shared background and promises him his freedom. Another resident is Consuelo, a woman considered crazy because she is waiting for an Austrian captain who years earlier had first seduced and then abandoned her. Mateo, the administrator, is writing his memoirs and recalls his service in the army. Through these characters different perspectives are portrayed, as well as the human consequences of the struggle. The myth surrounding Ascensión Tun's miraculous ascent is clarified, for he actually died at the hands of Consuelo, who "freed" him.

The novel, with its narrations by different characters, gives the impression of simplicity. However, it is complex and somewhat fragmented, with excerpts from the ancient Mayan *Chilam Balam*, visions, dreams, prayers, nightmares, and prophecies. In *Ascensión Tun*, Silvia Molina works with many sources to create a work of fiction that allows the reader to piece together and ponder a lesser known period of Mexican history.

Molina's third and fourth novels, *La familia vino del norte* and *Imagen de Héctor*, reflect the work of a novelist who has developed and polished her craft. Both works share certain characteristics. They deal with a woman's search to unravel her past—the history of her family—and at the same time to define herself and reinforce her identity. The autobiographical elements are few in *La familia vino del norte* and many more in *Imagen de Héctor*, in which the novelist creates a feeling of authenticity through the use of family photographs, archival photographs of historical figures, the narration of historical events, and references to published source materials. However, neither novel rewrites history or claims to offer a definitive version. They both question the official renditions that history has recorded and, in looking for answers, recreate historical figures and events, giving the reader a different point of view to consider.

La familia vino del norte opens and closes with texts external to the novel that tell the reader what the work is about and give it a documentary character. Significantly, there is a short quotation from the Russian writer Boris Pilnyak (1894–?) about the "fox," who, as the god of cunning and betrayal, is the god of writers. A prologue consisting of two letters follows: one from Dorotea to X, a journalist, in which she tells him of her plans to publish a double story, that of their personal relationship and a corrected version of his rendition of her grandfather's story; the other letter is X's response advising her to let the manuscript rest and to omit certain details that might be damaging to his career. The epilogue is a short letter from Dorotea to X telling him that he will be called Manuel in her novel *La familia vino del norte*. Framed by these letters is Dorotea's novel, appearing as a novel within a novel with several stories unfolding simultaneously. Composed of two parts, each preceded by a page of old photographs, the novel is narrated by different voices in the first person and also by an omniscient narrator in the third person. *La familia vino del norte* tells of Dorotea's search for her own identity as she learns about her family's secret. The death and funeral of her grandfather, General Teodoro Leyva—who had served in the revolutionary army from the state of Sonora and had supported the 1927 revolt of Francisco Serrano against the reelection of Alvaro Obregón to the presidency—sparks her interest in learning about her grandfather's past and in trying to make sense out of the fragments she had picked up as a little girl. She was particularly curious about why he had spent a year hiding in his mother's cellar. For Dorotea, her grandfather's death, rather than a closure, serves as an opening that will lead her along a circuitous route to her own freedom and independence.

Dorotea is a young woman of twenty-four, alienated from her family and its values, and unsettled in her profession as a biologist. She meets and later does some clerical work for a forty-six-year-old journalist, Manuel, a man who is arrogant, all-knowing, and very sure of himself. He is manipulative and wants to remake Dorotea. She innocently shares with him the little she knows about her grandfather, and the two set out to learn General Teodoro Leyva's secret. The story unfolds and moves both in the present and in the recent and distant past. Dorotea calls upon her memory of conversations with her grand-father in which he spoke of his service in the revolutionary army. In fact, he himself narrates a chapter that takes us back to Venustiano Carranza and the struggle over the succession to his presidency (1920). It is at that time that Leyva became a supporter of Alvaro Obregón. Dorotea tries to get more information from her grandmother, and by accident, she picks up some handwritten notes and photographs of her grandfather. She appeals to her father for the truth, for an end to the secrets and game-playing. He provides additional details about the grandfather's support of Francisco Serrano, who opposed Obregón's reelection. General Leyva, although a faithful supporter of Obregón, could not betray one of the principles of the Revolution—no reelec-tion. That position caused him to go into hiding to avoid arrest and execution by Obregón's supporters.

Dorotea shares her information with Manuel, who is pursuing leads on his own mainly through archival sources. At the same time, their relationship is undergoing significant changes as Dorotea realizes that Manuel is trying to control her and that his greatest interest is his own ambition. She declares her independence, moves to her own apartment, decides to study history, and becomes an avid reader of literature and history. She speaks of her readings that include Boris Pilnyak, a Russian writer, very much aware of the discrepancy between revolutionary ideals and reality, who disappeared in the purges of the late 1930s; Jean Rhys (1894–1979), a British writer whose *After Leaving Mr. MacKenzie* (1931) about struggling women left a marked impression on her; Martín Luis Guzmán (1887–1976), whose *La sombra del caudillo* (The Shadow of the Tyrant; 1929) is a classic novel of the Revolution and deals with the Serrano revolt; John W. F. Dulles (1913), whose *Yesterday in Mexico: A Chronicle of the Revolution, 1919–1936* (1961) covers the period of her research. And then Manuel, without telling her of his intentions or giving her appropriate credit for the research, publishes his version of her grandfather's story. For Dorotea, this is an act of betrayal.

Dorotea continues her search for the true story by transcribing her grandfather's notes, which turn out to be a diary, by learning more from her grandmother before her death, and by finally piecing together the puzzle with a detail supplied by the family cook. She then writes her version, appropriating Manuel's article and her grandfather's diary, thus recreating what history had denied or altered.

La familia vino del norte immerses us into the Revolution of 1910 and makes us relive the twenties and thirties with the important figures of the time. However, in addition to the historical events, there is an emphasis on the human consequences of how these events affected families for generations. Molina focuses on the Serrano revolt against the reelection of Obregón and the tragic outcome of Obregón's attempt to betray the principles of the Revolution. She also takes us back in history to Venustiano Carranza and forward to Lázaro Cárdenas. In doing so, she makes the past a present reality, even for a generation born long after the events portrayed. Dorotea, despite her rebellion against her family and its values, realizes that she is part of its reality and history. Through her research, she learned who she was and what she wanted to do with her life. Ironically, her grandmother's inheritance, which she had so scorned, gave her the freedom and economic independence that she as a woman needed. Manuel's betrayal had the positive effect of leading to her intellectual development and to her striking out on her own. As for history and truth, there are different versions. The historian, the journalist, the diarist, and the novelist, each writes with a different point of view and for different reasons. Even Dorotea pays tribute to the "fox," the god of writers, by consciously taking liberties in recreating her story.

As for any autobiographical elements in this novel, General Teodoro Leyva is a composite figure based on Molina's three uncles, brothers of her mother, who were generals. One of them, Manuel Celis, did hide in his mother's cellar for a year, and that anecdote is the basis for the story. The rest is fiction.

Imagen de Héctor is the most autobiographical work of Molina. In this novel, not narrated in the first person, the writer constructs the history and puts into focus the blurred image of her late father, Héctor Pérez Martínez (1906-1948), who died when she was a year old. The protagonist searches for her father in his own works, his diary, and his photographs. She consults official sources like newspapers and published interviews; she speaks with his relatives, friends, and colleagues. In doing so, she hopes to define herself, establish her independent identity, and relieve herself of the burden of being "la hijita de Héctor" (Héctor's little daughter). Molina, using the technique of metafiction, observes and describes her act of creation by presenting her readers with her research as it progresses and her portrait of Héctor as it develops.

The story is preceded by a quote from the novel *Imagen de nadie* (Image of Nobody; 1932) written by her father, Héctor Pérez

Martínez, followed by a brief section entitled "El problema" (The Problem). The problem is outlined in ten very short chapters of unequal length. In them we are told why she wants to find Héctor and make of the legend and the heroic figure a real story with a human protagonist. She takes us back to her childhood and her belief until the age of five that her father was alive but away on a trip. This belief was nurtured by her family that denied his death by keeping his bow ties and eyeglasses ready and displaying his photographs and books. The vague memories of her father and the myths that were perpetuated were everywhere, stalking her like a ghost. The novel itself is composed of two parts, separated by several pages of photographs, and concludes with an epilogue in which the writer puts an end to her search wondering what her father might have thought of the image his daughter had created of him.

Imagen de Héctor is narrated in the third person, and most of the family members are generally not referred to by name. The daughter who is gathering information about her father is called "la Hija Menor" (the Youngest Daughter) or "Ella" (She); her father is Héctor or "El" (He); her mother is "la Esposa de Héctor" (Héctor's Wife); her aunts are "las Hermanas de Héctor" (Héctor's Sisters); her grandmother is "la Madre de Héctor" (Héctor's Mother). Molina in this way creates an impersonal portrait of herself and her family, as if she were describing people not at all connected to her. The narration also moves forward and backward in time, sometimes projecting filmlike clips of incidents or events out of chronological order.

We observe la Hija Menor as she gathers information by going back to her recollections of childhood with a nanny, Miss Heidi, or to the time she sat in Héctor's closet among his clothes and books he had written, or to her trip to Campeche where her father was born and lived for part of his short life. She recalls a visit with la Madre de Héctor, a sweet old lady for whom time had stood still and whose memory, in the midst of its confusion, could reconstruct images of those long since gone. From her and from one of las Hermanas de Héctor she learned the details of her father's early years, first as a student at the Instituto Campechano and later at the Escuela Nacional Preparatoria in Mexico City, and finally at the National University where he studied dentistry, a profession he hardly practiced, preferring to devote himself to journalism. Then there were Héctor's friends, who provided the itinerary of Héctor's life as a journalist and writer. She learned of his work on the newspaper *El Nacional*, the books he wrote and published, and his increasing interest in and concern about Mexico's social and political problems. He was named federal delegate for the state of Campeche (1937) and elected governor of Campeche (1939–1943). What gave her a deeper insight into her father was his *Juárez, el impasible* (Juárez, the Dispassionate One; 1934), a biographical work that portrayed a human Benito Juárez. Almost by chance, she learned how her mother had met and married Héctor in 1934. Héctor's library revealed him as a true bibliophile, and the old newspapers stored there finally clarified for la Hija Menor that Héctor had died of cardiac arrest as a result of progressive heart and kidney disease.

Whereas the first part of the novel is entitled "El mito" (The Myth), the second is "La reconstrucción" (The Reconstruction). The "reconstruction" begins with a close examination of Héctor's library that la Hija Menor had transferred to her house. She records her observations in a notebook—Héctor was a stutterer, he had a lover, he was an honest and uncorrupted politician, he was genuinely concerned about the welfare of his state and its constituents. In her notes she sometimes refers to Héctor as "mi papá" (my father), words that rang hollow because they had no context. The library revealed the existence of a diary, which proved to be a disappointment for la Hija Menor. She had hoped for an intimate document, but instead found a political one dealing with the governorship of Campeche. The personal correspondence revealed that Héctor had political enemies. At the end of his term as governor, Héctor returned to Mexico City and was appointed Undersecretary of the Interior by President Manuel Avila Camacho, and then Secretary of the Interior by President Miguel Alemán. There was evidence in the correspondence and other documents that Héctor was aware of his failing health, which took his life at forty-two years of age.

Imagen de Héctor became Molina's portrait of her father as a counterpoint to his book *Imagen de nadie*. What kind of image did she draw? One that was unfinished and subject to alterations because she realized that he, like everyone else, was the result of all that came before, that any search for truth was open-ended and variable. La Hija Menor puts an end to her notes and to her obsession, feeling relieved of the burden that she had borne for so long. She wonders what Héctor might have thought of her image of him and concludes wistfully that he probably would have wondered who his Hija Menor was, for he never got to know her.

Not only does *Imagen de Héctor* immerse the reader in the family of the writer, because much of the narration is based on the life of Héctor

Pérez Martínez, but the book is grounded very solidly in the history of Mexico of the thirties and forties. Politicians, writers, presidents, and governors pass through its pages giving the reader more than a glimpse of the political and intellectual life of the period. We as readers can form our own image of Héctor Pérez Martínez, who seems to represent the possible but rare union of politics and intellect. And through this novel the writer has revealed something of herself. Consciously or unconsciously, Silvia Molina is a link in the generational chain, and her reality was formed in part by her father.

Molina's three collections of short stories—*Lides de estaño, Dicen que me case yo*, and *Un hombre cerca*—primarily depict women as they face or cope with the problems that contemporary society inevitably forces upon them. Her women are young, old, little girls, married, single, faithful and unfaithful wives, mothers, and daughters. Each confronts a different problem, many of which, having no solution, give rise to bitterness, loneliness, or fantasies.

From the collection *Dicen que me case yo* (which includes most of the stories of *Lides de estaño*), "La casa nueva" (The New House) portrays the bitterness of a young woman who, even many years after the incident described, cannot forget the cruelty of her father. When she was a little girl, he took her halfway across the city to see their new house, a dream house. He showed her its many bedrooms, the bathroom, the kitchen; he assigned rooms to the different members of the family. It was everything she had always wanted but had never had. Then, dragging her away abruptly, he shattered the illusion by telling her that the house will be theirs when they win the raffle.

"El regreso" (The Return) is the poignant story of a young woman who returns to Campeche to deal with her grandfather's inheritance. It quickly becomes clear to her that her greedy uncles are doing all they can to complicate the distribution of the estate. Finally, to put an end to the constant fights, she agrees to accept an old house as her inheritance. When she goes to look at it, she realizes that a poor, deaf-mute woman whom she had run into a number of times lives there. Now she truly has a problem.

In "¿Qué hubieras hecho?" (What Would You Have Done?) Molina presents a painful picture of two women—the lady of the house and a maid. The lady, feeling uncomfortable and guilty, goes to the Plaza de San Jacinto, a place where those looking for work gather. She has mixed feelings as she observes the crowd of men and women offering their services to those who drive up in their cars seeking domestic help. It reminds her of a slave market, but she moves forward in the line and announces that she is looking for someone to work in the kitchen and care for a small child. Her offer of six thousand pesos is rejected by one woman, but another gladly agrees and jumps into her car. Something about Manuela Sánchez is disconcerting: she doesn't look or dress like a maid and she seems somewhat aggressive. When the lady arrives at her home, she calls her girlfriend, the one who had suggested she seek help at the Plaza de San Jacinto, and the rest of the story is a telephone conversation, a monologue, in which she describes her fears and suspicions. The phone of Manuela's only reference was always busy, she behaved almost as if she were the lady of the house, she liked classical music, she knew some English. When she asked to borrow two hundred pesos to repay a loan, it seemed like the perfect opportunity to be rid of Manuela. However, she returns in a very cheerful mood, and it becomes evident that she has been drinking. When the lady insists that she leave, Manuela begs to be allowed to tell her that she isn't a nobody or a thief. She presents her husband's identification card from the Ministry of Public Education with her photograph and another picture of her two daughters. How could someone sink so low? What would you have done?

"Recomenzar" (Starting Over) is a moving story told by María López to an unidentified listener. In it she reveals her struggle to survive after a cancer operation and her simultaneous struggle to be her own person. Faced with the specter of death, she becomes strong and determined to live her life on her terms and to stop living and behaving as she had been taught. She is tired of being a teacher, of having her mother-in-law as a visitor in her apartment, of letting others make decisions for her. Her husband, Santiago, can't accept her attitude nor cope with this new reality. In a fit of rage, he tells her that she is going to die anyway, to which she calmly responds that whatever is left of her life she will live in her own way. Recollections of her childhood come back to her—a father who abandoned the family for another woman, a great-grandfather who, with advancing age, lost his sight and the ability to recognize others. María fights to cling to life, as former friends fade into the background and as she and her husband separate because the woman he married no longer exists. María wants to start over and be herself.

"La pulsera" (The Bracelet) concerns a woman who has just given birth to her first child in a hospital and is frantically trying to reach her physician by phone. She has noticed that the plastic identification bracelet on her wrist bears the name López, and hers is Mendoza. No one seems to care as they take her to Mrs. López's room, have her put on the other woman's nightgown, and try to give her the other woman's medication. Mrs. Mendoza is frantic because she wants to make certain that the babies haven't been exchanged, but everyone treats her as if she were a child and, with a pat on the head, tells her not to worry since all babies wear bracelets as well.

From the collection *Un hombre cerca*, the story "Domingo" (Sunday) depicts a woman, separated from her husband, who is having an affair with a married man. When she awakens without him at her side, memories of fear and loneliness come back. She recalls how frightened and alone she felt after separating from her husband, how boring Sundays had been with him. This memory triggers others of how as a little girl she spent Sundays with her parents and grandparents eating breakfast in a restaurant and strolling in the park, and of how as a university student she spent Sundays with friends exploring places of interest nearby. Usually her lover spends Sundays with his family, and she shuts him out of her mind. But this Sunday he comes back to be with her.

"Hospital" deals with the problem of an aging father and his relationship to his adult daughters. One daughter, Luisa, has lived with her father since the death of the mother. The other daughter, who is the narrator, never got along with him and resented his treatment of her mother. When her father falls and is hospitalized for surgery, Luisa calls her, and they both stay at the hospital to care for the old man. At his bedside, the narrator is overwhelmed with mixed feelings about her father, who had reduced her mother to a passive woman without self-esteem, and she silently wishes that the mother were in the hospital so that she might care for her. The father, when he awakens, rejects her completely and asks for Luisa, who knows she is the only one who can really care for him.

In "Mentira piadosa" (White Lie), Molina touches upon several themes of today's society. Carmela, after a lapse of some twenty-five years, runs into Eugenia, and the memories come rushing back. Eugenia—pretty, well-developed, and different from the other girls—entered the third year of secondary school at sixteen. Carmela, barely fourteen, tries to befriend her and notices bruises and lacerations on her arms and legs. Supposedly, Eugenia's mother hits her with a belt because she disapproves of her boyfriend. One day Eugenia persuades Carmela to accompany her to "the dentist," who turns out to be an abortionist. Carmela, still very much a child, can't cope with this experience and feels betrayed by her friend, who took advantage of her friendship and ignorance. It is only after meeting Eugenia twenty-five years later and having dinner with her that she demands to know what the abortion and Eugenia's disappearance shortly thereafter were all about. And so Eugenia, still very attractive, relates the sad story of her adolescence—a stepfather who knew that a married friend of his was forcing her to drink and was abusing her sexually, a mother who beat her, school girls who shunned her. She finally escaped and married at seventeen, after which she had two more husbands. Carmela can't forget what she has heard, just as she never forgot what had drawn her to Eugenia so many years earlier.

Silvia Molina has been working at being a writer all her adult life. Realizing the chasm between wanting to write and doing it professionally, she studied the craft by working with its practitioners and by intensive reading. Not only does she write for herself and for what it tells her about herself, but she brings the world of literature and reading to others. In furthering this aim, all her activities complement one another. Whether writing her own fiction, running a publishing company, or producing children's books, Molina is emphasizing the importance of literature and trying to bring it to a wide reading public.

Molina's fiction, especially her novels, demonstrates her breadth of vision, her incursions into Mexican history and anthropology, and her creation of women characters in search of their identity. Whether the characters are autobiographical or not takes second place to their struggle to strike out on their own and break away from traditional families and conventional roles. They symbolize today's women and point in the direction of self-realization and independence. In her short stories, Molina depicts many of society's problems. These may be relationships between husbands and wives, parents and children, or lovers. Her stories often reveal feelings of despair and bitterness or contradictions. As in her novels, she uses a simple and unadorned prose style to make her point and let the problem or action speak for itself.

Silvia Molina is committed to her profession and can be counted on to continue making a contribution to literature. The novel she is currently working on about a relationship between a man and a woman through an exchange of letters promises to be another challenge to Molina's creative and narrative skills.

Conversations with the Writer
AUGUST 10, 1992; JANUARY 9, 1994

How and when did you begin to write?

I began writing as a very young girl, but when I was in preparatory school I wrote my first novel, which was never published. It was called *Esos fueron los días* [Those Were the Days], and I wrote it after reading José Agustín's *De perfil* [In Profile; 1966], because for the first time literature became something I could identify with, something that could happen to me, in my neighborhood, in my city, and to my friends. By the way, my title was taken from a song, "Those Were the Days."

I had been accustomed to the Mexican educational system that distanced us from literature. As children we used to read *Don Quixote* [1605, 1615], the classics, literature for which we hadn't been properly prepared. And almost always we were given texts that we couldn't understand, that we couldn't feel. And when I read José Agustín [1944], I got so excited—I felt that he was talking directly to me and about my city—that I wrote my first novel from beginning to end. For two months I sat and wrote, never realizing that I would be a writer some day. But I had a story to tell, and I sat down to develop my novel, which really had very little to do with the literature of José Agustín and with his use of language. I thought that José Agustín wrote as he spoke, and that is not so. Obviously, José Agustín was a writer who polished his texts constantly. I didn't have any idea about the craft of writing, but I felt that I had something to tell and I told my story, in what was for me a natural tone of voice, about what was happening to me at that time, with my friends, in the city in which I happened to live. It wasn't until many years later that I wrote my first real novel.

And why didn't you publish Esos fueron los días?

I didn't publish it because I wrote it out of a sense of need, as an impulse. I think I had a lot built up inside of me, and I let it all out in that novel. But later, much later, in 1976, I joined a writing workshop because I heard that José Agustín was teaching there. At that time literary workshops were very much in fashion in Mexico. However, when I got there I didn't meet José Agustín. But anyway, it was in that workshop that I really learned the craft of the writer. And I realized that my novel was very poorly written because I had sat down to write it from

75   Silvia Molina

beginning to end without paying attention to grammar or to structure or to anything else. I simply threw myself into that first book. That's why I never published it.

When and how did you begin to publish?

When I went into the writing workshop in 1976, Elena Poniatowska [1933] and Hugo Hiriart [1942] were the coordinators. At that time, there was a short-story contest that I wanted to enter with a story of mine that I thought had a very good theme, and I began to write what would later become *La mañana debe seguir gris*. But I kept on thinking that I didn't know how to write a short story, never realizing that I was writing a novel. I had filled up many pages and still I couldn't finish telling all that I wanted and fit it into a short story. Then, of course, I didn't enter the contest, far from it. But I was very far along in my text.

When I finished the novel I gave it to Hugo Hiriart to read, and he told me to take it to Joaquín Díez-Canedo, the director of the publishing company Joaquín Mortiz. I didn't feel that I was a writer. It was natural for me to write but without pretensions to being a writer. But Hugo convinced me, and I went with him and Elena Poniatowska—they both accompanied me—to leave my novel with Joaquín Díez-Canedo. Don Joaquín told me, "Call me in a month," and I didn't call him because I thought that he would say, "Come and pick up your manuscript." But then they called me for an appointment, and I realized that they were going to publish the novel. Don Joaquín was very nice and said, "Silvia, anything that you write from now on, I will publish for you, I will be your editor." And my book was published very quickly, and for that novel I was awarded the Xavier Villaurrutia Prize. That's how I got started.

I never planned that "I am going to be a writer and I am going to publish this novel," but I also wrote that novel because it was something that I wanted to relate to myself. I wanted to understand certain things and modify others. It is a novel that has some autobiographical aspects. However, it is very much reworked. What I narrate is not what happened in real life. It is my way of understanding some things in my life that I had lost somehow.

My problem after that was that I was a very poor reader because of what I mentioned to you earlier. As long as the Mexican educational system is not revised, what it does is distance students, both children and adolescents, from the pleasure of reading. They don't teach us that literature is something in which we can see ourselves reflected, that it is something through which we can understand ourselves; but rather it is made into a very difficult chore.

It was after that I knew that I wanted to be a writer—I was very frightened when they gave me the Villaurrutia Prize—and I decided to enter the university and study literature, because through force and discipline, I would have to read what any student of literature had to read. It was going to be very necessary for my profession, and there at the university I got my degree in literature. And without intending to, I put a book together at that time as well. A teacher, Huberto Batis [1934], who for many years had been directing cultural supplements and literary magazines in Mexico, was giving a course called "Methods and Techniques of Research." I already knew how to do research and always liked it a great deal. He had us prepare index cards about literature, and I decided that instead of cataloguing roses or carnations, I would catalogue one single animal for the assignment: the turtle. And by the end of the semester I had finished another book. Once again I showed it to Hugo Hiriart, who said it was very nice. He also told Martín Casillas, of the publishing company Martín Casillas Editores, and Martín published it for me.

What book was it?

It is called *Leyendo en la tortuga* and is something like a dictionary. It deals with the turtle in mythology, magic, religion, literature, and old dictionaries. And afterward the same publisher, Martín Casillas, published my *Ascensión Tun*. I didn't submit it to Joaquín Mortiz because, although he is a lovely person, he really doesn't make much of an effort to promote his books. Even though I had gotten the Villaurrutia Prize, my book wasn't in any bookstore. Later I was lucky to have my novel *La mañana debe seguir gris* become part of the collection "Lecturas Mexicanas" [Mexican Readings] published by the Ministry of Public Education, and then it was really distributed widely. Some thirty or forty thousand copies were sold. Afterward it was republished by Cal y Arena, and now it is used as a textbook in high schools and preparatory schools. That might also be because of my use of language. I had two books published by Martín Casillas—*Ascensión Tun* and *Leyendo en la tortuga*. That's how I started.

As part of your literary training, what writers did you read?

As part of the normal preparation of any Mexican student, I read all the classics of Spanish literature. But I really became interested in literature through the writing of young people and not through the classics. That is to say, the generation of José Agustín, Gustavo Sainz [1940], Parménides García Saldaña [1944–1982], etc., opened the world of literature to me. When I began to read them, I became excited about literature, and from then on I began to read different people. At that time I read a lot of poetry—Jaime Sabines [1925], for example—and afterward, while studying literature at the university, I reread with greater depth everything that was literature, especially Spanish American literature.

But in my training I think that the work of Elena Garro and that of the English writer Jean Rhys [1894–1979] have been particularly important. The first work of Elena Garro [1920] that I read was *La semana de colores* [The Week of Colors; 1964]. I really understood that here was a very intelligent writer who was telling me a lot about the life of Mexicans in rural and urban areas, but with a special kind of magic that I didn't find in texts written by other Mexican women. There was something in her writing that made literature interesting for me. And afterward, when I read *Los recuerdos del porvenir* [1963; *Recollections of Things to Come,* 1969], I almost fell in love with the magic of Elena Garro's writing. I had met her when I lived in Paris when I was fourteen and admired her a great deal as a woman. I even met her here later on when I was fifteen, and she called me from her hotel and asked me to visit her. But at that time I hadn't read anything of hers, I wasn't interested in literature. I hadn't been trained as yet. And when I read *Los recuerdos del porvenir*, I realized that literature was more than simply wanting to tell a story. I understood that one had to tell a story, but that stories had their narrative voices.

On the other hand, Jean Rhys is very basic for my work because she is a writer who has always invented herself. She is no longer alive; she died in 1979 at the age of eighty-five, quite old. But she wrote nine books. For me the most important ones were *Good Morning, Midnight* [1939], *After Leaving Mr. MacKenzie* [1931], *Sleep It Off, Lady* [1976], and a novel called *Quartet* [1928]. I thought to myself, I know Jean Rhys, I know her inwardly. And I realized that it wasn't so, I realized that Jean Rhys had invented herself and had made me, as a reader, believe that I knew her. What I was doing was simply becoming part of her game of creation. And it really struck me because I was doing the same thing in my work. That is to say, everyone believes that my work has a great deal to do with my autobiography, but it doesn't. What happens is that I play a game of inventing myself in each one of my works.

Everyone confuses me with the narrator. On the one hand, it is a very playful way for me to write, and on the other, it allows me to experience things that in everyday life we don't experience. It is an interesting game; literature has really become for me a game with complicated rules, which as in all games, like tennis or any other sport, one has to follow. Therefore, I think that for me, Elena Garro and Jean Rhys have been the two fundamental writers.

Which writers influenced your prose?

As writers, I really wouldn't know. I don't remember having read the works of many writers to see how they wrote. I remember having read, for example, Martín Luis Guzmán [1887–1976], Jorge Ibargüengoitia [1928–1983], Vicente Leñero [1933], Octavio Paz [1914], etc., but just for pleasure. I don't think that I ever stopped to analyze their use of language or to analyze the structure of their works. I really can't answer that question because I don't feel that I was influenced by anyone. Nor do I feel that any writer has in any way triggered my work.

Do you prefer European, Spanish American, or North American writers?

I read many writers, women writers, above all European and American, even Canadian when I can. Of course, I have read all the Latin American women writers. That is also why the work of Jean Rhys interested me, because we Latin American women are used to viewing ourselves with a bit of caution, with a bit of compassion. We are used to being in the period of our infancy, with a certain amount of nostalgia. And I believe that the American and European writers have gone beyond this stage. They view women with harshness, even themselves with a degree of cruelty or little compassion. That's why their writing is more authentic for me. I mean that it reflects more of what can happen to me than those days of happy endings and all that nostalgia about one's infancy. It is precisely for that reason that they interest me because they are more attuned to the world in which we live. The stories of other Mexican or Latin American writers often seem to concentrate on the family and are very traditional.

What do think of the women writers of your generation?

I think that in my generation there are truly interesting women writers—María Luisa Puga [1944], for example. What is interesting about her is that she began to write outside of Mexico. Although many of her plots are set outside of Mexico, specifically in her early novels, in some way she is talking about Mexico. She is talking about Africa, but since it is third world, she creates a bridge between Africa and Mexico. She is an intelligent writer, her work is provocative, and I like it a great deal. Then there is another interesting writer, Aline Pettersson [1938]. They are the only women writers of my generation who began to publish at the same time and are more or less the same age. I may be the youngest. Of my generation, Puga and Pettersson are the two writers that interest me most.

Is there a Mexican literature "written by women"?

I always have problems with the term "feminine." Even I—and I don't feel that I'm a feminist or anything—recognize that in my work there is perhaps a feminine point of view. The critics, in particular, have said that my work is very subtle and that my use of language is transparent, very delicate. But I always have something of a problem with that term. I prefer not to talk about feminine or feminist literature but rather about literature written by women.

Do you attribute the success of your novels to their themes, style, or to the fact that their author is a woman?

I think that in *La mañana debe seguir gris*, which was my first novel, I caused a breaking away. I myself didn't realize it until now that I am thinking about it. There was a breaking away from the work that was being done before. Just as José Agustín and the writers of his generation broke with the previous generation, I believe I also broke to some extent with the earlier generations, because for the first time a woman's voice writes in first person and, in addition, uses the real names of the real characters in her novel. For that reason I think that my first novel was more of a commercial success, because although I was doing a recreation of an event—if not, the book would have been a memoir or a chronicle—it was something that hadn't been customary in Mexico at that time. What I mean is that we writers all use reality as a point of departure to relate something, and that reality is then transformed. But few writers leave the names of characters taken from real life and allow one to identify them. And I believe that it is difficult to do what I did, because although I am not telling a verifiable truth, I have to be credible when creating characters who use their own names. It doesn't matter if a Chinese person reads the novel and doesn't know who the characters are, but if a Mexican reads it and knows them he can say, "So-and-so wasn't like that."

I don't think that I can attribute my success to the fact that I am a woman, since writers like Elena Garro, Elena Poniatowska, Luisa Josefina Hernández [1928], and Rosario Castellanos [1925–1974] had already opened the doors of literature to us. I also believe that we are a product of the writing workshops, of the closeness and growth that occurred after 1968 with regard to the writing of the young people.

I think that in reality the success that my work may have had—I don't know if I am mistaken or if I haven't thought about it until now—could also be because my women are somewhat rebellious, women who are trying to break away from their family traditions, from society's traditions, and who are seeking authenticity in their identities, in their professions. I am a simple and straightforward person. That is reflected to some degree in my writing, which is not very complicated. I don't dwell on creating the metaphors and images of a masterpiece. Rather I try to have my language emerge as clearly as possible. My craft has always consisted of pruning and refining rather than adding. It could be for that reason, but I don't think because I am a woman.

Has being a woman made your career difficult?

No, not really for me. I can't speak for other women writers, but I don't think that it was difficult for the others of my generation either. I believe it was so for the generation of Elena Poniatowska and Rosario Castellanos, because they were the first women to have the drive. But no, for my generation it wasn't difficult any longer. It is as hard as for any contemporary writer, because in Mexico we writers cannot yet live from our writing and we always have several occupations. In that sense, yes. But I am fortunate in a way that perhaps some of my colleagues aren't, because I can work at something I really like, which is producing books. But as I mentioned, my first novel came out very quickly, and as a result, the doors of publishers were opened to me. Afterward, Océano (now Cal y Arena) asked to publish my novel *La familia vino del norte*. Even before I had finished the novel, Océano told me that they would publish it, which was unbelievable for me. Therefore, I can't say that I really have had a problem.

Is there a relationship between your journalism and your creative writing?

No, none. Maybe there was at one time, because after I studied literature at the university, I did devote myself to literary criticism for a while. I wrote literary criticism for some of the cultural supplements, but I didn't do news reporting. No, my writing really has nothing to do with journalism.

Do you think that there is a feminine way of writing that is different from a masculine way of writing?

I don't think so. I think that people write the same way. I do believe that there can be a feminine point of view and a masculine point of view. But I also believe that both men and women are capable of appropriating one another's point of view. That's why novels like *Anna Karenina* [1875–1877] about female characters have been written by men, or why women have written about men from the masculine point of view.

Are there any autobiographical elements in your narrative works?

Some, yes. But as I have said before, I always play at inventing myself. I almost always start from a reality. In my first novel, *La mañana debe seguir gris*, it is true that I took that trip to England and that I met José Carlos Becerra [1937–1970], a Mexican poet who died in an automobile accident in Italy. And after that, it is anyone's guess what really happened between us. But what I wanted to relate is in that book. What is very interesting is that the female narrator is nameless, and she doesn't have a name because it is not me. Had it been me I would have left my name, but I was creating a character there. It got to the point that the producers of an audiocassette here in Mexico gave my name to the character. Instead of just calling the female narrator, "narrator," they said "Silvia," and I stopped the circulation of the audiocassette. It's not that I care what they say, but what bothers me is that they are negating my work of creating a character. It's not me. That it may sound like me is fine, as long as what I say is believable.

And then, for example, in the character Dorotea of *La familia vino del norte*, it may also be that there is something of me, perhaps my tone of voice. But I don't have that grandmother, nor did I have that grandfather, nor did I know Manuel, nor anything else. I am simply playing. It is very easy for me when I understand the character and she is part of me, because then I can let her come out more easily. You might say that little by little I become the character. Then I can play at doing many things that I couldn't do in real life. Another thing that concerns me a great deal in my work is that it must be believable. I play a lot with rules of reality to make things credible in my work. Perhaps that also has something to do with the confusion between the narrator and the author.

Are you working on something new?

I am working on another novel. I don't know yet what it will be called or when I am going to finish it because it will take me a while. But I have finished a number of children's books, one called *El misterioso caso de la perra extraviada* [The Mysterious Case of the Lost Dog; 1992], published by the Ministry of Public Education, and distributed to all the schools in the country. Another, *Mi Familia y La Bella Durmiente cien años después* [My Family and the Sleeping Beauty a Hundred Years Later; 1993], won the Juan de la Cabada National Prize for Children's Literature.

How did you become interested in children's literature?

In Mexico we don't have a tradition of children's literature as they do in other countries. There were neither readers nor publishers who concerned themselves with children's literature. And I found myself working for a publishing company that imported many collections of children's books from Spain to sell here in Mexico. I then realized the variety of things that could be published for children and the importance of having our children read texts written by Mexican authors. What was happening until that time was that we were importing from Argentina or Spain, but those books were not adapted for Mexican children, and there are language differences. That is when I began to become interested in the field of children's literature.

Later I was the director of a different publishing company, and there I learned that no Mexican writer wanted to write for children. All of them viewed—and many still view—the genre of children's literature as a subgenre. A story for children was something they didn't tackle because it lacked prestige. And I came to the realization at that time that, although writing for children was exceptionally difficult, it was very noble and well remunerated. Faced with the problem of getting appropriate texts for children, I told myself, "Well, you can do it yourself." And that is really how I began to write for children.

Does your interest in writing for children have something to do with your own reading experience as a child?

Yes, a great deal. I read many things with my daughters that I should have read as a child. I took special care that they read as children, but there was really very little I could offer them. The books available were few or were very poor translations. That also prompted me to become involved in the field to the point that I am now an editor of children's books. My publishing company has put out several collections of books for Mexican children, and I am very interested that Mexican authors write for them.

What Mexican writers are writing children's books?

Those who are writing are María Luisa Puga, Aline Pettersson, David Martín del Campo [1952], Juan Villoro [1956], Carmen Boullosa [1954], Vicente Leñero, Eraclio Zepeda [1937], José Agustín. All of them have produced texts for children. More recently a group of young writers who are not yet recognized has appeared. Other contemporary Mexican writers usually do not write for children because they don't want to, because they can't, or because they don't like it. It is a pity that many real writers don't want to devote some of their passion to write for children.

Going back to the novel you are working on, does it have a historical theme?

No, it doesn't have a historical theme. It is something like a game of letters, of correspondence in which we never see the correspondence. It is about a man who receives a letter signed with a pseudonym. The woman who sends the letter wants to begin a correspondence with him and asks him to tell her things. And he at this time is seeing an attorney because he is getting divorced and has certain problems to resolve. He consults the attorney about whether he can answer the letter, because he is interested in playing the game. The attorney tells him, "Either the woman is a maniac, because there are many of them, or it is someone who knows you well and is playing a game with you." And they make certain with the lawyer that she register the pseudonym and that she can't use the letters to blackmail him. And he begins to have a correspondence with her, but in truth no one ever sees the letters. He keeps a kind of diary—sometimes a monologue in which her letters appear—commented on by him in the second person, but his letters don't appear with them. And an entire relationship is begun in which the two can lie to one another about what they are saying.

In Mexico there has been a generation of notable women writers before yours. Which ones do you admire and why? Do you believe that the presence of that group helped those that followed them?

As I have said before, I admire Elena Garro and Rosario Castellanos above all. I don't think my novel *Ascensión Tun*, for example, is *indigenista* like the work of Rosario Castellanos. But there is something, some influence, but from another perspective. However, what I considered the best of Rosario Castellanos were her short stories. I was really trained at Elena Poniatowska's side, I was in her workshop. She is a very diligent and hard-working woman, and I particularly admired her skill in producing her very special kind of journalism. There is another important writer, Luisa Josefina Hernández [1928], who is very well rounded because she has written theatre, novels, etc. Also Inés Arredondo [1928–1989] and Guadalupe Dueñas [1920]. I think that generation would be made up by them.

When do you write and how do you relate your writing to your other responsibilities—domestic, professional, family?

I usually write at night, because I am a nocturnal person. I am more lucid at night. I wake up as the day unfolds, and I write at home; I need my study, I need my space in order to write. I can never write in an office or in a public place. I really need my own space. Then I write at night. When I am not working on a novel or a short story, it may happen that a week or two goes by without writing. However, when I am writing—I am a very disciplined person, most likely because of my upbringing—I am deeply involved. Even if I am not sitting at my typewriter or computer, I am writing mentally in my car, in the supermarket, sort of coexisting with my work. What I mean is that I don't write every day. And if I am not writing a novel or short story, and I have to prepare a lecture or a book presentation, or I am asked to write the introduction of a book, then I sit down to write. Many of these things are commitments that one has to carry out. But I keep on thinking about my own creative work. Then two weeks may go by, and I haven't been at the typewriter. But all that time I am thinking about how the problems can be resolved. Because writing involves a lot of problem-solving, of putting one's all into the discourse. That's why I am always reflecting.

I have two daughters who are already grown up and independent, and I go to my office in the morning. My work there has a lot to do with my writing, because I am in constant contact with all the writers of my generation. I have to read literature all the time. My husband, a geologist, is very respectful of my work. I believe that I am one of the few women writers of my generation who has such a companion. He has always been supportive of me, he is very considerate of my work. He views it as my profession, as important for him as for me. For that reason I am free.

Is there anything else you wish to add about your own work or about contemporary literature written by women?

The only thing I want to say about literature written by women is: in most of my short stories and novels the main character is a woman, although in *Ascensión Tun* the young boy is the main character. In *Imagen de Héctor* the main character may be Héctor, but usually a female character takes the lead. I think I write about women because I am a woman, and it is natural for me. I know the world of women somewhat. And also because I read women writers more than men. Those women help me to know myself and help me to know other women, to understand them. To know ourselves is the biggest problem we have. It takes us our entire life and who knows how many years of psychoanalysis. I like to read books written by women, because they always offer a way to get to know the inner world of women. In the same fashion, I want to get to know the inner world of men in novels written by men.

Do you believe you have had any influence on younger writers?

Perhaps, a little. For those who are of the generation of José Agustín and later, my generation managed to take the solemnity out of literature. And besides that, we narrated our everyday stories in a very direct and uncomplicated way. I have attracted a large number of readers. My novels and stories are used as texts in secondary and preparatory schools. Also I have trained many students in the literary workshops that I coordinate for those who have won scholarships from the National Institute of Fine Arts or other agencies. Therefore, in a certain way, I feel I have had some influence on younger writers.

How would you summarize your contribution to contemporary Mexican literature?

I feel that I did something very interesting that, at the time, was not well understood. What I really think I did was to have written my first novel, *La mañana debe seguir gris*, in the first person using the real names of the characters that existed. There are characters that never existed and are fictitious. I broke a taboo in Mexican literature at that time. Everyone writes about reality and transforms it. That is, all novels start off from reality, and then there is a transformation and the characters undergo change. What I tried to do in that novel was the opposite. I started off from reality, and I tried to preserve the real characters, more or less in keeping with their reality in life, and I used their names. That didn't sit well with some critics because it had never been done before in Mexican literature.

Representative Selections

The New House

["La casa nueva," from *Dicen que me case yo*]

To ELENA PONIATOWSKA

Of course I don't believe in luck, Mama. Now you are just like my father. Don't tell me he was a dreamer; he was sick—forgive me for saying so. What else can I say? For me, good luck is either there or it isn't. Don't give me any of that stuff about winning the lottery. What lottery? No, Mama. Life is not an illusion; it is life, and that's it. It is okay for children to believe in everything: "I am going to get you the little bed," and after waiting so long they begin to forget. Although let me tell you. Sometimes time goes by and one refuses to forget certain promises; like that afternoon when my father took me to see the new house in the Anzures neighborhood.

The trip on the bus from our neighborhood, San Rafael, seemed different to me, Mama. As if it weren't the same as always... I was paying attention to the trees—they are called ash trees, he insisted—and the flower beds filled with orange and yellow flowers—they are sunflowers and daisies, he said.

We had gone along Melchor Ocampo thousands of times, but never as far as Gutemberg. I liked the spaciousness and cleanliness of the streets more and more. I didn't want to remember San Rafael, so sad and so old: "It isn't dirty, it's just old," you always used to reprimand us, Mama. Do you remember? Nor did I want to think about our toilet without privacy and without running water.

My father paused before going in and asked me:

"What do you think? A dream, isn't it?"

It had a white railing, recently painted. Through it I saw the new house for the first time... A man in uniform was caring for it. It seemed to me so... just like when you buy a piece of fabric: an odor of newness, freshness, making one want to feel it.

I opened my eyes wide, Mama. He led me by the hand from here to there. When we went upstairs he said:

"This is going to be your bedroom."

His chest had puffed up with pride and it even seemed that his voice was choking with emotion. Just for me, I thought. I wouldn't have to sleep with my brothers and sisters any longer. As soon as I had opened the door, he rushed over to say:

"Here is where you'll keep your clothes."

And honestly, I put them there, fitting very nicely on the shelves, hung up my three dresses, and put my treasures in the drawers. I felt like jumping up and down on the bed with delight, but he stopped me and opened the other door.

"Look," he whispered, "a bathroom."

And in my imagination, I stretched out in that enormous tub, with my body relaxed so that the water could cradle it.

The he showed me your bedroom, your bathroom, your dressing room. He twirled his mustache as when he was anxious. And I, Mama, pictured the two of you embracing in that big bed—it didn't look at all like yours—where you could do your things without us, your children, listening. Afterward, I imagined you coming out, freshly bathed, smelling of peaches, apples, clean. Happy, Mama, very happy to have embraced him alone, without the commotion or the crying of my brothers and sisters.

We went through the girls' room, pink like your cheeks, and saw the twin beds; and then, Mama, through the boys' room where "you'll see, here they are going to put their toy cars and soldiers." We walked through the living room, because it had a living room, and through the dining room and the kitchen and the laundry room. He took me up to the roof and then took me down quickly because "you have to see the room for my drafting table." And in my imagination I locked him in there so he could work on his designs without shouting and fights, without children being shushed because their father was working, working at all hours as a draftsman to put food on the table for us.

I never wanted to leave there, Mama. Even locked up in there I would be happy. I would wait for you to come, I would look at the smooth walls, I would sit on the tiled floors, on the carpets, in the upholstered living room; I would take a bath in every bathroom; I would go up and down the stone and the spiral staircase thousands of times; I would bake lots of breads to enjoy them very slowly in the dining room. There I would wait for your arrival, Mama, for Anita's, Rebe's, Gonza's, the baby's, while writing a composition for school: *The New House.*

In this house my family is going to be happy. My Mama won't ever complain again about the filth in which we are living. My Papa

won't go to the bar; he will come home early to draw. I am going to
have my own room, mine, just for me; and my brothers and sis-
ters . . .

I don't know what came over me that I let go of his hand, Mama. I
ran upstairs, to my bedroom, to see it once more, to take a good look
at the furniture and the big window; and I touched the bed to make
sure it wasn't just one of so many of my father's promises, that everything there was as real as I was, when the man in uniform ordered me:
"Come on down, we are going to close."
I almost tumbled down the stairs, my heart beating wildly:
"What does he mean they are going to close, Papa? Isn't this my bedroom?"
Not even time has allowed me to forget: it was going to be ours when
we won the raffle!

89   Silvia Molina

What Would You Have Done?

["¿Qué hubieras hecho?," from *Dicen que me case yo*]

To SALVADOR MILLÁN

She felt an intense heat when she finally saw the Plaza de San Jacinto. Her hands were perspiring, but she refused to admit that it was out of a feeling of insecurity, since she was ready to follow her girlfriend's instructions. She looked around in the small open area visible from where she was, searching for the women who, according to the instructions, could be found in that place at that time. But she could only make out a kiosk selling books and a newspaper stand amid the dense crowd that was waiting for transportation.

Next to her, a lady holding a child by his hand crossed the street and a boy on a bike disappeared among the buses that were going up to Tizapán. She went a little further. The big colonial houses with their serene facades facing the Plaza were hiding those who lived there, protecting them from the commotion.

She had been looking at the very old trees, the ground cover, and the roses beside the paths of the plaza; but all at once the enthusiasm the landscape aroused in her was lost, when with one glance she took in almost the entire place and instantly analyzed the sinister part of what she saw and her own presence in that scenario.

It was then that she realized that she herself was a part of that ritual, set in a small plaza of San Angel, and the spectacle was humiliating.

It was a winter morning, free of icy gusts of wind, whose brilliant rays of sun shone over the cobblestone streets and hit the interior of her car. Suddenly she realized that it was impossible to go back: hers was but one more in that line of cars moving slowly toward the same place, one of an organized caravan in which the confidence of the drivers—all women like her—that they would find what they had come for made the wait tolerable.

Then she questioned her decision and tried to find an excuse. "I am here," she repeated to herself, "out of necessity." Her maid's long absence had made her certain that she wasn't coming back; and her own absence from the office would end up in her dismissal, something that would make the housework even more unpleasant. Well there she was, she told herself, despite her shame, pushing aside her scruples as if it were impossible to retrace the steps that had brought her to the threshold of a slave market—that was the word for it—where everyone was his own boss and offered himself to the highest bidder.

Her car moved forward a bit. The servants who were piling up at one corner of the plaza, opposite the market that on Saturdays made the atmosphere more casual and festive, swooped down on a green Datsun like a flock of magpies. They spoke very fast, spilling out words that from where she was were incomprehensible.

Little by little she was able to make out the features of those mestizas, of those Indian girls, of those dark-skinned farmers with jet-black hair, without beards. One girl proudly showed off a braid that reached her waist; another wore a checkered apron over her floral print dress that was spotless; another one was pushing along a teenage girl in plastic shoes; she must be her daughter, she thought, because she was pushing her to the car while talking—obviously—in her behalf. The rays of the sun showed off the tanned and well-formed arms of the gardeners who displayed their lawn shears in one hand while hiding their gazes under their wide-brimmed straw hats.

As if trying to convince herself, she thought it was too late to escape. Why was she thinking in terms of escape?—she wondered. A kind of fear forced her to have doubts about her own courage. Why courage?—she asked herself again. Can it be, she told herself, in order to put off even longer ironing the pile of clothes that was waiting for a skilled hand that wasn't hers. A hand tired of confronting the clumsiness with which it performed any domestic task although in an office it could type letters and memos with great skill. Nevertheless, when she was a couple of yards from the corner, she detected in the expression on her face a feeling of anguish: the lady in front of her had put a woman into her Renault and was taking off.

Now it was her turn; the crowd milled around next to her window. No one had gotten out of the car.

"A cook, ma'am?"

"A laundress?"

"A day worker?"

"Are you looking for a servant?"

"Do you want a nanny?"

"A gardener?"

"A chambermaid?"

They didn't let one another finish, and every syllable that came out of those mouths sounded like birds desperately flapping their wings. Engrossed in all kinds of thoughts that didn't take shape in her mind, she anxiously turned toward a young girl:

"Someone for the kitchen who can help me with a three-year-old child . . .," she couldn't finish her sentence, because at that moment two women were fighting to get ahead of one another.

There was a brief silence; then, the young girl asked:

"How much are you offering?"

"Six thousand," she responded categorically, because that's what her girlfriend had suggested to her.

"Imagine, just look at her! Here, and for less than ten thousand."

That answer jolted her, bringing her back to reality: a perfectly strange woman could be insolent, vulgar, disrespectful. Should she make an agreement with a strange woman? She felt she ought to withdraw from the battle although she wouldn't go away defeated; she would wait for her girl another week, after all, she was respectful and honest. Surely she will come back after the fiesta in her town—she thought. When she stepped on the gas, the crowd had flocked to the car behind her; but someone shouted:

"Did you say six thousand?"

Stepping on the brake she uttered an automatic yes, as if it had come out against her will.

"For the kitchen?" asked a woman who had remained standing very far behind.

"For everything. There are three of us," she emphasized to discourage her.

"I'll go with you," she said, coming a bit closer.

She observed her features, a snub nose, thin lips that turned into a smile, grayish eyes, and her dark complexion. She was wearing a brown jacket that looked like fur—perhaps one of those perfect imitations, she thought—and the hands that she had waved in order to speak didn't look rough from the use of detergents. Then, all she could ask was whether she had a letter of reference.

"Yes, ma'am. I worked for a couple that just got divorced. I stayed with the gentleman for a few weeks because he was very nice; but I couldn't get used to being without the lady of the house. You can speak to the man, a lawyer; here is his telephone number."

She offered her a typewritten piece of paper. There was no way to tell her that her appearance was disconcerting; it looked like she also had gone there to find a maid.

"Are you sure you'll be satisfied with six thousand pesos? I can't pay more," she said while looking for an excuse to reject her.

"Yes, ma'am," she answered with a smile.

"Well, in that case I'll give you my address so that . . ."

"I would prefer to start right now; I have my things here with me. The fact is I have some debts . . ."

She didn't give her any time to reply because the girl was already walking toward the other door of the car. At that moment she read the paper again: Mr. Montero, Miguel Angel de Quevedo 3978, 584-63-90. Her step did not seem urgent, she carried a plastic bag tied with a knot and a black leather pocketbook under her arm. When she was getting into the car, she tried to explain to her that she was not accepting her definitively.

"When I get home I am going to ask for your references."

But it was as if her words were lost, as if they were vanishing among the offers being made to the little Ford behind her.

In the car on the way home it was the maid who began the conversation.

"What kind of food do you like, ma'am?"

She had been observing her out of the corner of her eye: she noticed her sitting almost elegantly; she spoke with her hands a bit and then folded them gently over her legs. It seemed that she had a strange odor, but she couldn't identify it. Her clothes weren't of good quality and looked quite wrinkled, although not in bad taste.

"Simple."

"Do you know how to give orders?"

She didn't like that question. What did she want to imply with that? Wasn't she the one who should be asking if she knew how to cook? It upset her not to know anything at all about the person she was bringing to her house. That woman didn't have the slightest resemblance to a maid.

"What is your name?"

"Manuela, my name is Manuela Sánchez."

"What do you mean by that question, Manuela?"

"Well, there are women who don't know how to give orders. They only say, for example: make some spaghetti; but no, here we like it this way. And they explain how."

"Spaghetti," she had said "spaghetti" and not "espaghetti." She thought that she was one of those thieves who come into your house and in half an hour empty it out after gagging the family. She couldn't think of anything else; she couldn't think of how that day would end. She believed she had the strength to tell her to get out of the car. Get out, I don't like you. She didn't know how to give orders? She was confused and panic-stricken at the same time, which didn't let her act naturally and made her pretend to be calm so as not to show her panic.

When she had almost reached the superhighway, at Toluca Avenue, she spotted the kites that the children of Tizapán fly in the winds of November and December. She tried to calm down by watching them in the air, rising up defiantly. She thought about her son. Why had she gone to the Plaza de San Jacinto? She wished that her girl were back, that when she arrived she would open the door with the child in her arms and tell her: "He just woke up." She searched for a firm voice:

"Look, Manuela: Before I order you to do anything I am going to ask for your references, OK?"

"Yes," she replied tersely.

It had been a horrible day. She stretched out on her bed for a moment, taking advantage of the silence in the house when the child was asleep and her husband locked in his studio working. She thought about him, always working, she would have wanted a less distant husband. She decided to phone the girlfriend who had recommended that she go to the Plaza de San Jacinto: She needed an excuse to pinpoint the experiences she had been undergoing—that was the word, she told herself.

The first thing I did when I got home was to take Pablito out of the crib. He was still asleep, but the idea of leaving him alone with that woman in the house frightened me. Sitting in the room adjoining the dining room, holding him in my arms, I dialed Mr. Montero's number several times. Manuela— what nerve!—had picked up a photo album from the table and as she paged through it was exclaiming:

"How nice you came out here. Your husband's mother, right? The baby's first birthday!"

Her curiosity made me nervous, or perhaps it was the familiarity with which she was prying into the album. No way to tell her to leave it alone. It looked like we were having coffee together! So I went to show her the maid's room so that she could leave her bags there, and then I showed her the kitchen. I didn't want her to see anything beyond the room adjoining the dining room. I showed her where I kept the saucepans, the frying pans, the pots, the silverware; well, everything. I wanted to keep her busy, and I realized that after ordering her to prepare what we were going to eat, I had said: "Here we usually do that this way," and had explained to her how. I felt as if Manuela were beginning to dominate me; then I tried the phone again.

"Manuela, the number you gave me is still busy. Do you know the number of Mr. Montero's office?"

"No, ma'am. He has just moved; but he stays at home on Mondays to take care of his personal affairs. That's why the line is busy. Be patient," she answered me indifferently while washing the rice.

While Manuela was speaking, I heard some very faint background music; she had the radio set to one of those stations that Raúl, my husband, likes. It seemed to be a concert or something like that. I have never understood anything about music.

"You don't have to leave it on that station, Manuela. You can change it," I suggested, wishing to please her; how obsessive. I think it was my nerves.

"It's okay, ma'am. Don't worry, the lawyer I worked for also likes that kind of music; I am used to it," she answered without taking her eyes off the vegetables she was peeling.

The phone was still busy, and since Pablito had woken up, I went up to change him and called Raúl from my bedroom.

". . . I'm telling you she doesn't look like a maid; she pronounces spaghetti like the Italians and she likes classical music. Come right away, please, I am frightened. I can't tell her to go, what if she does something to us?"

At around one o'clock Manuela came into the room adjoining the dining room: I had completely stopped struggling with the phone number 584-63-90; I was just entertaining Pablito with his toy cars. She looked happy, as if she had adapted herself, as if she had been in the house for years.

"The meal is ready, ma'am," she said looking at me ironically.

I heard her without knowing what the devil to order her to do; mute, completely speechless. She remained pensive a few minutes and then added:

"Can I ask you a favor?"

I felt my heart beating rapidly but I replied without showing my alarm.

"What do you want, Manuela?"

"Can you lend me two hundred pesos? I owe it to someone who gave me breakfast in the San Angel market. Believe me, I didn't have a dime on me," Manuela said all that emphasizing the believe me.

But what I believed was that this was my chance to get rid of her. As a lesson to myself, this had been more than enough. I had decided to stay alone, completely alone; I even thought about leaving the office for a time; I even convinced myself that it was best for Pablito.

"Look, Manuela. I am going to pay you for your day right now and that's where this matter ends. Mr. Montero hasn't gotten off the phone (I didn't dare reproach her for giving me a phoney telephone number), and the best thing is honesty. You did your job and I am going to pay you."

"No, ma'am. You don't understand. I told you that I owed money. I told the person in the market that if I found work I would repay him today. Lend me the two hundred pesos and I'll be back in half an hour."

I really imagined that she wouldn't return, although I was sure that she would steal something; perhaps the electrical appliances from the kitchen. I wasn't going to stop her, I was resigned to her taking anything she wanted as long as I wouldn't see her again. Her presence terrified me; how idiotic. I gave her the two hundred pesos.

"It's okay if you don't come back, Manuela," I insisted.

When Manuela left, I locked the door and checked the kitchen. Everything was in order and not even a teaspoon was missing. I walked to the maid's room to see if she had taken her things, but the bag with her clothes was still on the bed although untied. The room had a strange smell; I thought it was due to the dampness and to having been closed. I left the door open to let some air in.

I had finished feeding Pablito when the bell rang. From the dining room window I saw Manuela next to the street door. I ran to dial 584-63-90 but to no avail. Carrying Pablito I called Raúl's office: he was on his way home.

Why did I let her come in? First she went to her room to leave a little package she was carrying and then she appeared in the kitchen. I asked her to sweep the courtyard and I went to set the dining room table. Suddenly I heard Pablito's laughter; he had gotten away from me and was playing with Manuela, whose voice was becoming more and more euphoric and cheerful. Pablito was laughing his head off. Then Manuela said to him:

"This is a ball. A ball. Say: ball."

"Raúl!" I shouted distressed when I saw him. "She also speaks English," I whispered to him.

Well, you know what Raúl is like, all that matters to him is his work; he said that having been cooped up in the house for so long had made me hysterical.

"I saw her already. She is not an evil princess. Haven't you ever seen light-skinned peasants with green eyes?" he said, laughing at me.

But Manuela was different, she was educated. We sat down to eat; Manuela was like a waiter from the White House. Raúl insisted that her former employers must have trained her very well. At any rate, I begged him not to go back to his office; I was beginning to feel hysterical.

In the afternoon, I played with Pablito. Suddenly I remembered that I hadn't ordered Manuela to do anything: iron the clothes, sweep here, dust there, mop the hallway. Manuela was probably thinking that I didn't know how to give orders. I then went down with the pretense of giving the child his supper. The kitchen was immaculate but had a penetrating odor. The maid's room had smelled of the same thing. I thought that Manuela needed a bath. Just then she came in:

"Do you need anything, ma'am?"

She had a strange expression on her face and was smiling somewhat sarcastically.

"We have supper at around nine. Usually, the same thing we had for lunch. When it is ready you'll call us," I didn't even say please, I was only wondering what Manuela might be thinking about.

Raúl, as always, didn't come out of his study at all; it was as if he were and weren't at home. I had gone in to watch TV and suddenly I was surprised to see that the ten o'clock show was already on. I went down to speak to Manuela. She came in reeling. Then I understood:

"Manuela, do you drink?"

"No, ma'am," she had the nerve to answer.

"What do you mean you don't drink. You're drunk," I was no longer afraid.

"Only two little beers . . ."

"Take your things and go," I ordered her, now with a confident voice.

"Don't fire me, ma'am. I have nowhere to go, nowhere to sleep: it's already very late. Wait, wait, I am going to show you who I am; I don't want you to think that I'm just a nobody, I am not a thief, wait . . ."

She staggered toward the maid's room, and I ran to get Raúl.

It is still hard for me to believe; to believe that Manuela . . . She handed us an ID from the ISSSTE in the name of Ricardo López, from the Ministry of Public Education, Class "C" Director of Student Services. He looked very middle class, "decent," as they say. Underneath was Manuela's photograph: Maribel Chignioni de López, wife, 11/6/46; and the photos of two girls, their daughters, with Manuela's coloring and eyes. Looking at her I wondered how it was possible that she had sunk so low. What can change the direction of a life so drastically? Of four lives?

She had gone to San Angel to buy herself a bottle with the two hundred pesos that I gave her. Manuela got on her knees hugging my legs, begging me: "I have nowhere to go." She smelled of whiskey and sweat, she disgusted me.

Raúl pulled her away from me. "Just tonight, I'll go tomorrow," she kept on saying. Her tears revolted me and the terror in her eyes seemed obscene to me. Tell me: You, what would you have done?

The Problem

["El problema," from *Imagen de Héctor*]

I

Her search for Héctor didn't come about merely by accident, but because of a more powerful reason: Héctor was her father. A father She didn't remember because He died when She was a year old.

Until She was five, She was brought up with the idea that Héctor was alive; but one afternoon, when She was going into the house of a neighbor, Efraín Aranda Osorio, The Sweet-smelling One, then the governor of Chiapas, a child cornered Her:

"How does it feel not to have a father?"

"I have one, but He isn't here."

"They say He died."

The Youngest Daughter neither refuted nor contradicted him. That child wasn't lying. Héctor had died, and in her house no one accepted it. They hid the truth, they kept it silent.

II

Although some things made Her suspicious of that long absence; when She asked about Héctor, they told Her He was traveling.

Then She used to picture Him going around that globe that was the earth that the Older Children had in the bedroom. A metal globe with designs in color, not good at all for playing ball.

"The blue," insisted Miss Heidi, "is the ocean."

She didn't understand that it was the ocean, but Héctor was certainly sailing in a boat like the scale model in the library, exactly like the pirate ships that several times attacked a place called Campeche.

Campeche seemed to Her as intangible as Héctor in every sense; but everyone spoke of both as if they were right there, around the corner, as if they were one and the same thing: Héctor—they said—was from Campeche originally and by nature friendly. What would Héctor be like, his real voice, his look, his laugh? What would that place called Campeche be like? What would his land, his people, his ocean be like?

She didn't like that relationship, that inseparable couple, because it was incomprehensible to Her and because it was similar to the smell of mothballs. An odor that imposed itself and impregnated the entire house; that clung to the wood of the dining room, to the paint of the pictures, to the brocade of the living room furniture, to the walls of the bedrooms, to the fabric of the curtains, to the linen of the sheets. And She, the Youngest Daughter, didn't sleep well because the odor stuck in her stomach.

Héctor's essence didn't diminish or disappear even if She left the window open and the rain stirred up the camphor of the eucalyptus trees in Chapultepec Park, a half block from her house.

III

And even if no one said it, the Youngest Daughter felt intuitively that the future was made of quicksand and no one was teaching Her how to walk safely in that world that never stopped holding on to Him, or mentioning his name, or inventing Him.

A world that was enclosed within itself, that let no one out and was beginning to suffocate Her.

Perhaps in Campeche—She thought—Héctor was being held prisoner by the pirates, because He didn't come to save Her from that monster that was stalking Her everywhere.

But Héctor wasn't returning, He had never come back. In his place, treasures arrived that perhaps He had taken from Lorencillo, Peg-Leg, Bluebeard, the pirates in the games of the Older Children. Someone was sending boxes of bounty from that distant port: red mangos, creamy avocados, big cashews, juicy *nances*, tender *zaramullos*, very white custard apples and black sapotas, candied sapodillas, and strange star apples and *pitahayas*.

Campeche was also part of that blue spot on the globe that filled the freezer with giant shrimp, moro crab, crayfish, and lobster; with fish they didn't have at the corner market: snapper, yellow jack, mullet.

And even if Miss Heidi used her index finger to point out a pink spot surrounded by blue on the metal globe, assuring Her that it was the state of Campeche, with its capital city Campeche and a tranquil and transparent ocean, She couldn't give it form or meaning inside of Her.

The same thing happened to Her with Héctor; She couldn't manage to make Him into a person of flesh and blood, who might have made a mistake like the rest of the people around Him. For the Wife, He was "the best husband in the world"; for the Older Children, "the best father on earth"; for the brothers and sisters-in-law, "a magic key that had opened many doors"; for his acquaintances, "the Secretary of the

Interior of President Miguel Alemán"; for his friends, "the Friend, really, the Friend, or the Writer or the Historian or the Journalist"; for his sisters, "He, the one who had brought them up"; for his countrymen, "the best governor of Campeche"; for the Spanish refugees . . .

IV

"For Héctor's little daughter!" Merle Oberon, the wife of Bruno Pagliai, said in a special tone of voice when they spent Christmas at that big house in Lomas Altas. "For Héctor's little daughter!" she repeated at least ten times, taking boxes from the foot of that tree loaded with ornaments, colored lights, and gifts; and then she saw with those beautiful eyes, with that beautiful hair, with that beautiful smile, with that beautiful dress of a famous Hollywood actress, how the Youngest Daughter sat near the door of the terrace looking over the fabulous gifts that She wouldn't get from the Wife of Héctor even if She cried the whole year, and that were being given to Her only because She was Héctor's little daughter. And Héctor's little daughter knew it and left the dollhouse, the little store, the skates, the electric stove, the American doll with its crib, chair, tub, carriage, and walker on the terrace and ran out to play with the Dalmatians that were barking in that immense garden filled with echoes, sounds of insects, hills, shrubs, fountains, and daisies.

V

Héctor, no doubt about it, had been an important man; proof of it was that fantasy that surrounded Her, the set of a film in which the beauty of Merle Oberon was eclipsed by personages of primary importance whose pictures were in *Excélsior, Novedades, Tiempo.* Click: important public officials. Click: the richest men in the private sector. Click: writers and journalists of the left. Click: Spanish refugees. From General Lázaro Cárdenas to Adolfo Ruiz Cortines, from Justo Fernández to Bruno Pagliai, from Luis Cardoza y Aragón to Fernando Benítez, from Juan Rejano to Arturo Souto. Nevertheless for Her, for the Youngest Daughter, Héctor never ceased to be the portrait that was in a silver frame in the living room of the house (from there He followed Her with his gaze toward any angle, although She would hide to avoid it); Héctor never ceased to be that unique voice that emanated from the recording that the Youngest Daughter put on the RCA Victor phonograph; that voice that sang while accompanying itself on the guitar, like an ominous premonition:

> *Where will it go,*
> *quickly and wearily,*
> *the swallow that is leaving from here...*

Héctor was also a series of pure silk bow ties, brand new, that the Youngest Daughter saw moving on the back of Héctor's Wife's closet door when someone opened it. It looked as if they were ready for Héctor to put them on at any moment, just as his reading glasses were ready on the night table at his side of the bed, and on his desk the filters for the mouthpiece and the tobacco for his pipes.

VI

Héctor was like those white mothballs that She found in suits, vests, hats, shirts, coats, shoes, papers...; He rolled around all over, but She couldn't touch Him because He was intangible even though others were determined to preserve his existence.

VII

That's how things were: Campeche was becoming an Ithaca, and Héctor, the hero who would return home after a long and mysterious journey.

VIII

Perhaps it won't be difficult to understand the fear that the certainty of a death that everyone denied caused Her, Héctor's Youngest Daughter, and her anguished confusion brought on by the constant presence around Her of a ghost.

Anything at all that competed with the need to know more about Him, about Héctor, made no sense to Her. For a long time She put aside the swings and her bicycle, and although the Older Children needed Her for their games of baseball or soccer, her time was spent in Héctor's library navigating through the very blue seas of her imagination in that scale-model boat into which She almost fit; rummaging among incomprehensible papers, photos of unknown people, gold-pointed pens, small pre-Hispanic figures, albums of fragile records, stamp collections, files of correspondence written on paper with a little eagle in the upper left-hand corner, innumerable books.

IX

One day She asked herself the first question: What had Héctor written?

Through the polished glass, She looked for his books in the old bookcase; and after turning the key in the lock, She took out a big one, the thickest one, the one with a pink binding.

She opened it. She hadn't been more frustrated in a long time. That book that her hands were holding, was, nevertheless, completely out of her reach.

She satisfied Herself with looking at the illustrations: a picture of an Indian was among them. An Indian. Perhaps Héctor had written a book about an Indian.

She went to the oak desk and made Herself comfortable squatting in the swivel chair. An impulse forced Her to take the pen out of the holder and scribble a lot of pages. In tears, She went looking for Miss Heidi:

"When am I going to understand?"

X

Understanding took Her years. She still doesn't know if She has understood, but She tried to make of the legend an ordinary story; and of the hero, a human being.

This novel is that, her search for Héctor. The problem is obvious.

Bibliography

Publications

La mañana debe seguir gris. Mexico City: Joaquín Mortiz, 1977; subsequent eds., Mexico City: Cal y Arena.
Leyendo en la tortuga. Mexico City: Martín Casillas, 1981.
Ascensión Tun. Mexico City: Martín Casillas, 1981; 2d ed., Mexico City: Corunda, 1993.
Lides de estaño. Mexico City: Universidad Autónoma Metropolitana, 1984.
La familia vino del norte. Mexico City: Océano, 1987; subsequent eds., Mexico City: Cal y Arena.
Dicen que me case yo. Mexico City: Cal y Arena, 1989.
Imagen de Héctor. Mexico City: Cal y Arena, 1990.
Campeche: Punta del ala del país. Mexico City: Consejo Nacional para la Cultura y las Artes, 1991.
Un hombre cerca. Mexico City: Cal y Arena, 1992.
Circuito cerrado. Mexico City: Textos de Difusión Cultural/UNAM, 1995.

Children's Books

El papel. Mexico City: Patria, 1985.
El algodón. Mexico City: Patria, 1987.
La creación del hombre. Mexico City: Trillas, 1989.
Los cuatro hermanos. Mexico City: Corunda, 1991.
Leyenda del Sol y de la Luna. Mexico City: Trillas, 1991.
El misterioso caso de la perra extraviada. Mexico City: SEP, 1992.
Los tres corazones. Mexico City: Corunda, 1992.
Las dos iguanas. Mexico City: Corunda, 1993.
Mi Familia y La Bella Durmiente cien años después. Mexico City: Corunda, 1993.
Así soy (mi autobiografía). Mexico City: Fideicomiso Para la Cultura México–U.S.A./Corunda, 1995.

Translations

"Autumn." Trans. Margaret Sayers Peden. *Scents of Wood and Silence: Short Stories by Latin American Women Writers.* Special issue of *Latin American Literary Review* 19, no. 37 (January–June 1991): 123–125.
"I Confess." Trans. Elizabeth Gamble Miller. *Manoa: A Pacific Journal of International Writing* 4, no. 2 (Fall 1992): 98–102.

"Starting Over." Trans. Russell M. Cluff and L. Howard Quackenbush. *New Writing from Mexico*. Special issue of *TriQuarterly* 85 (Fall 1992): 135–147.
Gray Skies Tomorrow. Trans. John Mitchell and Ruth Mitchell de Aguilar. Kaneohe: Plover, 1993.
"An Orange Is an Orange." Trans. Paul Pines. *Pyramids of Glass: Short Fiction from Modern Mexico*, 77–80. San Antonio: Corona, 1994.

Brianda Domecq

Brianda Domecq ⁽¹⁹⁴²⁾

About the Author and Her Writing

Conversations with the Writer

Representative Selections

Balzac ["Balzac," from *Bestiario doméstico*]

In Memoriam ["In memoriam,"
from *Bestiario doméstico*]

Galatea ["Galatea," from *Bestiario doméstico*]

Bibliography

About the Author and Her Writing

Brianda Domecq is direct, forthright, and self-confident about herself, her work, and the significance of contemporary women writers. Having realized her long-held desire to become a professional writer relatively late, she compensates for the lost time with an increased intensity. This characteristic is apparent when one meets and speaks with Domecq, reads her work, and muses upon her ideas and opinions. It is as if she had reflected on her views over a long period of time and then refined them to the point where they can be articulated clearly and forcefully. However, Domecq is not close-minded; she makes room for different ideas and interpretations. Most important, she always allows her sense of humor to enter in no matter how serious the subject. Thus, whether she is talking about herself or about traumatic events in her life, or whether she takes on controversial issues such as women's writing or the cult of virginity, her special kind of humor always befriends the reader, making the subject no less serious but rather more palatable. Domecq knows how to use language, working with it as if it were clay to form the straight lines, mold the curves, and create the textures that constitute her art. Perhaps this sensitivity can be attributed to the fact that for Brianda Domecq, Spanish is her second language.

Brianda Domecq describes her recollections of the first thirty years of her life in *BD/De cuerpo entero* (BD/In Full View; 1991), a short autobiographical book. She tells us she was born in New York, the first child of a Spanish father and a North American mother. Even her birth by Cesarean section—with the umbilical cord wrapped around her neck—under the sign of Leo was of significance. To Leo she attributes her rebelliousness and the lack of discipline that manifested themselves early on and that she portrays with tongue in cheek. Her literary bent she ascribes to her father, who, in those carefree years in New York and Connecticut, made life into an endless novel with stories about knights and battles, adventures and romance, both told and acted out. Her curiosity was awakened and her imagination knew no bounds in that world of magic created by her father.

She suffered her first trauma at the age of six when her mother presented her with a baby brother. The competition for attention caused her to become obstinate, untruthful, and angry, and to long for the time when she reigned as queen of the house. This insurmountable obstacle, coupled with her entrance into elementary school, where she was taught how young ladies are expected to behave, made her rue the day she was born female. One can only guess that this early experience is the root of Domecq's feminism. Her maternal grandmother, recognizing that her granddaughter was jealous of her brother, took Brianda to her home for weekends and holidays so that she could be an only child again. This woman, with her feet planted firmly on the ground, taught Brianda about real life and offered a vision of reality as opposed to fantasy. The grandmother listened to Brianda's stories, gave her a notebook and pencil, and declared that some day she would be a writer. It was then that she began to write things down, a habit she continued when the family moved to Mexico when she was nine.

Although her North American roots quickly dried up, no Mexican roots grew to take their place. But despite being a marginal student, she kept on filling notebooks with stories and verses. At age fifteen, Brianda Domecq returned to the United States to attend a boarding school in Massachusetts, and resumed her relationship with her grandmother. Now they were able to discuss politics, social issues, and women's liberation. After finishing high school and studying for two semesters at a college in New York, Domecq returned to Mexico. Beset by a feeling that she didn't belong, she once again searched for her place. She tried social work and took an interest in religion. Then she married and had two children. After some years she went back to writing, first in English, and then made a complete break with thinking, speaking, reading, and writing in English. Spanish was going to be her instrument of communication. At age thirty, with the children and the household attended to, Brianda Domecq entered the National University to study literature. This move and her conscious decision to write in Spanish were major turning points in her life that would pave the way for her career as a professional writer.

BD/De cuerpo entero is by Domecq's own admission not a completely accurate account of her first thirty years, but it is probably close enough in its general outline to give us some clues about this writer. Unlike those writers who knew or felt that literature was to be their profession, Domecq seems to have grown into her calling gradually and then made a serious and irrevocable decision. Her thrust is twofold: her own creativity and the promotion of women writers and writing. She is equally passionate about both activities, which complement each other. Her output to date can be classified into fiction and essay. As a writer of fiction Brianda Domecq has published two novels—*Once días...y algo más* (1979; *Eleven Days*, 1995) and *La insólita historia de la Santa de Cabora* (The Unusual Story of the Saint from Cabora; 1990)—and a volume of short stories—*Bestiario doméstico* (Domestic Bestiary; 1982). Her essay writing includes *Voces y rostros del Bravo* (Voices and Faces of the Rio Grande; 1987), a photo essay on the flow of life and history on the Rio Grande; the introductory study to her *Acechando al unicornio: La virginidad en la literatura mexicana* (Stalking the Unicorn: Virginity in Mexican Literature; 1988), an anthology of brief pieces written by Mexican writers since colonial times on the cult of virginity and the hymen; *BD/De cuerpo entero* (1991), her autobiographical essay; and *Mujer que publica...Mujer pública* (Woman of Words, Woman of the Streets; 1994), a compilation of her essays on women's writing and women writers.

Several threads run through all this work, giving it a sense of wholeness and unity. First among them is the theme of women: their history, the myths that surround them, their place in a patriarchal society, their struggle to free themselves from a repressive family and society, and their desire to be and behave as they choose. Brianda Domecq brings to this broad theme her understanding of history, her reading of literature, and the analysis of her own life and background. The other dimension that permeates her writing is her exceptional facility with language. She is able to work with prose in different ways to amuse, cajole, distract, and convince the reader. She uses puns, appropriates titles of other writers' works, incorporates sayings, and, in general, plays with language. This sensitivity may well be the result of her conscious decision to use Spanish as her instrument of communication. In doing so, she manages to engross the reader in her text and articulate her message forcefully.

An atypical work by Brianda Domecq is her *Voces y rostros del Bravo*, whose large size and extensive use of photographs and illustrations make it a coffee-table book. However, this is a serious collaborative effort between a photographer and a writer, providing image and text about the Río Bravo, the Rio Grande on the North American side of the border. The book is the product of a nineteen-day trip between Ciudad Juárez and the Gulf of Mexico during which the photographer captured the beauty of the terrain, with its flora and fauna, while the writer collected images, impressions, and anecdotes about the history, myths, and legends of the area. The border, with all that it implies in the relationship between the United States and Mexico, is a topic of appeal to Domecq, who, having traversed it both literally and figuratively countless times, understands its importance. Her text alternates between descriptions that complement the photographs and a series of facts and anecdotes that trace the ebb and flow of the river over time, especially since the 1848 Treaty of Guadalupe Hidalgo, which reduced Mexico's land by more than half and established the Rio Grande as the country's northern border. Once a symbol of defeat and a political, economic, and social barrier, the river has changed not only its course but also its significance. For Domecq this border is where the two cultures have met, fused, and formed a third—Mexican-American—culture that despite the strong influence from the north still clings to Mexican traditions.

The subject of virginity as well as the many myths surrounding it is one that Domecq takes on with particular fervor. Here she combines her study of the subject from a sociological perspective with her readings of Mexican literature from colonial times to the present. The result is an anthology composed of poems, short stories, and chapters of novels whose central theme is virginity. *Acechando al unicornio: La virginidad en la literatura mexicana* is preceded by an introductory essay tracing the subject and its treatment by writers, both men and women, over the centuries. Toying with the dictionary definition of "hymen" as that membrane that preserves a woman's *integridad*, defined literally as "wholeness" and figuratively as "integrity" or "virginity," Domecq amuses herself by pointing out that a man considered *íntegro* is honest and upright, whereas a woman considered *íntegra* is one who is whole, without missing parts, and it is only the lack of a hymen that renders her "incomplete." To her mind, this conceptual morass results from the confusion of a minute physical phenomenon with an exaggerated sociocultural and moral one. Having no known physiological function, the hymen serves only as a warranty of the moral integrity of women, making virginity a perfect state and creating a cult of the hymen.

Among the indigenous populations of Mexico prior to the conquest, Brianda Domecq finds a variety of customs and rituals associated with virginity. There was a general emphasis on premarital chastity for both sexes, often accompanied by educational traditions to prepare young people for sexual maturity. In most groups, women had to prove their purity at marriage or suffer the consequences of shame or even of return to the parental home. Control of sexuality through celibacy or abstinence was an individual and mostly male responsibility, an exercise in self-control, proof that one was not a slave to one's instincts. If one could restrain oneself, then one might aspire to exercise power over others. With the arrival of Christianity in the New World, sexual repression was universalized for all Christians. Slowly, responsibility shifted from the individual to the clergy, who acted as overseers, and concurrently the burden of sexual responsibility became woman's. Sin was viewed as the result of the temptation provided by woman's flesh, not man's lack of ability to control his instincts. Therefore, celibacy, the denial of one's instincts, constitutes Christian perfection. With time, the Spanish concept of honor attached itself to indigenous customs, giving virginity additional importance in Mexico.

Domecq asserts that Mexican literature, with the exception of works by Sor Juana Inés de la Cruz (1648–1695) in the colonial period, did not approach the theme of feminine sexuality until after the war of independence in the nineteenth century. Then the subject became part of the interest in customs so prevalent in the letters of that century. Certain themes have persisted over time: the contrast of virgin and prostitute, the double standard for men and women, the cult of the hymen, the eroticism of deflowering, the parental role in preserving the daughter's virginity, the question of honor. The preservation of the hymen led to the creation of two literary stereotypes—the chaste, good, and pure virgin as opposed to the immoral prostitute. These two forces of good and evil struggle to conquer or ruin man. However, Domecq points out, the passage from one to the other is accomplished through a simple act of tearing, either by force or choice.

As Mexican literature moved into the twentieth century, the act of losing one's virginity was judged more by the sentiment that accompanied it. Innocence and naiveté were admirable; promiscuity immoral. The double standard became a constant in Mexican literature. The man who seduces is a winner; he triumphs. A woman seduced is a loser. Two standards also prevail among different classes. The demands of chastity are not as stringent for lower-class women as for those of the middle and upper class. With time the portrayal of the pure, innocent, and ethereal maiden gave way to the woman who experienced the enjoyment of sex and even the loss of her virginity. However, men continued to be portrayed as desirous of women physically pure, almost asexual creatures who accede to the act of love out of sentiments all but sexual. Women who choose to remain virgins are rare, and after reaching a certain age, being a *soltera* (single woman) is viewed as shameful and humiliating. Virginity is erotic among the young but carries a stigma later on. Literature has in different ways removed the sacrosanctity of virginity and viewed it from different perspectives. More recently the emphasis has shifted from what society thinks or expects to what women feel and to the importance they may or may not ascribe to virginity. Thus literature now allows women to express themselves biologically as well as socially—a positive step toward changing men's views and creating lasting and fulfilling relationships.

The selections that follow in the anthology are representative of the entire history of Mexican literature, from early chronicles, legends, and popular songs through well-known works of nineteenth- and twentieth-century poets, novelists, and playwrights. Both men and women are included, giving the reader the additional stimulus to think about whether the attitudes portrayed are gender related.

Humor, that ingredient that Domecq uses so well, is not lacking here either. Her own story "In memoriam," autobiographical in nature and included in *Bestiario doméstico*, is among the selections illustrating the theme. She relates matter-of-factly how, as an eighteen-year-old on an evening's outing to the beach, she lost her virginity in a motel room. Describing the mixed feeling of anticipation and martyrdom, she confesses she went through the motions expected of her. Most amusing is her description of her boyfriend, who had armed himself with a condom, which for her was evidence of a cold and calculating person. However, everything went as expected, and she didn't feel a thing. What left the most lasting impression were the blood stains on the sheets, thus confirming what she had formerly believed were only old wives' tales. So that her tranquillity might not be confused with the detached attitude of a prostitute, she burst into tears and preserved her image of decency. The next day it was as if the previous night had never occurred.

Domecq's interest in the theme of virginity is but one aspect of her concern with women's position in Mexican society, their portrayal in its literature, and their acceptance as writers. A number of the essays included in *Mujer que publica...mujer pública* deal with the broader theme. When invited to participate in a session at the Feria Internacional del Libro (International Book Fair) held in Guadalajara in 1990 on the topic of "Sexualidad, sensualidad y erotismo" (Sexuality, Sensuality, and Eroticism), she was impressed with the fact that women are generally not asked for their opinions on what are considered masculine topics. She viewed the invitation as a definite sign of progress and delivered a talk called "Puta, re-puta, re-puta-ción" (Whore, Super-Whore, Reputation). The title, a play on the word *puta*, not generally used in a public forum, served to shock and concomitantly to draw attention to what was being expressed. Women writers do not have a good reputation. The three words—sexuality, sensuality, and eroticism—denote pleasure, an unacceptable feeling for reputable women who define themselves by their function and relationship to others, such as daughter, sister, mother, wife. Women writers form a sort of third gender—the supposed mothers of the sexuality of their literary daughters to whom they lend their voices in their texts to show a feminine vision of sexuality. Domecq reviews a number of texts by women writers about women to illustrate her point. There are "decent" women, portrayed as those who see men as savages and feel persecuted; others described as asexual even within marriage so as not to fall under a cloud of suspicion; those who hypocritically feign virginity or revulsion at sexual enjoyment; and some who defy society and engage in premarital sex.

Domecq's concentration on literature written by women has led her to the conviction that there is undeniably a Mexican "literatura femenina," separate and distinct from that written by men. In her essay "Hasta no verte, literatura mía," a play on the title of Elena Poniatowska's novel *Hasta no verte Jesús mío*, she outlines her reasons and reasoning for arriving at that conclusion. She starts from the premise that Mexican literature is literature written by men. Just as all facial tissues are known as "Kleenex," "Literature" with a capital L is that written by men. They are the ones who write, review, classify, and extend recognition. Women's writing is the exception, not integrated into the corpus but tacked on to it as if with pins. Many women writers themselves claim they don't write "literatura femenina," and some have attached themselves to "la Literatura." Others, often compared to well-established and renowned writers, will in time be forgotten. Domecq feels strongly that literature written by women cannot continue to be treated as an isolated phenomenon without its own context.

Domecq pinpoints the year 1950, the year Rosario Castellanos published *Sobre cultura femenina* (On Feminine Culture), as the date that marks the full participation of women in literature. She reasons that there have been four generations or decades of active women writers with a sufficiently voluminous production to be considered a corpus independent of the masculine corpus of the same period. This corpus will create the basis of a tradition of literature written by women and provide a context for studying feminine works. Domecq disagrees with those women writers who deny that literature has gender and with those who are afraid to say that they write "literatura femenina." As for women critics, they too are so involved in the patriarchal academy that they deny the existence of "literatura femenina" and prefer to cling to the masculine corpus. Domecq maintains that women's writing without the recognition of a corpus will continue to be a subgenre, a passing fashion. However, as a corpus, women's voices will be heard, and their originality, freshness, and subversive potential recognized. Theirs is a new form of writing literature, not an outgrowth of masculine literature.

Brianda Domecq's first novel, *Once días...y algo más*, in many ways sets the parameters of her narrative skill and facility with language. It is a novelized version of an incident in her life when she was kidnapped and held captive for eleven days in 1978. Meeting the challenge to turn this material into a novel, Domecq marshaled all her storytelling ability to relate this traumatic event in a manner that keeps the reader thoroughly engrossed and hanging on to every thread of this suspenseful tale. The book, written so soon after the event depicted, seems to capture Domecq's life as if on film and points to her future as a strong, independent, liberated woman.

The day of her kidnapping finds Brianda Domecq no longer in the flower of her youth, married, the mother of two children, upper middle class with servants, attending university classes, and feeling a certain amount of guilt about her bourgeois way of life in the midst of a society that for the most part did not enjoy her privileges. It was going to be a day free of all household obligations, capped by lunch at her parents' home in the San Angel section of the city. She drives off to classes and then to San Angel free and unburdened. In an instant all that changes as a car pulls in front of hers and another behind it, forcing her to a standstill. That moment, as she looks down a gun barrel and at a knife, is frozen in her memory and becomes a watershed in her life. The games she had played with her father so many years ago had taken on the seriousness of reality. Her first reaction was disbelief, followed by fear and denial. Blindfolded and unable to perceive the limits of reality, she feels the rational world disappearing and the horror of her predicament pushing her to the edge of madness. But this was an adventure she was living, one whose every moment she had to remember.

Making use of her intelligence, instincts, and imagination, she tries to make light of the situation primarily to keep a grip on her sanity. Her kidnappers are, in their own way, courteous and attentive, thus allowing their victim to establish a friendly bond. Clearly, their aim is ransom, and she was selected because of her family's financial situation. Giving her captors names—Santa Claus, el Jefe, el Cantinero, Oreja Parada, el Pícaro, el Barbas—she anchors her experiences to reality and amuses herself in the midst of her nightmare. Here her facility with language is a tool she wields to cajole, convince, disarm, and distract her captors. By judging how they treat her, she adjusts her tone of voice and her approach to them. The ordinary routines of daily living become obstacles to overcome: eating, smoking, bathing, sleeping. However, she manages to win over her captors enough that they help her and even give her some "privileges."

When Domecq was rescued physically unharmed, her reaction progressed from terror to disappointment, depression, emptiness, and finally sadness. Her freedom was her rebirth, and it would take time to become accustomed to life. Justice meted out to her captors gave her little solace and never compensated for her mental suffering.

Once días...y algo más is a fascinating book whose subject matter keeps the reader in a state of suspense and incapable of putting it down. The natural curiosity to find out how the nightmare unfolds, whether the victim will be harmed or freed, and whether the perpetrators will be caught makes for an exciting and completely absorbing novel. But more important, this work shows Domecq as a skilled hand at narrative technique. Each day of her captivity is captured in a chapter followed by a brief epilogue—*algo más* (something more). Narrated in the first person using names taken from the zodiac, the book includes intermittent flashbacks to conversations recalled or invented. Each captor assumes a different personality, and Domecq's attitude toward them varies. She finds herself almost taking a liking to them and reprimands herself for being so cooperative and docile. The ordinary becomes extraordinary as she is grateful for some face cream, a game of dominoes, a breath of fresh air. Survival and sanity are her goals. In the epilogue, marking the anniversary of her kidnapping, she talks of herself in the third person as Leo, reborn and adjusting to the world as she once knew it. She had seen her captors, but this time they, with their downcast eyes and sullen looks, hadn't seen her. She learned who they were—men with real names like Sánchez, Pérez, González—and about their families and criminal activities. She had been taken to the house where she was held and was able to put together the pieces of the puzzle—spaces, noises, doors, and walls. Reunited with her family, she experienced the catharsis of describing the world she had inhabited for eleven days and the multiple emotions she had gone through. But now she was a new Leo.

La insólita historia de la Santa de Cabora, Domecq's second novel, is the culmination of a seventeen-year odyssey, and the high point of her literary production to date. This work—long, dense, and complex—combines all of its author's interests and narrative techniques in creating (or recreating) a nineteenth-century historical figure, Teresa Urrea. In focusing on this woman, also known as the Santa de Cabora because of her healing powers, Domecq builds a bridge connecting her fiction to the history and literature of Mexico.

Teresa Urrea (1873–1906), the protagonist of this novel, is a monumental character who captivates the reader as much as she does her creator. Teresa appeared in Mexican literature in the 1906 version of the novel *Tomóchic* by Heriberto Frías (1870–1928), first published in serialized form in 1893. Frías had participated as a young soldier in the government's campaign against the rebellious inhabitants of the town of Tomóchic, where an uprising had occurred. The book was rewritten several times, and in 1906 for the first time mentions the Santa de Cabora, in whose name the people of Tomóchic had rebelled. Frías's book is among the early examples of what later became known as the "novel of the Mexican Revolution." However, what inspired Domecq was the character of Teresa, under whose banner antigovernment uprisings were recorded. The writer tells of her years of research, both archival and ordinary legwork, spent in tracing Teresa Urrea's history and establishing her as a real person. Having stumbled upon her in Heriberto Frías's novel, Domecq became obsessed with this woman who, for her time of the late nineteenth and early twentieth centuries, symbolized everything that a Mexican woman couldn't and shouldn't represent and prefigured the contemporary Mexican woman of a hundred years later. And for some seventeen years Teresa held a grip on Domecq's imagination until the novel was completed. Although *La insólita historia de la Santa de Cabora* is a novel that integrates reality and fiction, it is solidly grounded in history and supported by Domecq's painstaking research to learn all that was known and had been written about Teresa Urrea. The writer described and documented this in a talk delivered at a symposium held in Hermosillo, Sonora, in 1981, in which she confessed that her readings had always left her with nagging questions about this woman. Why was Teresa persecuted by the government? Was she really involved in the political uprisings of the time? Or was she but an innocent victim devoted to healing the sick and preaching love and kindness? What follows are the facts that she gathered.

Teresa Urrea was born in Ocorini, Sinaloa, in 1873, the daughter of servant and master, Cayetana Chávez and Tomás Urrea. Baptized Niña García Nona María Rebeca Chávez, she assumed her father's surname in 1888 or 1889, several years after moving to his ranch, Cabora, in the state of Sonora. A year later she suffered a cataleptic-type attack, leaving her comatose for two weeks and in a trancelike state for some months. Upon coming out of the trance, she was capable of performing miraculous healings and endowed with supernatural powers. Her fame spread among the sick and disheartened in an atmosphere beset by antigovernment uprisings. Thousands made the pilgrimage to consult her, mainly from the northern states of Sonora, Sinaloa, and Chihuahua, transforming Cabora into a meeting place not only for the physically infirm but for political malcontents. The government became concerned about the situation and sent agents to observe the activities. A series of events—a wave of religious fanaticism among Indian groups, a cult of the Santa de Cabora among the people of Tomóchic, an uprising under the banner of ¡Viva la Santa de

Cabora!—combined to convince the government that Teresa and her father were a threat, and they were taken to Guaymas to be exiled. Domecq points out that Teresa, with her magical powers, came to symbolize good as opposed to the evil and omnipotence of the dictator Porfirio Díaz. Her open anticlericalism and her protection of the indigenous groups who provided the labor of the region posed a real threat to the regime. As her fame spread so did the exaggerations about her power and activities.

In June 1892, Teresa and her father arrived in Arizona, and in 1893 the rebellion in Tomóchic took place, as well as other rebellions that invoked the name of the Santa de Cabora. Evidence seems to point to the fact that in Solomonville, Arizona, the Urreas were involved in the revolutionary activities of Lauro Aguirre—in his anti-Díaz manifesto, and in his newspaper of the opposition, *El Independiente*. In 1896, they moved to El Paso, Texas, from where small uprisings took place in which Teresa was implicated. The historical sources consulted by Domecq are not clear about Teresa's level of participation in these activities. In 1897, the family moved to Clifton, Arizona, but the stories of Teresa's involvement in rebellions continued. In June 1900, she married Guadalupe Rodríguez, who subsequently tried to kill her. Suspicions that Rodríguez was a Mexican government agent seem very strong, and whatever political activities Teresa may have been involved in came to an end. The remaining six years of her life were lived out in the United States, where she worked for a medical company, married John Van Order, the son of a friend, and had two daughters. In 1906, she died in Clifton, Arizona.

Domecq gathered, sifted, and weighed these facts to give her novel a solid grounding in history. But apart from the historical framework, there is a large amount of fiction that fleshes out the narration and makes this a novel. The protagonist took on characteristics and proportions that are more a reflection of Domecq's inspiration and creativity than an accurate portrayal of the woman Teresa may have been. Thus we are presented with two visions of reality that intersect and interact—the historical and the fictional. The figure of Teresa Urrea more than fascinated the novelist. She became obsessed with her, hearing her voice, dreaming about her, following every slim lead and trace until finally portraying her as one of the strongest female characters in contemporary Mexican literature. Teresa came to symbolize the Mexican woman and her evolution from illegitimacy to legitimacy in the broadest sense.

La insólita historia de la Santa de Cabora has a very definite structure corresponding to the different periods of Teresa's life. In Part I, consisting of twenty numbered and one additional chapter, "La caída" (The Fall), Domecq's technique is to alternate between an account of a fictitious researcher's trip to Sonora to track down certain leads and to discover others about the object of her research, and the story of Teresa from the time of her conception to the moment she fell into a cataleptic state. The researcher's account is filled with dreams, visions, flashbacks, and recollections of all the material she has gathered, heard, and studied over the years. Teresa's story is that of the first seventeen years of her life—her birth as the illegitimate daughter of master and servant, her desire to be a man, her rejection of all that is feminine, the realization of who her father was, and her determination to claim his surname and be accepted by him. In the course of this narration one learns that Teresa is a fair-skinned beauty with penetrating eyes, the hands of a man, and the ability to teach herself to read and write with the help of an old woman. She is rejected by her aunt and cousins, who consider her the fruit of her mother's shame, and finally abandoned by her mother. However, she has taken it into her head to make herself known to her father and succeeds in having him accept her as his daughter. Don Tomás Urrea had only sired sons, and Teresa's appearance in his unhappy family life seemed like a miracle. From a servant girl, doomed to a life of hard work and no future, Teresa became a *señorita*. Suddenly this free spirit, who roamed about barefoot in the company of men, played the guitar, and rode bareback, found herself corseted, coifed, and squeezed into shoes so as to fit into the lifestyle of the "big house." Although happy with her new life, she yearns for the old freedom and soon befriends la Huila, an old faith healer who teaches her to heal the sick, assist in delivering babies, concoct remedies, and to use all her senses in ministering to those in need. In one incident, when a woman in labor seemed to be dying, Teresa jumped on top of her, screaming at her to look into her eyes, upon which the woman's contorted body relaxed enough to allow the child to be born. Teresa lost consciousness and, after regaining it, came to the conclusion that she had absorbed the death of the woman in labor and that she would soon die. This feeling, accompanied by physical symptoms of impending death, drove her to jump out of bed, mount her horse, and ride off as if to escape. She fell from the horse, a fall described as a fall into herself, which is reflected in the researcher's fall while climbing down a hill from which she had viewed Cabora. There is a merging of the two characters in "La caída," in which time and space seem to lose their boundaries. The fictional researcher is possessed by Teresa, who takes over her life.

The second part of the novel, composed of sixteen chapters, describes Teresa's cataleptic condition, what seemed like her death, her resuscitation into a phantomlike creature—living in a trance, unable to attend to her own physical needs and functions, but endowed with healing powers. Thousands, having heard of the miracles performed by the Santa, throng to Cabora. After three months and eighteen days, Teresa came to herself, bereft of the memory of her trancelike state. Still capable of healing the sick and infirm, she becomes the focal point of Cabora, to which the crowds come for her blessing, miracles, and cures. Her father is torn between his love for his daughter and his ego that cannot accept being disobeyed or ridiculed. Teresa disobeys his orders to put an end to this cult, and his legal wife, who does not live at Cabora, showers him with insults, threats, and ridicule, and locks the bedroom door, depriving him of his rights. However, Don Tomás, at the urging of his friend Lauro Aguirre, comes to a working solution with his daughter that satisfies her needs and allows him to maintain his authority and dignity.

The country, especially the northern states, is experiencing political unrest and pockets of uprisings against the government of Porfirio Díaz. In some cases the name of the Santa de Cabora is invoked, attracting the attention of the official press. An uprising in Tomóchic headed by Cruz Chávez brings Chávez to Cabora to seek the Santa's protection. This man awakens something more than political sympathy in Teresa: her sexuality. She becomes preoccupied and depressed by all the death that surrounds her and feels guilty for having caused the deaths of some while saving the lives of others. Teresa's name becomes associated with antigovernment uprisings, and an order for her and her father's arrest and expulsion is delivered to Cabora. Her visions and premonitions are realized as she and her father are taken to Guaymas under military escort, imprisoned, and then transferred to Nogales with the proviso that they never return to Mexico. For Don Tomás, the loss of Cabora was a death sentence that his daughter had brought upon him. For Teresa, her anonymity and impotence in a strange country were humiliating and degrading.

Part III, composed of ten chapters, chronicles the last years of Teresa's life, beginning with her arrival in Nogales, Arizona. There she and her father are met by Lauro Aguirre and settle in a modest house in the Mexican part of town. Don Tomás had fallen into a deep depression, and Teresa couldn't cope with her powerless state. With Aguirre's help in promoting Teresa as a saint and the incarnation of kindness and justice, their situation improved and the family from Mexico joined them. Don Tomás even recovered some of his former strength and spirit. Teresa cooperated with Aguirre in his antigovernment activities, but the rebellions he planned failed. The family, after having moved several times, finally settled in Clifton, Arizona, a mining town, and agreed to the demands of the United States government to refrain from revolutionary activities so as to avoid extradition to Mexico. There Teresa lived an ordinary and tranquil life dedicated to the construction of a hospital that would dispense both traditional and nontraditional medicine. She fell madly in love with Guadalupe Rodríguez, a foreman from the mine, and, against her father's wishes, ran off to marry him. On the day of her marriage, Rodríguez went into a furious rage and attempted to kill her. When she returned home, a broken woman, her father refused to speak with her and fell into a deep depression. When an opportunity presented itself to travel to California and other states to work for a medical company, she asked her friend Juana to "lend" her one of her sons to act as an interpreter. The young man lived with her, and they had a daughter before they finally married. Later, after the birth of another daughter, they separated. Don Tomás died a broken man without ever learning of Teresa's marriage and motherhood. Teresa died at the age of thirty-three.

A short epilogue tells about a woman who in 1987 returned from the dead claiming to have come from heaven to bring justice and kindness to the world. It is Teresa in the body of her fictional creator.

Apart from the story, which captivates the attention of the reader with its strong links to the period preceding the Mexican Revolution of 1910, the characters of *La insólita historia de la Santa de Cabora* are unforgettable. Teresa, the product of lust and innocence, of the conqueror and the conquered, spends her life seeking her legitimacy, her real self, her empowerment. And yet when she achieves her goals—the desired recognition by her father, her dedication to the sick and infirm, her participation in the Revolution in the name of social justice, her complete domination of her father, and the assumption of the male role—she doubts her success and lets her emotions lead to poor decisions and to loneliness. Her sexuality is ambivalent. Denied at first, it is then aroused by Cruz Chávez, who goes off to fight for his people, and later by Guadalupe Rodríguez, who almost kills her. Both are relationships that are not consummated. Finally, she seems to fall in love with Juan Van Order, a much younger man, who prefers an easy life over family and responsibilities, but who gives her some happiness and two daughters. Don Tomás, the embodiment of the conqueror with a wife and a mistress and two families, is caught up in Teresa's powers and cannot deny her will. He supports her activities as a healer, allows himself to be involved in revolutionary activities, loses Cabora (that symbol of power and authority), goes into exile, and very late in life learns that an individual can play a role in the course of history. The many secondary characters, each in his or her own way, round out this novel and contribute to its structure and composition.

Domecq, in weaving in the story of a fictitious researcher who is the author herself, uses the technique of metafiction in which the writer observes and describes her own act of creation. Thus her novel is both the story of the research for her narration and the story of Teresa Urrea.

Brianda Domecq, who became a professional writer relatively late, is now completely devoted to her career. Her solid grounding in literature, especially the work of other women writers, has given her a perspective on literature written by women. Although not all her contemporaries will agree that Mexican literature written by women has withstood the test of time and is sufficiently voluminous to form its own corpus and tradition, she makes a convincing case for her point of view. Her interest in women's sexuality, clearly manifested in her anthology on virginity, shows Domecq's grasp of the history of Mexican literature and her delight at taking on a subject considered taboo. It is the underlying humor touched with malice that gives this writer's work a feeling of lightness and fun, even when the topic is heavy and serious.

As a writer of fiction, both in her short stories and in her novels, Domecq has concentrated on themes and created characters that preoccupy and haunt her. Whether it be a woman's loneliness, which permeates many of the short stories, or her struggle to be independent and free from a patriarchal and repressive society that expects her to behave according to its rules, seen so clearly in her second novel, Domecq molds these themes into solid works of fiction. *La insólita historia de la Santa de Cabora*, with its metafictional technique and its recreation of a historical character and period, is her best and most ambitious work to date.

Domecq's next novel, about several generations of women over a period of some 150 years starting in 1850, will portray the transformations achieved in their intimate lives and the external changes brought about by the movements of history. The theme, a challenging one, will call on Domecq's proven gifts for historical research coupled with her sharpened narrative skills.

Conversations with the Writer
AUGUST 5, 1992; JANUARY 11, 1994

How and when did you begin to write?

From the very beginning, writing for me has been as much a basic possibility in my life as a long process. As a possibility, it was awakened in me in by what we would call oral literature. My father used to tell me stories, especially when I was frightened and couldn't sleep at night, and not only did he tell me stories but we acted them out. We used to walk through the woods and pretend that the Indians were attacking us or that we were searching for a treasure, something like that. As I said in my autobiography, my father devoted himself to fictionalizing my life and from him I learned to translate reality into stories.

Ever since I can remember I wrote little stories; I always liked writing letters and stories. One of my hobbies when I traveled with my family by car was to take along a notebook and write down the entire dialogue that took place on the road. And then at night I read it aloud, and we all laughed a lot because there never failed to be an argument between my parents about whether we should go to the right or the left and then came my brother's funny remarks. I also remember how as a child and an adolescent I used to like to converse with the adults and take very controversial positions. My grandmother always told me, "You are going to be a writer, you will be a writer." However, I didn't write anything serious until after I was married. Of course, when I was engaged I wrote poems, and during my high school years at Dana Hall in the United States I used to write poetry and took classes in creative writing, but there was no rigor or craft.

At that time did you write in English or in Spanish?

I wrote in English until I was twenty-five years old. After I was married, I took a correspondence course at the Famous Writers School. And in those days I managed to publish my first short story in the United States, in an insignificant midwestern magazine called *Marriage Magazine*. They paid me eighty dollars, something that was like a dream. But that was the only story I ever published in English. Later I began to feel a lack of roots. I was trying to write for a public and a milieu in which I no longer had any roots, although I was born in the United States. I felt displaced, divided between two cultures.

Then my life took a turn, and I decided to adopt Spanish as my working language and Mexican reality as my point of departure. It was at that moment that I really began my apprenticeship as a writer. In those days I needed to earn money, and in 1968 I began to work for the Olympic Committee in the Publications Department. Afterward, I went to work at an advertising agency as a creative writer, and there I really began to become disciplined in the use of Spanish as my instrument of communication. Later on, because of the demands involved in having a young daughter, I devoted myself to doing translations from English to Spanish, a profession that came to an end with the translation of Norman Mailer's *Of a Fire on the Moon* [1970; *De un fuego en la luna*, 1971], about the flight of Apollo 11 to the moon. That experience taught me what a thankless job translations were. It was a book that fascinated me. I did the translation and then, regrettably, it was given to a copy editor who knew neither English nor Spanish, because he made corrections that were incomprehensible in any language. It is a translation that has always embarrassed me somewhat because they don't mention the copy editor in the book; they just have me as the translator.

When it was no longer necessary that I work, because my husband's business was going well, I gave up translating and I began to study language and literature at the National University of Mexico. I was then thirty years old. I got my degree and began to write short stories, essays, and I even published some poems in *La Palabra y el Hombre*. Afterward I devoted myself more to short stories. But still, I must confess that the idea of tackling a longer text like a novel put me into a state of panic. It was, without a doubt, my kidnapping, which I used in my first novel, that finally pushed me into writing a longer text and struggling with the problems of structure, narrative voice, the handling of time, and all that is involved in the complexity of a novel. And since then my texts have become longer. I have published a collection of short stories, an anthology about virginity in Mexican literature, two novels, and right now I am putting together a collection of essays on Mexican women writers.

These essays have already been published in newspapers or magazines?

Most of them, yes. Some were written specifically for conferences and published later either in the cultural sections of newspapers or in magazines. There are some that are unpublished. But I discovered that many traced an evolution from 1980 to 1992 in which the progression and the different modalities of the now-famous boom in literature written by women could be seen. Therefore, I do feel that they form a unit. One group of essays approaches the phenomenon in a general way, whereas others offer an analysis of a specific work. This allows one to see simultaneously the general development of the phenomenon and its particular manifestations over a period of twelve years. This "writing in time"—to quote Bárbara Jacobs [1947]—permits a progressive view that leads me to the conclusion that there exists a corpus of literature written by women in Mexico of sufficient proportions to be able to speak of the foundations of a tradition of literature written by women, separate from and independent of the tradition of literature written by men. At this time, if we divide the women writers into generations by decades, as of the 1950s we have four generations who are actively producing and one—the decade of the nineties—that is just beginning. With the exception of Rosario Castellanos [1925–1974], Josefina Vicens [1911–1988], and Inés Arredondo [1928–1989], all the women who began to publish in the decade of the fifties continue to write. To these we must add those of the generation of Elena Poniatowska [1933]; then mine that includes Aline Pettersson [1938], María Luisa Puga [1944], Silvia Molina [1946], and others who began to write in the middle and end of the seventies; the generation of Ethel Krauze [1954], Miriam Ruvinskis [1951], etc., that started in the eighties; and finally the young women who have begun to publish in this last decade of the century. Certainly in Mexico this new voice contributed by literature written by women is changing the face of Mexican literature.

There are those who argue that Literature written with a capital L has no gender, but I disagree: Literature with a capital L has always been literature written by men, and we women, when things go well, can aspire to see our little work recognized by the grace of "God our father" and tacked on with pins to the corpus of literature written by men. Our work is analyzed in comparison to literature written by men, it is squeezed—with a shoehorn—into masculine literary schools and movements, and in the end it is judged that we are either modernists or late avant-gardists or that we have taken it into our heads to imitate someone or other. The enormous disadvantage is that it permits one to arrive at the hackneyed conclusion that we women never create anything new and that we only know how to follow and imitate. The most obvious example of the damage that this produces is the case of Elena Garro's novel, *Los recuerdos del porvenir* [1963; *Recollections of Things to*

Come, 1969], which was pronounced to be a clear manifestation of the magic realism made famous by [Gabriel] García Márquez [1928]. The fact is that Garro's book was published several years before *Cien años de soledad* [1967; *One Hundred Years of Solitude*, 1970]. The work of contemporary women writers can be placed in its own category, within its own context, which is literature written by women, or feminine literature. Then if we recognize that there is a corpus of literature written by women just as there is a corpus of literature written by men, we can distinguish the good, the mediocre, and the bad within these two bodies, and from these two bodies the best of each will emerge to constitute Literature with a capital L, without writing off the literary production of an entire period, as has happened with literature written by women. That is why there is such a great attempt to recover the forgotten [women] writers of the nineteenth century because, if they weren't as outstanding as Nellie Campobello, who was recognized and accepted as a writer, the rest fell into oblivion.

As part of your literary training, what writers did you read?

My literary background is quite heterogeneous because I got started in American and English literature and I have continued reading both. Then during my university studies I read all of Spanish literature, later Latin American literature, and more recently literature written by women as a topic of research for my essays. I would say there is a little of everything in my background, from cheap, pornographic literature that my father used to hide in the closet to the all-time classics.

What writers influenced your prose?

This business of influences disturbs me a lot, and every time someone asks me that question my mind goes blank. My readings at the university were disciplined, but in general my readings are undisciplined and very random. I don't know, I think I don't write from the perspective of literature, and therefore it is difficult for me to know who has influenced me or not.

I feel that my readings have formed a kind of foundation within me, so that what literature has given me has neither title nor author but just emerges naturally. I can give you two examples that I didn't even realize I had used until long afterward. One of them is obvious, and John Brushwood pointed it out to me, which is the use of "el día de su segunda muerte" [the day of her second death] in *La insólita historia de la Santa de Cabora*. It is a technique similar to the one used by García

Márquez in *Cien años de soledad:* "Muchos años después frente al pelotón de fusilamiento . . ." [Many years later in front of the firing squad . . .]. It is a literary technique that I believe many authors have used, and I didn't connect it to García Márquez when I used it. The other example is, as a matter of fact, in my first novel, *Once días...y algo más,* in which instead of the real names of the characters I use their signs of the zodiac. Afterward I realized that this is what Norman Mailer [1923] did in *De un fuego en la luna,* the book I translated. Now whether this comes from Norman Mailer or doesn't, I don't know. It comes from that literary foundation that I have inside of me. I think this happens, although I can't be sure, with most writers unless one is involved in a literary milieu in which a kind of avant-gardism aimed at breaking with a previous tradition is being forged. Then one can say, "Well, I am starting from [Juan] Rulfo [1918–1986]," for example, "in order to go toward the next step" or "I am starting from [Juan José] Arreola [1918]" or "from [Alejo] Carpentier [1904–1980]." Everything good that I read I end up liking sooner or later or it fascinates me from the beginning. It is from there that one learns, one absorbs techniques and ways of writing that form part of that foundation and that, if the text demands, emerge and are used.

> *But it is not a conscious thing. It is a matter of having absorbed*
> *all these readings and afterward making use of what one has absorbed*
> *in one's writing.*

It is a little like learning the craft from the masters. And this business of influences I believe is always a matter of the critics, who when they read someone's work say, "Ah, look, this connects so-and-so to someone else." But I really don't know. In my case, it is not conscious. If it is a conscious and direct influence in the case of some other writer, then one could speak of imitation. For example, obviously in Isabel Allende [1942] there is the influence of the entire school of magic realism in her *La casa de los espíritus* [1982; *The House of the Spirits,* 1985]. But she breaks away and does something else. I was very annoyed with the critics who said that she was an imitator of García Márquez. Despite the fact that the first thirty pages of her novel are similar in tone to that of García Márquez, afterward she manages to break away and does something that is all her own. But it is easier to say that she took the formula from García Márquez than to analyze her real contribution.

Ever since I published my first book, I have been interviewed and always asked the same thing and I have never been able to answer. As soon as I am asked, I begin to grope. Who? Who? Carpentier? Here? There? Who? Rulfo? García Márquez? [Miguel de] Cervantes [1547–1616]? [Luis de] Góngora [1561–1627]? What I am really doing is mentioning writers that I like, but whether they have influenced me I don't know. Góngora's baroque sense of humor? Can he have influenced me?

Do you prefer European, Latin American, or North American writers?

Since my literary background has been a bit of everything, I prefer the author that gets to me and says something to me. A preference by group, no. I am fascinated by all that has been called magic realism in Latin America. I consider it a very important break. And also the "Boom" and the recognition finally that Latin America is producing literature at the international level that can be translated and read by people other than just Spanish speakers, the fact that Latin American literature is at last transcending its regionalism.

What is your opinion of the women writers of your generation?

I believe that, irrespective of the quality of their work, they are doing something very important. First, they are practicing the art of writing, writing literature professionally. All of them, even if not full-time writers because writing doesn't pay enough to live on, are steady writers. Of the women writers of my generation I have the fewest books, although I am not sure. Maybe not. But María Luisa Puga, Aline Pettersson, I, Silvia Molina, all of us have more than five published books, which can be considered as writing professionally. I believe that this is important. Each in her own way and within the bounds of her ability is leaving behind a body of work that will permit a study, that will clearly establish a woman's voice in literature. I believe our work is very varied, something that is going to give it even greater prominence. Sometimes there is a desire to see all of literature written by women as a block or school and to look for what unites all women writers. How do women write? This is like wanting to look at a period of men writers and say all write the same way. No. Those who belong to the romantic movement have certain characteristics in common. But the movement is established after the work has been written, so that when the critic sees it he says, "romantic period," and gives it its label. I think a bit of the same happens with the question of influences. It is more the work of the critic than the consciousness of the author.

For that reason I propose the establishment of a corpus of literature written by women, because I believe that women—those of my time, those who are coming afterward, and those who came before—are writing very diverse things. And each one starts off from her need for self-expression. I don't think any "mafia" at all has been formed. I believe that most of us are not members of literary "mafias," "mafias" in the good sense of the word, which are literary groups established by our male colleagues. I suppose that this will eventually be classified as a phenomenon of postmodernism. I believe that what is really happening is that individuals are being heard, and that is quite important. I believe what they have in common is that they are voices of women, that most are narrating from a marginal perspective, which gives them a point of view distinct from the male point of view, although they may be dealing with the same themes. I believe that what we are doing is very important and that there is work of great value there.

As for my personal taste, the work of María Luisa Puga is solid. Certain things I like more than others. I like *Pánico y peligro*. Her first book, *Las posibilidades del odio*, I find extraordinary. Her latest book fascinated me, especially because of its narrative point of view. It is called *Las razones del lago*, and the story is narrated from the perspective of the town's street dogs. The dogs describe the life of the people and their own lives in this town. Now that absolute marginality, since the dogs cannot influence the life they are describing but can only describe it, seemed sensational to me. The narrative voice fascinated me. It is an autobiographical story because María Luisa went to live near the lake of Zirahuén with her husband, and part of that experience is depicted there. But the narrative point of view is very, very interesting, very original. Nevertheless—and here you have an example of forcing a book written by a woman into a masculine classification—the novel was classified as part of the "great tradition of the rural novel" in Mexico. I believe it doesn't belong there, that Puga's literary intent was different, but it got lost. That slender novel, narrated from the point of view of street dogs, ended up as an appendage of the great tradition of the rural novel in Mexico and that's where it has remained.

In other words, the critics wanted to classify the novel within an already accepted category, the rural novel.

That's exactly the point, and they even put it on the cover, which didn't help María Luisa's book. The work of Aline Pettersson is all of one piece. All of her novels, though very different, have threads that unite them, recurring themes. Most of them deal with women, and the concept of death is evident in her work. Her writing is very important, and I believe that her work viewed as a whole is going to have a greater solidity than the individual novels. Silvia Molina's work is also very solid already. It is very varied and, in that sense, perhaps is similar to mine, which is also quite varied. There are no themes that unify it. No, that's not so. In my work there are—women and myth. They are the two basic threads, myth understood in the broadest sense of the word. But all of this means that my generation is fundamental because we are continuing the course of the great writers from Rosario Castellanos to Elena Poniatowska, and this continuity is necessary so that a tradition of literature written by women is established. I don't know if I have made myself clear.

Yes, and you have answered my next question—whether you believe there is a Mexican literature "written by women"— unless you want to add something.

Whether women use language in a different way has been debated a great deal. Whether women deal with themes differently from men has also been argued. I believe that these two avenues of questioning lead to a dead end. There is no way out because really the themes of literature are so few that it would be unusual if we didn't all talk about love, death, power, the concept of God. As for the use of language, obviously women make use of the established patriarchal language which is the working instrument we have. There may be linguistic transformations, but they appear equally among men writers.

Therefore, I believe that one can establish a literature written by women essentially because it is written by women, and forgive the redundancy. In that sense it can exist without demanding that it be different from literature written by men because of a particular characteristic, like the literature of the romantics differs from the neoclassics in its form, style, and approach. And the reason I believe that it should be considered this way is because if we view literature written by women within its own context, we are going to find many things in it—many common threads, much development, its own form of development— that we are not going to find if we try to compare it to literature written by men that comes to us through established literary schools or movements, the famous "isms" of literature written by men. Therefore, I believe that yes, it is important to consider the body of literature written by women as something independent, although at any particular moment the comparison between a work written by a woman and one written by a man is perfectly valid because obviously there are connecting links. All of us women writers up to the new generation have been nourished by literature written by men because we didn't have anywhere else to go.

To what do you attribute the success of your novel
La insólita historia de la Santa de Cabora?
To its theme, its style, or to the fact that its author is a woman?

No, I don't believe the fact that I, the author, am a woman has influenced its success or its reception by the readers. Basically, it is the theme and the handling of the theme that determine the success or fame of a book. The identification of the reader with the character, be it a man or a woman, is important. *La insólita historia de la Santa de Cabora*, unfortunately, did not become a best-seller in Mexico. I would have been delighted had that happened. But it has sold very well and has been very well received by the critics, which surprised me because I think it is fundamentally a book that undermines patriarchal values written, as my friend Aralia López González says, in the tone of "the law of the mother," which constantly undermines the law of the father. And frankly, Teresa really ends up "killing" her father when she seizes the power, when she assumes the authority within this patriarchal system. And her father ends up following his daughter and losing all the symbols of that patriarchal authority—his land, his wealth, his power, his recognition, and even his name—through his daughter, who little by little takes it away from him in order to practice a kind of black magic, a maternal medicine of the "law of the mother" that is more a product of the body than the intellect. Teresa actually "kills" her father because, although he dies of natural causes, he dies having disowned her when she commits the final treachery of abandoning him and going against his authority, against his law, and saying, "Yes, I am going with Guadalupe," and then goes.

I was surprised that the book was so well received by the critics, and especially by the male critics, given the fact that from a certain perspective it is feminist without being propaganda or ideologically feminist. I would hope that this reception was a reflection of the discovery of a depth in the book that leaves something with its readers—a new vision, identification with the character. It was really wonderful for me when several readers told me, "I didn't want it to end. I didn't want the book to end. I didn't want Teresita to die." That is the best review an author can receive. I do believe that its success can be attributed to the story, to the force of the personality of Teresita, who is certainly a magical character.

Is this character fictitious or does she have some historical basis?

She is a historical character, definitely historical. She was born in 1873 and died in 1906. The structure of the book is historical. All of Teresa's life and the basic facts are true. What is not historical is the development of the plot. There are secondary and tertiary characters who are entirely fictitious. The character of la Huila seems to have existed, but the way I develop the character is wholly my own.

Where did you discover Teresa?

In the novel *Tomóchic* by Heriberto Frías. The character of the researcher is autobiographical.

Yes, it was my impression that you were the researcher who had found a reference to Teresa in an edition of Tomóchic. *Is that the edition we read today?*

Yes, that is the edition we read today, the one of 1906, which, coincidentally, is the year of Teresa's death. And it is the first time that the chapter about her appears in Heriberto Frías's book. But I have always been wont to say that I didn't discover Teresa, but that she found me because something very strange happened to me with Teresa. She took hold of me suddenly and didn't let go for seventeen years. I carried her around in my head from 1973, when I first discovered her in a book, until the novel was published in 1990. As a matter of fact, I have an essay, written for the presentation of the book in Sonora called "La insólita historia de una novela" [The Unusual Story of a Novel; included in *Mujer que publica...Mujer pública*], which relates—from the moment I discovered Teresa—the entire evolution of how I followed her, how I went to all the archives, how I searched for her, all of my research, how I wrote four books during the period of time from my discovery of her until I began to write her story. This is my fifth book. Here they say that five is a lucky number. Teresa, by the way, waited to be the fifth. There is an entire magic behind my experience with this novel . . . fortuitous meetings. I would forget about Teresa for some time and do other things. I was convinced that I was never going to be able to write the novel, and then someone would come along with a bit of information, some clue, something that immediately told me "Teresa is calling me again." Then many years would go by and many unusual events, like being at a cocktail party where someone would say to me: "Oh, you're writing about Teresa Urrea. Well, my father or his grandmother did I don't know what . . . he knew . . . and look, why don't you go and talk with so-and-so, he knows." Well, there I'd go, but it was just by chance. I have always had the feeling that it was Teresa who was guiding me. I wasn't the one pursuing her, but she was saying to me, "Wait for me, you've gone away, come back again."

And once you finished the novel?

Then I was at peace. Well, more or less. I'm sure that if something is missing, she'll let me know.

Right now I am rereading your book and seeing things that I missed in the first reading, maybe because I am reading with greater attention. The use of language, for example, the way Teresa expresses herself. It is a dense book.

I believe that it is a book that has many levels and that can be read in many ways. It very much lends itself to interpretation. I think that explains why it wasn't received like *Como agua para chocolate* [1989; *Like Water for Chocolate*, 1992], because it is a book that demands more attention, it demands greater penetration into what is happening, although there is a story that one can read right through. But yes, I believe it has parts that, as you say, are dense. The entire suggestion, for example, that Teresa is stealing lives so that she can live: those of all the children who die when she is comatose, and then the life of the researcher who appears in Teresa's dreams. The researcher appears there, and Teresa doesn't know who that strange woman is. Well, there are many threads, a funny thing because I kept discovering these threads long after having written the book. Don't think that these were conscious things and that I said, "Ah, I am going to do this." It either comes through the process of writing, or perhaps after the book was written, I discovered many things that were put there unwittingly because writing has a large measure of unawareness.

That's what I have always believed.

There is spontaneity in writing, there is definitely a muse, and I believe there are unconscious functions. I don't remember the exact scene, but in a scene in which Teresita is speaking with Lauro Aguirre or with Don Tomás, it was only after I had written that scene that I realized that I hadn't imagined it. And, in addition, it explained things to me that I didn't know about another one of the characters—the very characters were explaining something about another character that I didn't know consciously. And another thing that happened to me was that when I reread what I had written the day before, many times I found entire sentences about which I said, "I didn't write these sentences." I didn't have any conscious memory of having written the sentences, and in general, they were very good, they were the ones that I kept.

But for me the first thing that presents itself is the story. I know what I want to tell, and my big struggle is how to tell it. I believe that every story has its own form and its own narrative voice, and it is the story that dictates to the author, it dictates to me. That's why my novels are generally the result of a series of trials and errors, of beginning to narrate and then suddenly running dry. If a structure or a narrative voice runs dry, then it is not working. An example is the novel that I am trying to form in my head now. The way I see it, it is going to be told from the perspective of the last woman in a genealogy, in a line of women, who, in addition, is unborn; she is the desired daughter who is never born because the next-to-the-last woman is sterile, she is barren. As I see it now, the unborn woman is going to tell the story, but I also had an entirely different idea when I began to write Teresita. The way I saw it then, Teresita was going to tell her story from her comatose state, from that space up there where she lived her past and her future at the same time. But obviously it wasn't told that way. Teresa didn't like it. Every story has its form, and coming upon that form is the most difficult task for me. I know that I have found the form and the narrative voice when the story begins to flow by itself.

Has being a woman made your career difficult?

Here in Mexico, the way things are, it has been more difficult because of my surname. I don't know whether being a woman has influenced my career or not. But since the surname Domecq carries with it all this business about the bourgeoisie, it is assumed that a bourgeois woman like me shouldn't be writing. I don't know whether it is because I am a woman or I am bourgeois, because Miguel Alemán's novels weren't well received either—because he was an Alemán and because they weren't very good novels. But as a woman I haven't felt that problem. The period from 1978 to 1981 is one during which several women begin to publish—Silvia Molina, María Luisa Puga, I, Aline Pettersson. One begins to see a greater reception of texts written by women. And from then on, by the end of the eighties, an editor without a book written by a woman is an editor living in the past. And now the texts written by women are almost fought over. Therefore, in that sense I haven't had any problem as a woman. Yes, I have found enormous resistance because of my surname. They didn't want to take me seriously.

Did it ever occur to you to use a pseudonym or another surname?

I began writing using my married name, which is Rodríguez. And a cousin of mine from Spain, the son of the poet Leopoldo Panero, said to me: "But you are a fool. Everybody's name is Rodríguez. You want to attract attention and have people buy your books even out of a sense of morbid pleasure, out of curiosity, or to hit you where it hurts. Use Domecq, don't be an idiot." And I listened to him and began to write with the surname Domecq. And my first book about my kidnapping sold like hotcakes because it was news. People wanted to know what had happened. There was a great morbid curiosity that propelled the sale of that book.

Is there a relationship between your journalism and your literary creativity?

I haven't devoted myself to journalism, but I did write a column for the cultural section of *Excélsior* three years ago. It dealt with a variety of themes, so varied that I didn't even attempt to collect all the articles for a book. Nevertheless, if there is a connecting thread, it is my interest in promoting women, in promoting literature written by women, in looking at questions of feminism. I think that is what connects all my literary and other basic activities. One of the things that I didn't mention when we were talking about influences is that often I am terrible and I read very little literature because my interests lead me elsewhere. I read a great deal of psychology, feminism, sociology, and anthropology books, everything that has to do with the reexamination of the great fields of human knowledge; the new reexaminations, the new perspectives that women are giving these fields of knowledge fascinate me. Therefore, you may find me reading more anthropology, more sociology, more theoretical feminism, more psychology written from the perspective of women than literature. I delved into all of that for my journalism, which I no longer do because journalism is exhausting. What I do is publish essays in cultural supplements.

We have touched upon the following question as well. Do you think there is a feminine way of writing that is different from a masculine way of writing?

No. I believe that we are going to find what is different in the perspective, in the view of the world a woman may have, not only because of her biology, which for me is undeniable—the experience of motherhood, of menstruation, of the female body, of her sexuality. They are different manifestations; they are experiences different from the experiences of men. As far as I am concerned, all of this has to have influence when one writes. And a woman's view of the world, because of her historically marginalized position, because of her historically confined position, obviously also has influence. A woman, even in a book as historical and as involved in a social situation as is Angeles Mastretta's *Arráncame la vida* [1985; *Mexican Bolero*, 1989], is a woman who is in her house, who views Mexican politics only from the sidelines. The same happens with Teresita. We are right in the middle of the Porfirian period, but how is this historical period viewed in the book? It is seen from the perspective of a woman isolated on a ranch in Sonora. Perhaps Don Tomás would have viewed it the same way, but I don't think so because Don Tomás read and was involved in politics. He and Lauro Aguirre took ideological positions with respect to what was happening. On the other hand, Teresa doesn't take any ideological position. Therefore, I believe that it is in this, in the view of the world, where one is going to find the real contribution of literature written by women.

Are there any autobiographical elements in your narrative work?

In all of it, even when it doesn't appear that way. For example, the "Trilogía" [Trilogy] at the end of *Bestiario doméstico*, the rewriting of "Genesis" with Adam and Lilith and Eva and Sammaël has much that is autobiographical. It is strange, the entire transformation of the feminine figure in Lilith and in Eva in that "Genesis" has its roots in my own transformation through psychoanalysis and in my own life, my own liberation through psychoanalysis. Therefore, I believe that everything I write has autobiographical roots. I wrote about Teresita not because her story seemed interesting to me but because it moved me. I identified myself, in a very unconscious way if you wish, with the figure of Teresa, with her struggle, with her search for herself, with her wish to understand her own powers and where her life was going. I believe that every work of literature has to have something autobiographical, even if the characters are from other worlds it doesn't matter, even if it is science fiction there is something there. Because you are writing from your own experience, you cannot write from someone else's.

Are you working on something new?

I already mentioned the book of essays. Also I have six or seven short stories, which will be the basis of another book of stories, and I have a novel in my head and written in part, the first quick narration of seven lives. It began originally about fifteen years ago with a text that I never finished entitled *Four Women*, which have increased to seven. It is a story that follows the lives of a lineage of women from 1850 to the year 2000 through the culture of New York and the United States and ending in Mexico. As you can see, there is the autobiographical line. The period from 1850 to 2000 is very significant in the development of feminism because the strong feminist movements began in the United States in the middle of the nineteenth century with the granting of the vote to women, with all the reexamination of women's roles, the temperance movement, and everything that marked the start of social and political activity for women. I want to use all of this as a backdrop to show how it effects my women characters in their intimate lives, in their interior beings, in their relationship to the outside world, to their husbands. It is something along that line. What is happening with women? Who are we? Where are we? Where are we going? In addition, lately I have undergone a process in which my emotional and psychological growth has come about through some extraordinary dreams. I want to use them the way Virginia Woolf [1882–1941] used waves in her novel *The Waves* [1931]. She divided the periods of the lives of her characters by the change of light as reflected on the waves and on the landscape. I want to use my dreams as a framework in my novel to show the development process of a woman who is me. I am not sure how I am going to integrate it all, but the pieces of the novel are beginning to come together. I hope it doesn't take me seventeen years, as it did with Teresita.

In Mexico there have been several generations of notable women writers before yours. Which ones do you admire and why?

Definitely the generation that encompasses Rosario Castellanos, Elena Garro, and—although it is later, I am still not of her generation—Elena Poniatowska. The work of Rosario Castellanos I believe is the first solid work. It is perhaps more solid than any work produced until now by the generations that followed, although, fortunately, if fate permits we will continue producing. I really believe that as far as women are concerned, just like Virginia Woolf was for English and world literature so is Rosario Castellanos for Mexican literature. She is the precursor, she is the mother of Mexican literature written by women, and she represents the woman as a professional writer. For me, Elena Poniatowska is a leading light, little recognized for her literary contributions and more so as a journalist. Her *Hasta no verte Jesús mío, Querido Diego, te abraza Quiela,* and *La "Flor de Lis"* fascinate me. I believe they haven't been given proper recognition. I was fascinated by *La "Flor de Lis,"* which is also very important within literature written by women. There is an entire line of literature written by women that is a return to infancy, and there is something else very important and that is the rediscovery of the mother. The mother in literature written by men does not have the same function as in literature written by women.

All of Ethel Krauze's work—in her short stories and her novels—is about the mother, the search for the mother. Ethel's work is extraordinary. Here is another case like that of Aline Pettersson where I feel that her work viewed as a whole is much more important, has greater density and weight than any of its parts. I have just finished a long essay about how the work of Ethel Krauze [1954] traces a woman's development in all its stages, from infancy up to the mature woman who takes a lover. But all these experiences are there in her stories. And throughout infancy and adolescence the presence and importance of the mother is most significant. Let me get back to your question.

We were talking about women writers of earlier generations.

Ah, yes, I went off talking about Elena Poniatowska because I believe she hasn't been treated justly.

That may be the case here in Mexico, but in the United States Elena Poniatowska is very much recognized and admired.

But here in Mexico she is looked down upon somewhat for being bourgeois. Elena Poniatowska is a member of an aristocracy or something like that. I don't know whether it is because she is a woman or because she's bourgeois. Here we have another such example. But she has transgressed everything that is patriarchal: politics, repression, machismo. Elena is one of our great women and great writers.

Do you believe that the presence of different groups of women writers has helped those that followed?

I think that Rosario Castellanos's perhaps more than the others, because Rosario had the advantage of being recognized as a writer in her time. I may be mistaken, but I have the feeling, an intuition, that some of the others have become better known now with the increased interest in the literature that came afterward. More studies have been devoted to them than before. When I studied at the university, which wasn't so many years ago since I was an older student, we didn't analyze the work of any woman, not even in courses on Mexican literature. I don't believe we even read anything of Rosario Castellanos.

How about Sor Juana Inés de la Cruz [1648–1695]?

Sor Juana is the exception that confirms the rule. Sor Juana is the only one. But it is only now that they are beginning to analyze Sor Juana as a woman, as work written by a woman, and they are beginning to find very interesting things. But her work had never before been viewed from a feminist point of view, but rather her work had always been seen as of the stature of Góngora or [Francisco de] Quevedo [1580–1645], of that school imitating the great men writers. But her very special woman's voice, I believe, has just been discovered now in our time.

You began at the university some twenty years ago, and in the 1970s they didn't read any women writers in Mexican or Spanish American literature courses?

With the exception of Sor Juana, no. I don't even know whether we got to the period of Rosario in Mexican literature.

And now?

I don't know. I haven't gone back. But I suppose so, because I have a friend, Gloria Prado, at El Colegio de México in the PIEM—Programa Interdisciplinario de Estudios de la Mujer [Interdisciplinary Program of Women's Studies]—and she is using my novel *La insólita historia de la Santa de Cabora* in the Universidad Iberoamericana. And she has also used *Bestiario doméstico* a lot. Women's Studies is ten years old at the PIEM, and from there the teachers have brought the works of women writers to the universities where they teach.

Are you saying that it is the women who are bringing this work to the classroom? And the men?

I don't know. I can't give an opinion because I haven't returned to the university. I personally don't teach and I devote myself to being the perpetual student. Studying fascinates me and I get involved in studying all that I can. That's why I can't tell you what is happening today in university classes on Mexican literature. I don't know if they are beginning to give courses such as "Mexican Literature Written by Women" as an appendage to Literature. But it would be interesting to do some research on the subject to find out what is happening.

*Let me tell you that in the United States, to offer, for example,
a course on contemporary Spanish American literature
and not include women is impossible.*

That is as it should be, and fortunately, thanks to that we are beginning to have a voice, we are beginning to publish, to move ahead, to count in this world.

*When do you write and how do you relate your writing
to other responsibilities—domestic, professional, family?*

I generally write from eleven to two and then from four to seven. Fortunately, I have just freed myself from all my maternal responsibilities. Instead of having the empty-nest syndrome, I have the full-flight syndrome and I feel liberated, marvelous; I can devote myself body and soul to myself. My husband of thirty years complains bitterly, but I tell him that for thirty years I was at home trying to combine my professional life and interests with the needs of my children and my house and now, frankly, I want to be a little freer. It is hard to combine all those things. I still remember when I was going for my degree, when my children woke up at 6:30 in the morning, I was doing my work. I used to work through the night because it was the only time I could work comfortably. Not now, now I work during the day very peacefully.

But I do think it is difficult for a woman. And in Mexico it is definitely difficult if that woman has to earn her living, because writing doesn't pay, unless you have a best-seller like Laura Esquivel [1950]. The film has just come out and it has been an enormous success, which pleases me no end because I think she fully deserves it. To my mind, *Como agua para chocolate* and *Arráncame la vida* are two books—both best-sellers—that are on the same level. They are very accessible to the average reader, but they have depth, they are very well handled. All this business about the youngest daughter who can't marry because she has to care for her mother is absolutely true, and to this day people will comment to you about it. People who are a little older than we are will tell you, "Well, my younger sister, no, she was the one whose job it was to care for Mom." It is a terrible existential drama, that of poor Tita trying to break loose. Laura Esquivel's success gives me great pleasure. At a conference, a round table we had a little while ago, I heard the men writers talking about popular literature with enormous disdain. I see that as envy, but real envy. They are green with envy because they have to work, teaching and doing other things, since writing doesn't pay them enough to live on, and with a family it is even more of a problem.

How would you summarize your contribution to contemporary
Mexican literature?

I believe that together with other women writers who, in my opinion, are producing important works, my contribution is the vision of the world of women, of the intimate world of women told with a greater consciousness, with greater veracity, through this looking inside of oneself that has been the task of every intelligent woman from my generation on. We have all—and I consider myself part of this—contributed to the view of women as thinking beings, as feeling beings, who are not men, whose vision is not the masculine vision of reality. In that sense I think that my work *La insólita historia de la Santa de Cabora* brings a different vision of a world that has already been seen, that of the Porfirian period. Or, for example, the presidency of Manuel Avila Camacho viewed from the perspective of Angeles Mastretta doesn't resemble what any male writer could have told about the same period. In my book, the vision is oblique, marginal. Also I brought to literature a character who is extraordinary. Teresa, despite everything, triumphs; she makes herself politically visible; she is a character that moves the world. There aren't many women characters in Mexican literature who move the public world, and Teresa achieves heroic stature. Her life was a complete triumph in the feminine sense, in which to triumph is to know oneself rather than to be successful in one's struggles. Because in her revolutionary struggle and in her personal one, triumph slipped out of her hands. Nevertheless, in the sense of understanding herself and her life, I feel that Teresa triumphed. That is important, as there aren't many role models in contemporary Mexican literature. Generally, it is the submissive woman who is portrayed or one who rebels in a nonaggressive way, but not the woman who assumes her legitimacy. In my novel, Teresa assumes her legitimacy and stands out as a truly significant figure.

Representative Selections

Balzac

["Balzac," from *Bestiario doméstico*]

They bought him to fill an incipient menopausal emptiness in their marriage and because he had inordinately long ears, reddened and droopy eyelids that gave him a very sad look, and properly deformed legs, typical of his misshapen and woeful breed. A distant literary nostalgia suggested his name to them.

While a puppy, he filled the house with tenderness and amusement, the carpets with urine, and his owners' trousers with hair. They, like doting grandparents, put up with everything. But from one day to the next he reached sexual maturity, and his puppylike pranks degenerated into a state of constant excitability bordering on madness. His owners, having long forgotten the power of instinct, contemplated with horror the erotic contortions of the animal desperately seeking satisfaction from any object solid enough to withstand the weight of his body. The couple, dusting off old memories of their own adolescent children, felt that the dog's excitement would die down by itself once he got past this period of emotional conflict, and they used every occasion when the dog was exhausted to pat him platonically on his ears and belly. Far from calming the fiery Balzac, these innocent strokes set off renewed hunts for a female that, ever more violent and frantic, expressed themselves in wild racing around the garden and absurd attempts to squeeze himself through the one inch of space under the door. This canine frenzy destroyed the garden and was about to play irreparable havoc with the peaceful marriage when Balzac discovered the pail.

It was a beautiful blue soft plastic pail with a golden handle, bought on sale because it was slightly longer and narrower than the ordinary ones. During the day it was used to soak the wash, and at night, to divert Balzac's violent instincts. The narrowness of the pail's torso, the resistant smoothness of the plastic, and the fact that lying on its side it could be mounted perfectly were for the delirious male unmistakable female characteristics. He never had a thought about the problem of the blue color or the capriciousness of siring a litter of long-eared pails.

All day long he prowled around the servants' courtyard, stalking the slender pail that, upright and filled with soapy water, was driving him crazy and prevented any approach. He lost his appetite when he couldn't understand the cold indifference of such a sweet-smelling pail in the presence of the suggestive wagging of his tail. He grew thin out of despair. Rather than race wildly around the garden, he waited, lying on his back in the servants' courtyard, letting his eyes follow the irresistible twistings of the blue provocation. The couple observed the dog's new serenity and thought he had gotten over his adolescence. Once again routine reigned in their house.

In the servants' courtyard Balzac learned to wait for nightfall with calm desperation while, stimulated by delayed desire, his snout broke out into a cold sweat. Sometimes he suddenly had to roll over on his belly to hide an erection when the maid would repeatedly lift and lower the beloved pail; reach into it up to her elbows, putting in or removing the wash from its tender insides; or simply handle it without any respect. In the light of day there was nothing to be done. But when night fell, the pail would be emptied and turned upside down to drain. Balzac would endure his growing tension and wait for the precise moment when the lights of the house were turned off before approaching the object of his desire. Then he would lick it from top to bottom, removing any trace of detergent, and gently seduce it. With a playful little push of his snout he would get it to turn on its side and roll mischievously and coquettishly beyond the reach of his passionate paws. Then he would try to grab hold of it tenderly, but the pail continued its playful resistance. The lively pail eluded the amorous advances of its long-eared seducer, rolling from here to there and barely letting him lick it, which for Balzac was the height of desire. The panting dog would finally manage to move it to a level place in the courtyard, and the pail would let itself be mounted in desperate spasms that caused it to roll over, throwing its lover onto the cold concrete. Balzac's patience would then turn into virile barking that demanded cooperation and tenderness, only to echo in the hollow and cold emptiness of his beloved pail. The tireless coquettishness of the soft plastic forever frustrated the erotic efforts of its canine lover. The bottom of the pail flatly resisted penetration, and Balzac felt his desire was in a constant struggle against his sanity.

One dark night of mad desperation and unpredictable wantonness Balzac couldn't stand it any longer, and with his ferocious and frustrated teeth, he lunged at the beloved plastic, bursting afterward into ear-piercing howls over the blue fragments of his passion that now lay beneath his paws. A week later, the couple had to call the veterinarian to put the poor animal to sleep in order to silence his unbearable wails and to retrieve the golden handle of the broken pail that he jealously guarded in a dark corner of his kennel.

In Memoriam

["In memoriam," from *Bestiario doméstico*]

HYMEN. (FROM THE LATIN HYMEN AND FROM THE GREEK
MEMBRANE.) M. MEMBRANOUS FOLD THAT REDUCES
THE EXTERNAL OPENING OF THE VAGINA WHILE PRESERVING
ITS INTEGRITY.

What is lost usually remains in the last place one leaves it and is found in the last place one looks for it; therefore, what was mine must still be in that sordid, fly-by-night motel at the seaport, because I never went back to look for it. Frankly, it did me no good either before or after, and I really don't understand what is meant by "integrity" since nothing of mine disintegrated. I certainly would have preferred to lose it on a secluded beach, bathed in splendid moonlight and rocked to the rhythm of passionate waves, or in a messy but artistic bachelor's apartment among pages of amorous poetry, or under a luxuriant tree on a soft bed of leaves, touched by the light of a slow and passionate dusk so as to at least endow the memory with a certain romantic air, but wherever it happens, it happens.

Neither can I embellish it with passionate confusion nor with an unforeseen moment of weakness, because both of us knew perfectly well—although we didn't say anything—why we were going to that secluded moonlit beach, and if not, somebody better explain to me why he took a bottle of tequila and I a blanket.

John was part of the inevitable series of awkward and fiery love affairs of normal adolescence, accompanied by petting in the back seat of the car; kisses so intense that they end up in mutual suffocation; shyness and insecurity that serve as a stimulus for a passion of completely illogical proportions; dreams, illusions, and plans for a future fortunately distant and vague. But we liked each other well enough, and for some strange reason we both sensed intuitively that the time had come to cast aside fear and shame and become adults all at once.

I think I told my parents about the evening on the beach, forgetting to mention the fact that we were going alone. I recall that we drove in silence, each of us lost in our own thoughts or doubts. It never occurred to me that he might be afraid because it didn't suit me to think so, and I didn't feel very nervous either, since I had erased from my conscience all thought of what we were going to do and was heading for the beach wrapped in perfect and virginal innocence. I believe that we women have the innate ability to feel ourselves seduced beyond all resistance at the slightest excuse, or to commit an act of our own will without assuming any responsibility for the consequences. It is a matter of survival. I, for one, had no problem that night accommodating in the same compartment of my brain a shaky enthusiasm and the conviction that I was being led to the slaughter like a martyr without salvation. Educational perversions.

After two tequilas to build up my courage, I tuned the radio to the hit songs of the moment and tried not to worry about the only thing that really worried me: What would John think of me afterward?

When we got to the beach, we stopped the car, took out the blanket and the tequila, and walked awhile until we found a place from which to admire ocean, sky, and palm trees all at the same time without having to lift our heads; it was a silent complicity to make the ordinary and trivial memorable. We spread the blanket over the still warm sand, under a moon that should have been unforgettable and which for the life of me I can't remember, and we sat down to have a little more tequila for our nerves. The appropriateness of demanding a promise of marriage—in the future of course—occurred to me, but I rejected the idea for fear he might agree to it and that would create problems in the long run. Instead, I embellished my seduction a bit with the conventional phrase, "I love you," something I wasn't very sure of either, except when we were apart and there was the distance necessary to allow for fantasy.

He laid me down on the blanket without any problem and began kissing me with his usual awkwardness. I became the image of languor par excellence, lest any movement be misinterpreted as cooperation. I don't remember having felt anything, neither excitement nor desire, nothing, because I was too busy being the passive victim of a situation from which it was too late to escape, and struggling to make myself believe it. I recalled all the stories that we girls used to tell each other about the agonizing testicular cramps that men suffer if suddenly frustrated, and I decided to sacrifice myself for poor John, who wasn't to blame for his irrepressible impulses.

We were already making progress. He was fondling my breasts and feeling my vagina, while I was letting out little moans to convince him that I was beyond any question of right or wrong, with my will completely shattered. The last thing I remember was the weight of his body on top of mine, both of us still dressed, and the surprising sensation of his erect penis between my thighs. I suffered a kind of internal faint and lost my breath just as an inopportune wave vented all its salty fury on us. We jumped up, coughing out sand and dripping water from head to toe. The bottle of tequila had been swept away; the blanket now sheltered tender little crabs, surprised at finding themselves under such a watery canopy; and John and I looked at one another halfway frustrated and relieved.

That's where it should have ended, and if we had had a sense of humor, that's how it would have been. We would have laughed readily, accepting the tragicomic end to our plans and postponing the consummation of the act till a more propitious and drier time. But it was September and I was eighteen and Elvis Presley was singing "It's Now or Never," so that when John asked me if I wanted to go to a motel to try again, undoubtedly it was the force of my original decision that permitted me to ignore the questioning tone, accept what was being asked as an irrevocable order, and prove once again that we women are always victims of circumstance because our mothers never knew how to prepare us for anything.

Silence is consent, and thus we arrived at a musty and dubious motel whose entrance—a dark and obscene driveway—was just a few yards from the noise and bright lights of the main street. John made me crouch down in the front seat of the car. I suppose it was to protect my honor, but all he managed was to exhaust what little remained of my drenched dignity while he bargained with the clerk to let us have a room until 3 a.m. for a hundred pesos. I thought my virginity had sold very cheaply, and I feared that my initiation—now public knowledge—would become a masturbatory fantasy for all the motel's shady employees.

The room, showing unmistakable signs of innumerable one-night stands, pitted the dreary brown color of its walls against the lewd orange of the bedspread which, for some strange, unconscious reason, made me feel like the tragic heroine of a class-B movie. But I didn't say anything since from the outset it had already been too late, and at this point even money was involved. The sheets, at least, appeared to be clean, but the beach had been a princess's bed compared to that lumpy mattress. I made myself as comfortable as I could in the worn-out memory of other bodies.

We were already going at it when, suddenly, I remembered that we couldn't go on. I felt a wave of relief and a bit of guilt because of John's frustration.

"John! Suppose I get pregnant!"

He looked at me with feverish eyes and, reeling with disbelief, got up and reached for his pants. I thought he would be furious. I was about to look for my stockings when I saw that he was taking out his wallet and from it, a small white envelope. I watched with horror as he opened the envelope, took out a transparent and moist object, and slipped it over his erect penis. I wanted to die. How could he have been so cold, so calculating, so cautious, and so lacking in passion as to have provided himself in advance with that unspeakable object! I despised him. I knew that this was it and I gave in to the inevitable.

Well, everything ended as it had to and I, what can I say, felt nothing. Of course, in those days I was also expecting the San Francisco earthquake. What I did experience was surprise. I took advantage of John's trip to the bathroom to look at the sheets, and to my shock, I discovered the historical and hysterical little red stains. Then it was true! The stories about the hymen had never convinced me nor had the one about the bedsheets that were used to discredit nonvirgins. To me all of that had always seemed like old wives' tales to frighten impetuous young girls. But no: there were the bloody traces of what had been lost, a presence only felt in its absence, a silent testimony of what had been, and suddenly, I thought I should cry. It's not that I felt like it, but it began to seem like the right thing to do. Actually, I felt very calm, a little disappointed by the complete insignificance of it all, but composed. And in some corner of my subconscious, being calm was associated with being a whore, which caused me to burst into such uncontrollable sobs that John came running to put his arms around me and swear never again to do what produced so much suffering and so little pleasure. Because of the contrite tone of his voice, I realized that my reaction had been appropriate to salvage for my image in his memory the last vestiges of questionable decency, and I kept on crying awhile longer.

I allowed myself to be cuddled the entire way home, and we ended the night swearing eternal love to one another and painting the future a platonic shade of pink. I went up to my room, slipped between the fresh, immaculate sheets, and fell asleep immediately. The following morning I opened my eyes and thought: I am no longer a virgin. I waited. Nothing. No change, no emotion, neither guilt, nor euphoria, nor anything else. I shrugged my shoulders, put on my bathing suit, and went down for a swim.

Galatea

["Galatea," from *Bestiario doméstico*]

I don't want to begin to imagine the dreams and the fantasies, the fears, deliria, and secret anxieties locked up in that gilded cage where the canary lived during the time she was with me. I would even like to forget her name, Galatea, "harder than marble, icier than snow," that I myself gave her, inspired only by her immaculate white plumage. But my memory of her remains here, in my mind and in the guilt of that last egg infected with a slow and incurable madness.

Truth be told, they sold her to me as a male, a mistake justified by the dazzling beauty of her feathers, her broad breast, and the way she always held her head erect even in her last days, perhaps out of excessive pride or because of a wicked determination. I had harbored the illusion of gracing my loneliness, first imposed on me and later assumed consciously, with the passionate song of a solitary male, but a little while after hearing the monotonous "chirp-chirp" of my acquisition, I accepted the idea of sharing my monologue with another of the same sex and fate. It didn't take us long to grow fond of one another. She mesmerized me with her stark whiteness and, besides, turned out to be a flirtatious and intelligent companion. She didn't rebel in the least against her isolated confinement and quickly learned to take seeds from my hand and even from between my lips as if giving me little kisses. She relieved me of the foolishness of talking to myself and, trying to be understood, responded to the sound of my voice with repeated "chirps." Every morning her cheerful call would wake me. It was inevitable that I got into the habit of revealing to her my most intimate thoughts, my memories full of resentment, and the thousand carefully chiseled reasons for my being an old maid, all repeated with the clarity of a secret bitterness.

How many months was it? August, September, October, November . . . Toward the end of January, with the beginning of spring, Galatea began to display noticeable variations in her routine of hop-chirp-hop-chirp. She showed signs of a sudden increase in appetite, especially for fresh lettuce and cuttlefish bones, and began to alternate her time on the perches with long sessions of scratching and pecking in the gravel on the bottom of the cage. By the middle of February, she had completely forgotten about the amusing swing, had abandoned the top of the gilded cage, and devoted herself body and soul to shredding the protective paper that was on the floor and to picking out soft little feathers from her breast in an inordinate and unmistakable desire to build a nest.

After much harsh questioning and painful analysis, I understood the injustice of imposing my spinsterhood on Galatea and went out in search of a male. I recall feeling an ephemeral illusion of a family. I found a white and tufted beau that I felt completely met the needs of Galatea with his clear and passionate song, and proceeded to fall in love with him vicariously, sensing exactly how the canary would give in to his male charm. I set up a small gold box for the nest, and I let the male loose inside the virginal enclosure, not without suffering certain palpitations and a strange tickling sensation. Then I sat down at a prudent distance to observe the union.

Galatea was appropriately modest. She looked over the male with reserve and kept on shredding paper. Her beau flapped his wings ostentatiously, spruced up his feathers with unquestionable male vanity, tilted his head flirtatiously, and let out a deeply felt trill that Galatea ignored completely. It was obvious that I was in the way and so, entertaining images of passionate matings and soft sensations of fertility, I moved away into the kitchen. I forced myself not to go through the living room until the next morning. That night, in my dreams, I made mine the uterine fantasies of my beloved canary.

The following day, the cheerful chirp-hop-chirp of Galatea woke me, and I went to the living room harboring illusions of being a grandmother. The canary was hopping frivolously from one perch to the other calling to me as usual. For a moment I didn't see the male, and then I discovered him crouching on the floor of the cage under the feeder, trembling and visibly plucked. Completely bewildered, I sat down to watch. After a while, the suitor, driven by his undying instinct, came out of his hiding place, hopped unsteadily onto the perch, and approached Galatea squeamishly before she could move away. She glared at him with instant rancor; her beak took on a life of its own and struck the head of her suitor with a tremendous blow. Then, with unaccustomed speed, she held down her surprised suitor with her beak and claws, and let loose a barrage of lashes with her wings that filled the air with feathers and blood. In one leap I reached the cage.

"Galatea!"

The canary immediately dropped her prey and looked at me, almost smiling: "Chirp?"

Horrified, I picked up the motionless and bloody little body. I cradled it for a long time in the palm of my hand. He was still alive. During the twenty-four hours that I fought to no avail to save the canary's life, I didn't respond even once to the growing desperation with which Galatea was calling me with her stupid chirp-chirp. Finally I approached her cage, and opening my hand abruptly, I filled her wild little eyes with the guilt of the vanquished dead body. She froze on her perch, looked at the handful of blood and feathers, and let out a sudden and unusual song that lasted until three in the afternoon. It was the last sound she emitted. The following morning the first egg appeared, white, immaculate, and completely empty: a small infertile ovulation expelled onto the floor of the cage. It saddened me to see it and I threw it into the trash immediately. On the following day, the second one appeared, identical to the first. I sensed the beginning of my anguish in the translucent emptiness of that small white shell and threw it away also.

That's how Galatea's incurable derangement began. During the day, she thrashed around in a frenzy of nest-building, tearing the paper of her cage into shreds and plucking mercilessly at her feathers. At night, a dark nymphomania took hold of her that, in less than a month, expelled the perverse sum of fifty-three empty little eggs, all of a perfect and virginal whiteness. My anguish was transformed into impotence, insomnia, fear, hatred. I felt unprotected in the face of that cruel and barren production, but every attempt to stop it was in vain. During the entire maddening egg-laying episode Galatea never deluded herself. She never once tried to hatch those violent castoffs. She only deposited them, night after night, in her mad ritual of ovarian atonement, while I was suffocating with nightmares about infertile ovulations and death wishes.

It was obvious that the perverse egg-laying couldn't go on indefinitely. That slow uterine suicide had to come to an end. One morning Galatea awoke motionless, lying on her side on the floor of the cage, her small and wretched existence blocked by one last and disproportionately large egg that couldn't be laid. I took her body into my hand and squeezed it: the egg appeared. It had a strange copper color and an irregular shell, totally opaque. It had a definite weight, as if it were sheltering something inside of it.

Galatea landed in the trash without tears or remorse on my part, but for some strange reason I couldn't get rid of the egg. Every attempt to throw it away produced a paralyzing mixture of anguish and curiosity, and I would place it back on the enormous white cushion where, every day, I sit on it awhile in the feverish hope that some day it will hatch and reveal its awesome secret.

Bibliography

Publications

Once días...y algo más. Xalapa: Universidad Veracruzana, 1979; 2d ed., Mexico City: HARLA, 1991.

Bestiario doméstico. Mexico City: Fondo de Cultura Económica, 1982.

"Teresa Urrea, la Santa de Cabora." *Temas sonorenses: A través de los simposios de la historia,* 139–169. Hermosillo: Gobierno del Estado de Sonora, 1984.

Voces y rostros del Bravo. With photographs by Michael Calderwood. Mexico City: Jilguero, 1987; 2d ed., 1988.

Acechando al unicornio: La virginidad en la literatura mexicana. Selection, study, and notes. Mexico City: Fondo de Cultura Económica, 1988.

La insólita historia de la Santa de Cabora. Mexico City: Planeta, 1990.

BD/De cuerpo entero. Mexico City: UNAM/Corunda, 1991.

Mujer que publica...Mujer pública. Mexico City: Diana, 1994.

"Teresa Urrea: La Santa de Cabora." *Tomóchic: La revolución adelantada,* 9–65. Ed. Jesús Vargas Valdez. Vol. 2. Ciudad Juárez/Chihuahua: Universidad Autónoma de Ciudad Juárez/Instituto Chihuahuense de la Cultura, 1994.

Translations

"Adelaide's Body." Trans. Carolyn Brushwood. *River Styx* 26 (1988): 80–82.

"The Eternal Theater." Trans. Carolyn Brushwood. *Latin American Literary Review* 19, no. 38 (1991): 96–99.

Eleven Days. Trans. Kay S. García. Albuquerque: University of New Mexico Press, 1995.

Carmen Boullosa

Carmen Boullosa (1954)

About the Author and Her Writing

Conversations with the Writer

Representative Selections

III ["III," from *Antes*]

Mary, Why Don't You?
["Propusieron a María," from *Teatro herético*]

Bibliography

About the Author and Her Writing

Carmen Boullosa is a woman of intense drive, passion, enthusiasm, and sensitivity, and these qualities stand out singly and together in all that she does. For her, being a writer is all-consuming and all-encompassing. Although it may seem contradictory, Boullosa is totally absorbed by her writing and at the same time she embraces many diverse activities that are essential components of her craft. On the one hand, she sequesters herself during part of every day so as to write undisturbed by the demands of daily life. Yet she seeks out and relishes many things that might well distract another writer. She delights in the role of wife and mother; she enjoys participating in literary symposia and gatherings; she travels widely to give lectures; she has learned the art of typesetting and bookbinding; she directs and participates in theatre; she does poetry readings so that her words can be heard as well as read. All that she does becomes part of her, because she is convinced that writing requires the participation of her entire being.

Soft-spoken, even-tempered, and patient, Carmen Boullosa is straightforward and frank in her opinions and uninterested in popularity or in being identified as a woman writer. To her mind, writers have neither gender nor nationality. Although completely devoted to her profession, she is concerned about and actively involved in environmental and political issues because of her deep preoccupation about the survival of the universe and of Mexico.

Unlike those writers who through their work share some autobiographical details with their readers, Boullosa does not. Even though she believes that writers make use of everything in their work, including their most personal, hidden, and private feelings, they must subject them to the order of the book. To her, a book is a work of art with its own rules and exigencies that must be met if it is to achieve an autonomous existence. Therefore, the reader who is searching for clues about Boullosa will have to look very closely to find an occasional autobiographical reference or to discover an issue that preoccupies her. Her first two novels, *Mejor desaparece* (Get Lost; 1987) and *Antes* (Before; 1989), have some very tenuous connections to her life. But curiously, she herself believes that it is in *Son vacas, somos puercos* (They're Cows, We're Hogs; 1991), a novel about pirates on the island of Tortuga where women are proscribed, that she used the largest number of elements from her personal life but transformed them completely.

Carmen Boullosa was born in Mexico City into a large middle-class Catholic family. Surrounded by books at home and at the parochial schools she attended, she experienced something akin to a spiritual calling to be a writer when she was about fifteen years old. She felt that her life without writing would be unbearable and not worth living. And so, driven by an unexplainable frenzy, she wrote poetry and prose firmly believing that merely wishing so would make her a writer. Only on her father's insistence did she attend a university, first the Jesuit Universidad Iberoamericana and later the National University.

It was at the Iberoamericana, under the guidance of her teacher Huberto Batis (1934), that she realized that it wasn't enough just to write, but that writing required discipline and practice. Batis persuaded her to switch to the National University, a step that became a turning point in her life. There she met other aspiring writers of her generation and was caught up in the general excitement of writing and publishing. Among her peers, who were also smitten by a spiritual calling, one thing naturally led to another and she published her first books of poetry—*El hilo olvida* (The Thread Forgets; 1978) and *La memoria vacía* (Empty Memory; 1978).

In 1980 she was awarded a scholarship at the Centro Mexicano de Escritores (Mexican Writers' Center), where, in the company of established writers like Juan Rulfo (1918–1986), Salvador Elizondo (1932), and Francisco Monterde (1894–1985), she learned how difficult and painful writing was. It was during that year that she completed her first novel, *Mejor desaparece*, but it was not published until seven years later.

Despite the impression that this writer's continuous list of publications may give, each of her creative efforts is the result of much pain, agony, rewriting, and time spent maturing in the drawer of her desk. Each work terrifies her, and she is beset by doubts about whether to part with it. Her involvement with her writing is intense, from the research she does when working with historical themes to the prose she works as if it were clay, trying to give it life, to impregnate it with the story as it unfolds, to let it stand on its own and affect the reader beyond the telling of the anecdote. Consequently, Boullosa's work requires the concentration and participation of her readers when the writer speaks to them directly, when she uses her texts to rewrite or recreate history, and when, in a subtle way, she asks them to piece together fragments to capture an image.

Boullosa has a light side that manifests itself in her prose. Numerous humorous anecdotes and scenes in each of her novels can stand by themselves as vignettes. This inclination toward the ludic, even in the most serious work, helps to bring the readers to a realistic plane when Boullosa has drawn them into a mythical or fantastic world.

For many years Boullosa was active in the theatre. She wrote plays and directed and produced her own works and those of others. Some were performed in a theatre-bar she owned, El Hijo del Cuervo, and others in various theatres of Mexico City and elsewhere. Having learned typesetting and bookbinding from Juan Pascoe, the editor who published her second book of poetry, she established her own workshop where she published a number of small editions of the work of various poets and several very limited editions of art books. More recently, except for her lecture tours and a semester at San Diego State University as a visiting professor, Boullosa is completely engrossed in her writing and the reading and research she devotes to it. For her, there is no greater joy in life than being able to write.

Carmen Boullosa's creative production has been constant and varied. Since her first publications of poetry in 1978—*El hilo olvida* and *La memoria vacía*—there have been several other small volumes: *Ingobernable* (Ungovernable; 1979), *Lealtad* (Loyalty; 1980), and *Abierta*

(Open; 1983). Most of this early poetry has been collected and published in a single volume, *La salvaja* (The Savage; 1989). Boullosa has written for the theatre, and three of her plays, all a blend of reality and fantasy, are in *Teatro herético* (Heretical Theatre; 1987). *Papeles irresponsables* (Irresponsible Papers; 1989) is a diverse collection of short prose pieces, and *Soledumbre* (Solitude; 1992) contains both poetry and short prose selections. Because of the very nature of the genre, this writer is most widely known for her novels. The first two—*Mejor desaparece* and *Antes* (which was awarded the Xavier Villaurrutia Prize)—are set in twentieth-century Mexico and deal in broad terms with the family. *Son vacas, somos puercos* and *El médico de los piratas* (The Pirates' Doctor; 1992) are both rewritings of history, telling the story of pirates in the Caribbean Sea in the seventeenth century. History also comes into play in *Llanto. Novelas imposibles* (Weeping. Impossible Novels; 1992), a work in which Moctezuma reappears in the Mexico City of today. Her novel *La Milagrosa* (1993; *The Miracle-Worker*, 1994) is a complex narration combining the life and deeds of a miracle-worker with contemporary political intrigue. The novel *Duerme* (Sleep; 1994), set in late-sixteenth-century Mexico, is an adventure story whose protagonist is a minor character, "Ella," of *Son vacas, somos puercos*; whereas the forthcoming *Que viva* (Long May He Live) is about a child who is the lone survivor of an earthquake in today's Mexico City.

Boullosa's fictional world is difficult to penetrate and does not lend itself to an all-encompassing or general description. Although there is no single unifying theme, there are a number of threads with which she weaves the fabric of her tales. Her concern with the family—the relationship between parents and children and between husbands and wives—does manifest itself in her writing. One also senses an underlying nostalgia for earlier times when there was a belief in a utopian world and when honesty and loyalty were the hallmarks of society. Her preoccupations with the environment and with Mexico's political system are increasingly noticeable themes in her works. Boullosa sees a complex and difficult reality, and her novels challenge the reader to grasp its true meaning. Part of the challenge is following the structure of the novel and the narrative techniques she employs to reflect the world she has created.

Mejor desaparece, Boullosa's first novel, is in a category by itself. It is fragmentary, made up for the most part of very short chapters, each relating an incident. These fragments, when pieced together, create an image of a disintegrating family and of a world on the verge of collapse. The incidents are not consecutive nor do they flow one from the other in any coherent order. There are lapses and ambiguities throughout. Boullosa tells us that her original aim was to write a work something like the gothic novels of the British writer Ann Radcliffe (1764–1823). She had in mind a novel of muted terror, suspense, and the supernatural, set in twentieth-century Mexico. As she was working, the novel, originally entitled *Dulces afectos* (Sweet Feelings), developed into an enormous work. Realizing that it was all wrong, she salvaged one of the female characters, made her into several others, and completed the book in 1980. However, gripped by doubts and fear, she didn't publish it until seven years later, causing her to view it with a certain strangeness because of the time that had elapsed since writing it.

Mejor desaparece brings us into a world of the macabre, a world of horror that borders on the insane. In the novel, objects take on an independent existence; death is contagious; dreams are shared; mysterious letters are delivered; nature dries up and vanishes; the past becomes extinct. This world is inhabited by a widowed father, his four daughters, and the father's new wife, each of whom narrates a different part of the novel. Boullosa depicts this family in crisis, leaving a painfully stark image of its alienation, rejection, loneliness, and disintegration as a social unit.

The fragmentary narration is preceded by an "Explicación" (Explanation), a description of the father screaming like a scalded cat for his children to come out and look at something. That something turns out to be "*eso*" (that thing), a disgusting object one would rather ignore or kick away as if it were trash. But the father introduces it into the house, and with the appearance of *eso*, everything changes. The father is obsessed with it, moves it around, and gives it a name, all of which frightens everyone. He also becomes obsessed with cleanliness to the point where he washes the apples with soap, burns the used tablecloths, boils the silverware, and dips the bread into alcohol before eating it. He makes fun of his daughters and considers them absurd and deformed in contrast to *eso*, which for him has taken on form, as has the youngest daughter who now looks and smells like *eso*.

Neighbors say the girls are the daughters of the one whose name has been forgotten. Their mother is dead; her death from unknown causes is contagious and has taken life from others. The house is infested with rats that have invaded every corner and that reproduce shamelessly. Signs appear on the outside of the house; graffiti covers its walls;

garbage is all over; strange people come and go. The father's lawyer calls the daughters to his office to sign a letter in which the father deprives them of their legitimacy and vows to destroy them. Nature has joined other forces to shun the family: the flowers in the garden disappear, the crickets hide, the pebbles avoid contact with their feet, and the earth is a charred ruin. The daughters lose their past when their father burns their birth certificates.

The novel concludes with the father knocking on a door but getting no response. He can't reach the lock or the window and finds he can't remember who he is. His children are no longer his; his house is nothing but walls; he can't recall his wife's name. He seems to be slipping without falling, unable to speak, but thinking it would be better to disappear than become trapped in the grass of the field.

Mejor desaparece is a novel far removed from the more traditional realist mode. Boullosa uses many symbols, macabre humor, bizarre events and descriptions to create a text that trips along rather than flows in order to show the crisis of society that she wishes to depict. We watch in horror as a family is torn apart, as it deteriorates and collapses under the weight of many forces. It is a crisis borne of mistrust, loneliness, rejection, and doubt.

Antes is a novel in which a young girl tells of her passage from childhood to adolescence. The young girl is speaking after having died at the age of eleven. It is a self-conscious narration wherein the girl informs her readers that she wants to start at the beginning, and addresses them directly from time to time. The work is composed of sixteen chapters, each of which is simultaneously poignant, strange, humorous, sad, magical, and touching. Here Boullosa calls on her memories, experiences, and imagination to create a powerful novel of the world of childhood. The young girl, embodying all the feelings of fear, suspicion, and doubt typical of children, lives in a world where reality and fantasy are in a constant struggle for control.

The narrator, the youngest of three sisters, tells of her birth in Mexico City in 1954 and how she invented memories to be able to fall asleep. She began to hear frightening footsteps that kept her awake at night, but lulled her to sleep during the day. In addition to the two sisters, the family is made up of her mother, Esther, her father, and grandmother. Without dwelling on the early years, the narrator moves quickly to elementary school, a Catholic school for girls. The amusing descriptions—the salute to the flag with words that are incomprehensible and meaningless, the awarding of prizes for achievement, the pranks of the older girls, the written warnings sent home, the inevitable visit to the principal's office for some infraction of discipline, the cruelty of the children to one another—show Boullosa's lighter side.

Boullosa depicts the narrator as a typical child, but there is another side to the girl, a layer of fear, torment, guilt, and persecution. While watching an empty lot burn, she sees bodiless faces looking at her; when sleeping at her grandmother's house, she hears noises that frighten her and keep her awake, sounds she could hear but couldn't name; in the garden, the eucalyptus tree becomes her enemy as its little cones fall apart in her hands and the trunk retreats from her touch; a wad of paper burns a hole in her nylon slip. She finds peace for a short time when she places little stones from a neighboring house around her bed and creates an island of safety and silence. She has premonitions of death when a framed picture of a landscape, which had been thrown into the garden and which she had taken to her room, disappears. During a trip to Quebec, she hears footsteps, and the world seems to crash around her like a waterfall. At home, the nights are filled with terror as she wanders through the house trying to escape from the noises. She dreams of saving her mother, Esther, from the noises, but Esther dies suddenly. She experiences and recounts her own death when, running from those who are pursuing her, she can't open the door of the house. Her body becomes weightless and is lifted into the garden, where she finds a beating heart and regains her weight. She notices blood streaming down her legs and staining her panties. When she lets go of the heart clutched to her body, she rises once more, accompanied by her pursuers. She sees her father find her lifeless in bed, the sheets soaked in blood. The doctor has no explanation for her death.

Antes is a simple yet complex text. Every reading reveals something that a previous reading may have missed. Boullosa touches on the tenuousness of the family unit—the death of the mother and the distant, unapproachable father. She describes not only the narrator's birth and death, but her becoming a woman, her passage from childhood to adolescence. Throughout the work there are allusions to the symbols of Catholicism, giving it another level of possible interpretation. Bringing together all these related threads is the narrator's conscious use of words, of language, to make the silences speak, to express the fears, to tell the truth. All through the novel the narrator addresses the reader directly about the story she is telling. In one instance she speaks of memories clamoring to be heard (*A*, 44). Later on she insists that everything she has said was true; she didn't fantasize or imagine her memories; she didn't falsify images or events (*A*, 68). At one point she discusses her choice of words (*A*, 70). This narrative, by referring to itself and to the elements which constitute it, is metafictional, a technique Boullosa uses frequently.

In *Son vacas, somos puercos*, Boullosa works with the history of seventeenth-century America, retelling the adventures of Jean Smeeks, slave, apprentice, healer, surgeon, and buccaneer. Also known as Alejandro Olivierio Esquemelin and as El Trepanador (The Trepanner), the narrator tells us that he, who has the eyes and ears of Smeeks, is writing a book that will draw the images and record the sounds of that time. His pages will be dedicated to the memory of Negro Miel, the gentle healer, and to Doctor Pineau, the surgeon, two men who taught him his skills and introduced him to the Ley de la Costa (Law of the Coast).

Son vacas, somos puercos has two parts, the first consisting of five chapters and an unnumbered chapter, and the second of fourteen chapters. Smeeks's story begins in 1666 when, as a thirteen-year-old, he leaves Flanders under contract to a French company on a ship headed for the island of Tortuga in the Caribbean Sea. Among the many escaping from the poverty of Europe and attracted to the fabled riches of the West Indies is a smooth-skinned, rosy-cheeked young man who is really a woman. A former prostitute, she is determined to begin a new life in a place where, she has heard, there is no private property, people do not lock their doors, and everyone lives together in harmony as brothers. The only law that prevails is loyalty, which means that one cannot be weak, cowardly, or a woman. This woman becomes "Ella" (She) in the imagination of Smeeks, and her memory haunts him all his life.

After thirty-five days the boat anchors in Tortuga, an island of constant sunshine and unbearable heat. The misery he suffered on board ship has its counterpart on land, where Smeeks witnesses the cruelty of the company that contracted him. However, the Europeans, called *vacas* (cows), are forced to withdraw by the forces of the Hermanos de la Costa (Brothers of the Coast). Smeeks is sold to the governor of the island, and his new life as the slave of a cruel master is far removed from the dreams he had harbored in Europe. Fortunately, his life was made more tolerable by the half-blind Negro Miel who occupied the adjoining room. This man showed him affection, shared his medical knowledge, and left him his memory as an inheritance. It is his story that Smeeks wants to preserve, the testimony of his adventures in the Caribbean Sea in the seventeenth century. He lets Negro Miel relate his tale in his own words, and we find out he was born in a valley where nature was perfection itself and where he learned the secrets of healing wounds and curing the sick. During a battle with a neighboring village, he was taken prisoner, sold to the English, and taken aboard a slave ship. The ship was boarded by French pirates, and through a stroke of luck, he was freed of his chains. Noticing that the captain had an open wound on his leg, he offered to heal it. Doing so with his herbal powders and honey and also attending to other ailments, he was admitted to the Fraternidad de los Hermanos de la Costa (Fraternity of the Brothers of the Coast) even before reaching Tortuga. Unfortunately, Negro Miel takes ill and dies. But before expiring he leaves Smeeks his legacy—that he be remembered forever and that Smeeks respect the Ley de la Costa.

Saddened by Negro Miel's death, Smeeks is sold to Doctor Pineau, a surgeon who wants to acquire the medical secrets of Negro Miel. Pineau takes him to a house of prostitution in Port Royal on the island of Jamaica. There he learns the facts of life and is initiated into sexual relations with a woman. He tells that he had relations with Negro Miel and remembers that many years earlier the village priest had made use of his body. From Pineau he learns surgical skills as well as an appreciation of the beauties of the island. Pineau, a Huguenot who had come to Tortuga to be able to practice his religion, was adamantly in favor of the prohibition of women on the island, believing that their presence would bring about the return of private property and cause rivalries and envy. Pineau is murdered one night by a group of men who call him *puerco* (hog) and themselves *vacas* (cows) and shout that they had poisoned Negro Miel and now it is his turn.

In the unnumbered chapter that closes the first part of the novel, the narrator, addressing the readers, tells us that Negro Miel was Negro Piedra and that he is tied to a waterwheel with a white strip of cloth wrapped around his neck. In addition, they have never spoken, and Negro Piedra's powers lie in his ability to interpret the present and predict the future. Although this fact contradicts the veracity of the story being told, one shouldn't rely on appearances because both stories are true.

The second part of *Son vacas, somos puercos* has Smeeks, now seventeen and called El Trepanador, in the house of prostitution in Port Royal enjoying sex and alcohol. His greatest desire is to find out who killed Negro Miel and Pineau. However, he signs a contract to join the buccaneers, under the command of the cruel L'Olonnais, and abide by their rules. Thus he begins a new life, no longer living like a "woman" (*SVSP,* 79) protected behind the walls of a convent, but now living one of constant changes and challenges. As a member of the Brotherhood, he was now also considered the heir to the wisdom and skills of Negro Miel and Pineau. Recounting the many anecdotes he heard on board ship, his first impression of the expeditions was one of grace and humor. The grim reality came later when he witnessed the torture of prisoners, the wanton killings, the mass rape of women, the plundering, and the destruction. He describes the expedition to Maracaibo and its neighboring city Gibraltar where the attacks, assaults, betrayals, tortures, mutilations, demands for ransom, and taking of slaves took place.

The narrator reviews his two months as a member of this expedition and realizes that he has lost his own body and is now in the bodies of those who had been maimed, killed, or healed. He returns to Tortuga with his share of the booty and money. An endless party takes place on the buccaneers' return, and at a gambling house run by a Frenchman Benazet, Smeeks and other members of the fraternity avenge the murders of Negro Miel and Pineau by stomping Benazet to death. Other expeditions follow, and on one Smeeks watches as the galley slaves on a Spanish ship eat an official alive. The adventures continue, some of the expeditions are less profitable, but the level of atrocity does not abate. L'Olonnais is taken prisoner, and the Indians of Darien have the women tie him up and view him before burning and devouring him limb by limb.

Life in Tortuga had changed. The governor had received fifty women to be sold as wives, thus displacing the authority of the brothers. In a cave, an old member of the fraternity, Pata de Palo, hands El Trepanador a bowl containing two pieces of paper rolled together just before three shots ring out, killing the old man. A shout is heard— "Seremos vacas, pero ustedes son puercos" (We may be cows, but you're hogs; *SVSP,* 134). The first paper reveals drawings showing sexual relations between men, between men and women, between blacks and whites, blacks and whites with daggers in their chests, and a legend beneath the drawings referring to a prophecy: "If the women are not proscribed, the day will come when brother will kill brother and the power of the buccaneer will come to an end" (*SVSP,* 135–136). The second paper, the Ley de la Costa written by Pineau, made him realize that for all those years he was part of the utopia that "Ella" had told him about on board the ship to the Caribbean. Now Tortuga was no longer that place. The spirit of adventure had been replaced by gambling, and the dream had died. Smeeks signed the paper in his blood and lived another thirty years. That was his confession, written with the eyes, ears, and heart of Smeeks/El Trepanador in order to preserve the memory of a place where the earth reaches perfection.

Son vacas, somos puercos is based on a historical source, the Dutch *De Americaensche Zee-Roovers* (Antwerp, 1678) written by Alexandre Olivier Exquemelin (pseudonym of Hendrik Barentzoon Smeeks), which was translated into Spanish (1681) and English (1684–1685). Using this source, Boullosa created a fictional version of the pirate adventure and European colonial policy in the Caribbean Sea during the seventeenth century. She lets Smeeks, who is a character in her novel, write his own story of adventure and at the same time uses him as the instrument of memory. His writing is the preservation of the tradition of Negro Miel, who saw the utopia and harmony of the heavenly island. The narrator gives the reader a dual vision of the explorations in seventeenth-century America: the destruction, cruelty, and violence that existed side by side with a utopian vision of a society characterized by sharing and loyalty and where nature mirrored its beauty and harmony. The narrator, in reconstructing his memories, crosses both time and space in his writing. Very early in the novel Smeeks cites Negro Miel's story of his arrival in Tortuga and in the middle of the novel claims that he never met him. He challenges the reader with the question of veracity. Which version is true? Both? Later he rejects both the eyes and ears of Smeeks and requires his heart. However, the heart is rejected in favor of the memory, which can extend both forward and backward.

Of significance in this novelized version of history is the multiplicity of perspectives provided by the intertwining of European, African, mestizo, and Caribbean cultures. And the role of women is paradoxical. On the one hand, they are proscribed in Tortuga so as not to distract from or complicate the austere masculine world of loyalty and freedom. Yet they are pursued in houses of prostitution elsewhere and enjoyed even more as victims of violence and rape. Life in Tortuga was never the same after the arrival of women; yet without women life was a real nightmare.

El médico de los piratas is essentially a shorter and less complex version of *Son vacas, somos puercos*. In an edition geared to the younger reader, the novel is illustrated with a number of reproductions of drawings from the Dutch *De Americaensche Zee-Roovers* and other period pieces dealing with pirates.

Llanto. Novelas imposibles is a very different recreation of history in a novel set in 1989. It is a fanciful account of the supposed reappearance of the Mexican emperor Moctezuma in the Parque Hundido of Mexico City. He is picked up by three women who discover a strange-looking man lying on his back on a jaguar skin, a jade stone in his mouth, and covered with feathers. They take him on a tour of the city—the Paseo de la Reforma, the Palacio de Bellas Artes, the Templo Mayor—and then realize who he is. In this novel Boullosa makes use of some narrative techniques from her earlier ones—a fragmentary structure, multiple narrators, the interaction of real and fictional characters, dreams, and strange occurrences. In addition, there are intercalations of fragments from the early chroniclers. *Llanto. Novelas imposibles* revives the Moctezuma of the sixteenth century and has him confront the Mexico City of close to five hundred years later. By depicting an emperor who stood at the crossroads of the extermination of his culture, a period when his world with its customs and traditions was at the verge of collapse, the writer draws a parallel to the world of the twentieth century, a world that without a conqueror is conquering itself and bringing about its own destruction. Boullosa is deeply disturbed by the present world, which, through its cruelty and violence and the advances of civilization and technology, has devoured a large part of the planet. This novel illustrates the writer's growing interest in history and anthropology as well as her concern for the survival of humanity.

La Milagrosa, also set in today's Mexico City, is a very different type of novel. Using an unusual fictional character, a woman who has the ability to perform miracles, Boullosa is drawing a picture of the political situation in Mexico just prior to the presidential elections of 1994. It is novel of intrigue, political persecution, and murder that can be read as a metaphor of the political reality of Mexico or as a novel of suspense, mystery, and miracles.

Boullosa in this work distances herself from the narrator by using the stratagem of revealing the contents of a bunch of papers and a two-hour tape that were found in the hands of a dead body. These papers turn out to be La Milagrosa's, written in her hand, in which she explains her unusual gift and the routines she follows to be able to exercise it. People come to her to ask her to resolve impossible situations—physical defects, medical problems, amorous matters—and to fulfill their desires. La Milagrosa can only perform miracles through her dreams, and therefore she does all she can to be able to sleep and dream. Among the papers are some of the petitions of the supplicants, a litany of sad stories—one man wants to die because people will be happier for it, a widow has a son who dresses like a woman, a mother has a child who sniffs paint thinner, a twelve-year-old hasn't menstruated for five months and thinks she may be pregnant by an older brother, a woman is unable to free herself of an obsession that she is caught in a bottle like a fly and can't escape.

The transcript of the two-hour tape is the story of Aurelio Jiménez, a private investigator working for those who control the Textile Workers' Union. He has taped his story just in case something were to happen to him. His bosses have asked him to follow La Milagrosa because they suspect her involvement in union activities. They are looking for something that can destroy her. He records a day-by-day description of his activities. First he examined La Milagrosa's shack and took note of the signs, photos, and drawings covering the walls, as well as the long lines of supplicants. The following day he went to see Norma, the union bookkeeper, who had consulted La Milagrosa, and heard her strange tale of miracles. Norma was seeing an older man, Felipe, who went to La Milagrosa and asked to be made younger. The miracle was granted, and he and Norma made love in the dark. Norma then petitioned La Milagrosa to be made older so as to be closer to the age of her lover. Her wish was also granted, and again they made passionate love in the dark. The following night, with the lights on, Felipe walked out and never called again. Jiménez pursues his investigation by inspecting La Milagrosa's immediate neighborhood and talking with the neighbors. Instead of hearing complaints about crowds of sick and crippled people filling the streets at all hours, the neighbors are happy and seem to be part of the operation. They sell food and amulets; they keep the streets clean; they dispense advice to the supplicants; they attend to La Milagrosa's daily needs because she never leaves the house; they administer the contributions collected and use the funds for neighborhood improvements. The books are kept scrupulously, and there is no evidence of fraud.

The next day Jiménez joins the line of supplicants and by chance meets Felipe, Norma's lover. They enter La Milagrosa's place together, and Felipe asks her for a miracle to make him worthy of his wife's love. Jiménez in the interim is struck by the woman's beauty and her sensuous body. He can barely mumble a word, and she, telling him that he has a drinking problem, informs him that he'll return. The plot thickens as Jiménez is beaten up by thugs, healed by La Milagrosa, and almost murdered in his apartment. There is a shoot-out at the union building, and a man is killed. The secretary informs Jiménez that there is trouble with the textile workers in the north, and there are rumors that La Milagrosa is involved. The morning paper carries a photograph of a Felipe Morales, the same Felipe who had wanted to be younger and later worthy of his wife's love, now an independent presidential candidate. For Jiménez, Felipe is the country's worst nightmare, a has-been with aberrant ideas whose candidacy would please the party in power. After all, with the likely candidacy of Cuauhtémoc Cárdenas, the appearance of an independent candidate would be advantageous to the PRI, the governing Partido Revolucionario Institucional.

Jiménez goes back to La Milagrosa's house, where he learns that she, feeling betrayed by Morales and guilty for having in some measure given him credibility, has given up her dedication to the performance of miracles. They make love, he asks her to remove his aversion to alcohol, and she entrusts him with her papers. They take off in a taxi, and the driver talks about Morales's conservative ideas on AIDS, homosexuality, and birth control. At Jiménez's house they hear a report of a woman having been beaten, and Jiménez learns that the police are looking for him. Morales is on television commenting on the relationship between the rebellious textile workers and La Milagrosa, claiming that those who believe in her lack reason and intelligence. Jiménez wants La Milagrosa to dream the end of the nightmare, but she says that she has lost her gift. Norma is dragged off in a car, leaving behind her passport and two tickets to Madrid. Jiménez and La Milagrosa go to the airport, she hoping to be able to dream the end of the nightmare and he waiting for the taxi driver to bring his passport. Jiménez falls asleep in the airport bar and, upon awakening, learns that La Milagrosa has left with another man.

The narrator who has transcribed the papers and the tape makes a final commentary that expresses the doubts and the hopes of the reader. Who came to the airport? Who got on the plane? Is the dead body that of the investigator Jiménez? There was no identification and no alcohol found in the body. Is it the taxi driver who sacrificed himself? Who knows? Maybe some day this material can be read because there is a Milagrosa; perhaps she can fulfill the wish of others to destroy Morales; perhaps, as with his young lover Norma, on the third night the light will go on and he will be destroyed. The novel ends with a newspaper editorial about the death of Felipe Morales and the many questions surrounding the upcoming presidential elections. Can the PRI remain in power? Will Cárdenas run? Not even miracles can help the Mexican people.

La Milagrosa, a work of fiction with fantastic elements, is Boullosa's way of expressing her concern about the political reality of Mexico as it faced the 1994 elections. La Milagrosa, an enigmatic character, is perhaps the only hope for a people weighed down by myriad problems. Felipe Morales, the embodiment of the most conservative ideas, is portrayed as an instrument of the governing party in its desire to remain in power. The persecution, disappearance, and murder of the "opposition" are shown as entrenched in the system. In this novel, Boullosa has blended her narrative skills with her ability to use fantasy and has produced a complex work that questions the legitimacy of the PRI and makes a political statement.

Carmen Boullosa has also devoted herself to the theatre as a playwright, director, and producer. A volume of her plays, *Teatro herético* (1987), consists of three very different pieces: "Aura y las once mil vírgenes" (Aura and the Eleven Thousand Virgins), "Cocinar hombres" (Cooking Men), and "Propusieron a María" (Mary, Why Don't You?). The last play, the author tells us in a note, is a transcription of the final conversation between Joseph and Mary the night before her assumption. However, the play is set in contemporary time and is a questioning or rethinking of the ideal of the Catholic couple. Mary knows her destiny; she wants to rebel; she wants to be a real woman. She is not satisfied with her virginal role and proposes to Joseph that they change their relationship. Here Boullosa treads on sensitive ground, bringing in her own early Catholic upbringing and later rejection of it and combining it with her concern for the modern couple and the roles society imposes on it.

Carmen Boullosa is the consummate writer, having become more immersed in her craft and dedicated to her writing with time. The spiritual calling to be a writer that she experienced as a young girl has never left her, although she realizes that the desire or need to write is not sufficient. Boullosa is exceptionally well-read in numerous literatures and looks to other writers for inspiration. Yet her work is unlike that of her contemporaries or the many writers she worships. Her novels are complex and require great concentration, making them not easily accessible to every reader. The narrative techniques she employs, the movement in time, the mixture of fact and fantasy, the fragmented structure, and the increasing use of history and anthropology all make her work appeal to a more limited readership. However, hers is a very original voice that has aroused interest outside of Mexico. Translations are in progress in England, Germany, and the Netherlands, bespeaking her originality and lending support to her belief that writers have no nationality.

In her fiction, Carmen Boullosa creates complex realities that, if penetrated, open up worlds of magic and fantasy as well as worlds of authentic problems and serious concerns. She may be depicting a disintegrating family, a story of adolescence, a utopian world without women, Mexico before the destruction of the Aztec empire, or the political situation of today's Mexico, but underneath the many layers of the narration one will find profound problems and concerns.

Boullosa's forthcoming novel, *Que viva*, about a young boy who is the only survivor of an earthquake in twentieth-century Mexico City, and her novel in progress concerning an archeologist working on the Mayan ruins in Yucatán, promise to be further contributions to this writer's growing list of publications. Her more recent foray into essay-writing should provide us with much insight into her ideas on literature and especially her view of Mexican letters.

NOTE: Quotations or direct translations from Carmen Boullosa's works are cited using the following abbreviations: *A* (*Antes*); *SVSP* (*Son vacas, somos puercos*).

Conversations with the Writer
AUGUST 9, 1992; JANUARY 6, 1994

How and when did you begin to write?

I was fifteen. My elementary, high school, and preparatory education was at a parochial school run by Ursuline sisters, wonderful women, many of whom left the order years later. They left the convent in the 1970s, a very painful step because they weren't young any longer. It was an all-girls school for girls who were being educated in order to marry well. Besides a solid religious education and many lessons in the catechism, we had to read a lot both at school and at home. My father is a voracious reader; he reads absolutely everything, if somewhat indiscriminately. He likes many authors that I like, but he also likes things that I think are ghastly. And that is how it has always been. His literary taste is very uneven and so is his library at home, where he has all sorts of books. But at least there were books; I grew up surrounded by books.

When I was fifteen, I felt something that because of its intensity and inevitability was like a religious calling. I felt the calling to be a writer, I felt that if I didn't write poetry—poetry or prose because what I was writing at that time was neither, it was simply trash—I wasn't going to live. But I felt that if I didn't write, life had no meaning and I couldn't go on. It became something imperative. I associate it with three things: my education in a religious school, which gave me a different sort of spiritual training; the death of my mother a year earlier; and my entry into the adult world. I matured late, became a woman very late. I can say that I became a writer at the age when these three events came together: the loss of my mother, the imminent loss of the school where I had always felt protected, because my pre-university education was coming to an end—I had two years left, but I could already see the end coming—and the opening up of the world to me, the secular world of the street. And there I was with a religious training in the body of an atheist. I chose to be a writer.

As of that time I was certain of my vocation, which I no longer feel in the same way. That so-called religious calling has become more of a professional matter, but I still feel the same irrational attachment to literature. I am a professional writer; I write daily because I like to, because it is my work, because I cannot imagine my life differently. But

I no longer feel the feverishness that I did as an adolescent. And that is how I got through my adolescence, with the certainty that I was a writer. I didn't want to study anything. I didn't want to go to the university and only went because my father forced me to go. I left the private university I was attending after a year. I knew that I was a writer. That knowledge was completely stupid because I wasn't a writer; I didn't know how to write; I didn't understand that what I was doing had to become a book, that it had to have a rigorousness, that it had to have a craft. I read a lot, I wrote a great deal, and I felt that I was a writer. That is how what is now a matter of both hard work and professionalism began. The six hours that I spend at my desk every day hardly resemble the efforts of that feverish and romantic young woman who believed that devoting oneself to literature was an almost magical or religious matter. I no longer feel that way.

When and how did you begin to publish?

I first attended a Jesuit university, the Universidad Iberoamericana, to study Hispanic literature, a course of study chosen by marriage-minded young women. I wasn't looking for a husband, what I wanted was to be a writer. I was in a big hurry to find my own voice and to understand what it was to produce a work of literature. But I met a marvelous teacher, Huberto Batis [1934], who was very generous to me. He is now the director of a literary supplement, *Sábado*, as well as a research worker and university professor. Batis began to talk about writers, and I thought he was from another world, since he actually knew real writers. In my world, composed of a religious school and a bourgeois family, there was nothing that even came close to a writer, nothing at all. That didn't exist. Books existed, but writers were from another planet. In his classes, that teacher began to talk to us about writers, and I got up the nerve to approach him and show him my poems, which, fortunately, he tore to pieces. He led me to understand that it was necessary to have a craft, that one had to write well to be understood. It was he who published my first poem in a university journal. And, in addition, he was good enough to introduce me to people of other generations at the Iberoamericana, and finally, he convinced me to go the National University.

I switched to the Universidad Nacional Autónoma de México, and in the midst of the multitude, I began to see others wandering around there who also wanted to be writers. Without planning to, I got to know the writers of my generation: Francisco Hinojosa [1954],

Verónica Volkow [1955], Adolfo Castañón [1952], Manuel Ulacia [1953], José María Espinasa [1957], Francisco Segovia [1958], Pedro Serrano [1957], Juan Villoro [1956], Coral Bracho [1951]. And that is how I began to publish. One day I found myself with a small book of poems in my hand, and guided by a natural chain of events, I gave it to a friend of a friend, Federico Campbell [1941], who was doing a small collection of booklets very important for my generation: La Máquina de Escribir. Publishing seemed inevitable, without my even trying, like something that had to do with the most intimate and personal part of my being, since at that time I still felt the fever of a literary calling, something almost magical. My friends were writers, sometimes editors who published, and with them I shared my inexplicable passion for literature. My next book I gave to Juan Pascoe, a printer who produced his books by hand. He seemed like an editor-printer from another century, and with him I brought out my book *La memoria vacía*. And that's how, little by little, I began publishing, because it was natural, almost inevitable. The people I was surrounded by formed part of that adventure. Suddenly I was involved in a world of writers and editors that was taking shape by itself, almost without my realizing it. I never said, I never had time to say, "I want to publish a book." Before I had the desire to publish a book, I already had brought out my first book of poems, *El hilo olvida*.

My first novel I published in an entirely different way. In 1980 I had a scholarship from the Centro Mexicano de Escritores [Mexican Writers' Center] with the intention of writing a novel like that of Ann Radcliffe [1764–1823], but set in Mexico City in the twentieth century. It was going to be a novel of somewhat muted, not very frightening domestic terror with elements taken from Mexico City in the twentieth century. I began to work on the novel, but it was perfectly horrible, boring, and exceedingly long. I think I had some 870 pages written when, one day, realizing that I was completely mistaken, I had the idea of taking one of the characters out of all this anomaly. In that novel (called *Dulces afectos*) there was a widower, some ghosts, the girlfriend of the widower, and his daughter. I pulled out the daughter of the widower and converted her into a lot of characters and wrote *Mejor desaparece*. I wrote it in one sitting, which, though it may sound like an exaggeration, is true. I locked myself up in my house, I disconnected the telephone, I didn't open the door, and I didn't go out until I finished the novel. Now I really don't understand how I wrote it all like that, in one go, with one burst of inspiration, because it isn't the kind of novel that progresses in a straight line, but rather it is a novel that is in fragments.

Just when I finished *Mejor desaparece* and was correcting it, they gave me the scholarship from the Centro Mexicano de Escritores. The experience there was marvelous because we met once a month with Juan Rulfo [1918–1986], Salvador Elizondo [1932], and Francisco Monterde [1894–1985]. Also, Bruce Swansey [1955], Víctor Manuel Mendiola [1954], Héctor Perea [1953], and I got together to read one another's texts and comment on them. Since that time I suffer from the occupational disease of Mexican writers, which is paranoia (all of us feel persecuted and underrated). It was there that I had my first case of paranoia, because I thought that Rulfo and Elizondo were saying that my novel was very good because I was a pretty young woman. I was afraid that the novel wouldn't work out. To this one had to add that the novel was so important to me, so intimate that, not knowing how to confront it, I hid it in my desk. I finished it in 1980, the year of the scholarship, and published it in 1987, seven years later. I fantasized a lot about whether or not to publish it, becoming my own worst enemy. By the time *Mejor desaparece* appeared, I had already finished writing *Antes*, and my next novel was in my head. That's why I always have unpublished books in my desk, because it took me seven years to allow myself to publish *Mejor desaparece*.

On the day it came out I was very moved. The day of the presentation I cried all night. For me the publication was very, very important. With my poems there was no time for that to happen because the publication was always in-house. I wrote, my friends edited, we were all together, it was the same for all of us, but not so with *Mejor desaparece* nor with *Antes*. Every time a novel of mine comes out, I get very emotional. With *Son vacas, somos puercos*, I was enormously moved. And instead of feeling greater tranquillity with each book that I publish, I feel greater emotion. In that I am like a little girl, I get very emotional.

As part of your literary training, what writers did you read?

Which ones did I admire or which ones did I read?

There are two questions related to one another. What writers did you read? Which writers influenced your prose?

There are writers that I have always preferred, ever since I was a young girl, and one of them is Joseph Conrad [1857–1924]. I have just reread "The Shadow-Line" [1917], and what a marvelous writer. His narrations are perfect, they have a poetic depth, they say so much on different levels that I can't help admiring him always. Another writer I have always admired is Robert Louis Stevenson [1850–1894]. When I read *The Strange Case of Dr. Jekyll and Mr. Hyde* [1886] a million years ago, when I was sixteen or fifteen, it amused and moved me. When I reread it four months ago, it moved and amused me again and said new things to me besides. Stendhal [1783–1842] I began to read later, probably when I was twenty, and now I am rereading *The Charterhouse of Parma* [1839], and I ask myself how can he write like that? I like the classic novels very much, the traditional ones, but I also have a weakness for nonclassic ones, due certainly to my faithfulness to *Don Quixote* [1605, 1615], a novel whose possibilities have no limit.

Of course, there are also Latin American and Mexican writers that I admire. I admire Jorge López Páez [1922] a great deal. *El solitario Atlántico* [1958] fascinates and moves me a great deal. I admire Juan García Ponce [1932] to the point of worshiping him. And Tomás Segovia [1927]. I admire Josefina Vicens [1911–1988], Inés Arredondo [1928–1989], and Elena Garro [1920] a lot. Elena Garro has always impressed me as a great writer of fiction and continues to do so. *Andamos huyendo Lola* [1980] is an extraordinary book. But the writers I always read, those I got into without looking for them were Joseph Conrad, Stevenson, Ann Radcliffe, Stendhal, [Gustave] Flaubert [1821–1880], Jane Austen [1775–1817], the Brontës [Charlotte (1816–1855); Emily (1818–1848); Anne (1820–1849)], [Francisco de] Quevedo [1580–1645], [Miguel de] Cervantes [1547–1616], among many others. And among those I got into as an adult, those to whom I profess absolute veneration, those to whom I would build altars in my house if I still had a religious temperament, would undoubtedly be Marcel Proust [1871–1922] and Carson McCullers [1917–1967], whose extraordinary short stories fascinate me. They are the writers I always go back to.

And there are Latin Americans that I admire a great deal as well: those I already mentioned, some things of [Gabriel] García Márquez [1928] fascinate me, and the giants, [Adolfo] Bioy Casares [1914] and [Jorge Luis] Borges [1899–1986]. I have great regard for Adolfo Bioy Casares, I like his work a lot. He is like those who came before, a classic writer in the best sense of the word. When you go back to read his *Diario de la guerra del cerdo* [1969], *La aventura de un fotógrafo en La Plata* [1985], *La invención de Morel* [1940], once again you find the wonder and emotion of what makes a literary work. Borges, as you know, is *the* writer. And then there are the great Felisberto Hernández [1902–1964], Silvina Ocampo [1906], Clarice Lispector [1926–1977].

What writers influenced your prose?

That is very difficult to say. It is very difficult because that peculiar chemistry that is sparked from what one reads, what one experiences, what one writes, what one is, what one would like to be, what one was, is a very peculiar chemistry indeed. Whom I would like to resemble is another thing. In poetry, what would I have given to be like Ramón López Velarde [1888–1921], to be in his league? And in prose, I don't know. In prose it is very difficult because I know that I am very different from the style that I admire. Let me say that my style approaches that of [Louis Ferdinand] Céline [1894–1961] rather than resembling the writers I said I admire. I believe that words have to be alive to have meaning. I don't believe in the prose of best-sellers, which is used without giving it importance, without letting the words display their vitality and the stories their many meanings and their difficulty. I believe that prose must be alive, that books are alive, that prose must speak by itself, which doesn't mean that it has to be embellished, far from it. Embellished prose is a way of disguising lifeless prose. Words have to be alive, they have to infect the reader with the emotion of what is happening. The great master of that is Stendhal, of course. His prose is so perfectly delicate that it becomes saturated with the story that is unfolding, like the prose of Conrad; of [Lawrence] Durrel [1912–1990]; of Andrés Rivera [1928], the Argentine; of Quevedo; of Sor Juana [Inés de la Cruz; 1648–1695].

But going back to the question, whom do I resemble?, I don't know. Whom would I like to resemble?, I don't dare say. Perhaps my prose is wilder than I would want it to be, perhaps my prose is not faithful to my preference for the writer who is the master of restrained and transparent prose. That is my preference, but I realize that my prose isn't like that. It is a frenzied prose, always ready to take off, never calm.

Do you prefer European, Spanish American, or North American writers?

No, I prefer books. Where the writer is from makes no difference to me, because I believe that writers have no nationality. I believe that the only possible nationality for a writer is language. For example, Alvaro Mutis [1923]. People are going to tell me that Alvaro Mutis is Colombian. I believe, because he is my friend and I like him a lot, that he is Mexican. But I couldn't care less whether he is Mexican or Colombian.

The truth is that his nationality is his language, which is Spanish. Bioy Casares, is Bioy Casares Argentine? No, Bioy Casares is Mexican. Of course, he is not Mexican, he hasn't even lived here, but his nationality is his language. Alejandro Rossi [1932], the Venezuelan-Florentine-Mexican-Argentine-citizen of the world. Rosa Chacel [1898–1994], is she a Spaniard? No, she is Mexican. Of course, she did have a lot to do with Mexicans, but she never lived in Mexico. Rosa Chacel wrote in Spanish, her nationality is her language. And there is a higher form of nationality and that is literature. Then it may be that Alvaro Mutis or Alejandro Rossi are closer to French writers than to Japanese writers or perhaps not; perhaps they are closer to Japanese than to French writers. I really don't believe in the concept of nationality. I believe that one's nationality is one's language and that a higher form of nationality is literature.

What is your opinion of the women writers of your generation?

I believe that we are going through a very fortunate and very danger-ous moment, a moment that we women are not experiencing for the first time, a relationship that we are not enjoying for the first time, because we Mexican writers have a very peculiar tradition. The Mexi-can writer is not a pariah or an outcast. The Mexican writer is so involved in the world of power and public life that even the official state of the union address is made up by the intellectuals and artists. The position of a writer in Mexico is a very dangerous one because he is coveted by ministers, presidents, government officials—something that doesn't happen in the rest of the world. Those in power want to have the intellectuals on their side to give them legitimacy in Mexico. Everyone knows that since the public officials consider themselves democratic without respecting the vote, they must seek support from other quarters.

This is very dangerous for writers and their writing because their work can become filled with arrogance. I believe there are writers of fiction in Mexico that were doomed because of this, writers who could have been extraordinary but who could not be modest. It is very important that a writer be modest. A writer must disappear behind his story; if not, his narration is no good, it becomes a bad novel.

What is happening now is that it is not the men writers but the women writers who are important. There is an enormous desire on the part of the public to learn about the work of women writers. It is easy to publish if you are a woman. The books of women writers sell better than those of men writers. There is more interest in the work of women writers than of men writers, and I believe this presents a terrible danger because we may well fall into a kind of arrogance; it may well be that our work will become cheapened because it is too easy to publish. I am only mentioning the dangers, I am not saying that it happens that way. Since it is my view that the nationality of writers is their language, I also believe that the gender of writers is their language. Marcel Proust is for me the best woman writer in the history of the world. Marguerite Yourcenar [1903–1987], I don't know whether she is a man or woman writer.

As for their work, there are novels with tremendous charm, as is the case of Angeles Mastretta's *Arráncame la vida*. The first novel of María Luisa Puga [1944] is very interesting. There are very many that are interesting, such an enormous number that I don't believe I have even read them all. Hortensia Moreno's novel *Las líneas de la mano* [1985] fascinates me; it is a very beautiful novel. Also the women writers who are not exactly writing fiction, as is the case of Fabienne Bradu [1954]; her *Antonieta* [1991] is an excellent piece of work. And there are many women poets, some of them extraordinary, like María Baranda [1962], Verónica Volkow, Silvia Tomasa Rivera [1956], poets of the first order. There is an extraordinary number of women poets, as many as writers of fiction, if not more.

Is there a Mexican literature "written by women"?

I think that a sociologist would say yes, but if someone who loves literature or who likes the world of books were to answer, I don't know. If there were a label "Mexican literature written by women," I believe we would have to apply it to books with the least literary merit. I don't know.

*Do you think there is a feminine way of writing that is different
from a masculine way of writing?*

Of course there is a feminine way of writing, of perceiving reality, and of understanding life. However, this feminine way is not the exclusive province of women. There are women who have no access to it. It is a topic that intrigues me so much that I devoted my novel *Son vacas, somos puercos* to finding out what would happen in a community in which the feminine world were proscribed. *Son vacas, somos puercos* is a novel about pirates in the Caribbean Sea in the seventeenth century who live in a place where women are prohibited. A community, the Brothers of the Coast, seeks to live a utopian life in which private property is forbidden, no loyalty is owed to king or country, everything belongs to everyone, and the booty is shared equally. It doesn't hold that you get more because you are an admiral, and that someone of a lower rank gets less. Everyone is equal, and your lineage or family doesn't count. To me these seem valid intentions, but what happens if they are placed in a community where the feminine world is proscribed? Feminine feelings are proscribed, as is the feminine view of the world and of society and of intimacy, and the dream turns into a monstrous world. I wrote the novel as an inquiry into the feminine world in absentia, because the topic truly interests me a great deal. How can an idyllic world exist without femininity? The utopia becomes a nightmare.

There are completely feminine writers, one hundred percent feminine, both men and women. Katherine Mansfield [1888–1923] is a writer whose world is totally feminine; Vlady Kociancich [1942], that extraordinary Argentine, is an absolutely feminine writer; Carson McCullers is a feminine writer; Marcel Proust is a feminine writer; [Lord George Gordon] Byron [1788–1824] is a feminine writer; and so is Diamela Eltit [1949]. And there are women writers who I believe belong to the world of men.

But in those writers there is no conscious decision to suppress their other part. All of us are male and female, all of us have a male and a female part, and when writing, a writer can choose to use one of the two, or a combination of the two. I also believe that if one uses only the feminine side, the world becomes abominable. I would like to find a story in which all that is masculine has been suppressed in order to do this type of "research" in a work of fiction, in a novel, and to find out what happens in a world in which men are proscribed. I don't know . . . a story in which intelligence were prohibited, in which only feminine values, those considered culturally feminine, would be used. I'm afraid it would be an abomination. I don't know, I haven't done it, I haven't written it, I haven't thought about it.

On the other hand, there is a feminine world that is manipulated, that consists of the perversion of femininity and masculinity. It consists of the world of women seen by men and described by pseudofeminine women. The result is what can bring about the greatest success among readers. That which is classified as feminine by men, seen from the perspective of men, the sum of all the clichés about femininity, without any depth, and written by a woman. And that is the biggest best-seller that a publisher can have.

To what do you attribute the success of your novels?
To their themes, their style, or to the fact that their author is a woman?

I think I would have been much more successful—if success is measured by the sale of books—if I didn't concern myself with the themes that concern me. For example, a world in which there are only men, or the nonverbal and indefinite world of *Antes*, or the violent one of *Mejor desaparece*. I would have been more successful if I had produced a different sort of work, but I have no interest in success; I am interested in producing my work. The world of literature excites me too much to exchange it for anything else.

I believe that there is no greater gain, no greater joy in life than to be able to write. It is a wonderful profession. Life duplicates itself because one has one's own life and that of one's writing. One lives twice, life becomes fuller, it is a generous profession. And that has nothing to do with success. I am not a successful writer nor do I want to be, which does not mean that my books don't sell. My books do sell, I have been translated, the critics treat me inordinately well, but all of that has nothing to do with my work. Perhaps if I were to write different things my books would sell more, but so what? I have to do my work, not be successful.

Has being a woman made your career difficult?

In the sense that it is easier, yes. I told you already that it is easier to be a woman writer today than a man writer. But it really hasn't been difficult for me. I only have to be grateful for being a woman and having chosen such a noble and generous profession. With my family, it would have been awful had I been a man and said that I wanted to devote myself to literature, because they would have wondered what was I going to live on. However, a woman in that bourgeois tradition is considered useless anyway and is always supported by someone. I live from my work, but they would have believed that my work was useless.

When I was talking to Vlady Kociancich, the Argentine, she told me that she believes they pay less attention to her [in Argentina] because she is a woman, but I think Mexico is different, that more attention is paid to you if you are a woman. Publishing companies show greater interest, books by women sell a lot more, it is easier to publish, it is more likely that the critics will pay attention to you, and the treatment is very generous when one is a woman. And in all of this there is something very noble and generous, which one should support, and that is, in this period of disillusion in which one no longer believes in what one believed in before and in which the faith in values that there was in the 1960s has ended, the only thing people can rely on is the feminine world. There is a great interest in feminine themes. We have been approaching the end of humankind, we have acted against nature and against our own species with a cruelty so bestial that if we were to continue we would put an end to ourselves both morally and literally in a few years. There is a great interest in examining the feminine world to see a different side of things, and as far as I am concerned, that speaks very well for humanity and is a sign of hope. If only one were to hear more of what is the feminine world and were to choose a more feminine way of being for all humanity, that would give us some more years of existence on the planet.

Are there autobiographical elements in your narrative work?

The relationship between a writer and his work is always very intimate, more intimate with his work than with his personal life. A man or woman writer makes use of everything for his or her novels. We use everything for our novels, absolutely everything, even the private history of our parents, of our grandparents, our own, our intimacy, our deepest feelings, our most hidden concerns; things we wouldn't tell anyone appear in our books. But an autobiographical detail revealed just like that in a book is meaningless, as would be a historical fact let out in a book.

A book is a work of art and has to have its own rules, its own demands, its own rigor in order to exist independently. There is no personal life that can be used to create a book in that sense. That a writer may use his personal life is understandable. He uses it like he uses what he sees, what he has read, like everything he may come across to subject it to the order of the book afterward. Stendhal expressed it very well. In *The Charterhouse of Parma* there is a character who writes verses. Before that he worked as a servant in the house of a lady who pensions him off. She gives him money so that he can devote himself to writing poetry, and this character writes horrible verses. Stendhal reflects and says, "And once again one can see how feeling something or having something in one's personal life is useless, what a writer has to do is his work."

Of course I use my personal life, but later I subject it to the order of the book. I always tell lies for the good of the book. Oddly enough, in my novel about pirates I used the greatest number of elements from my personal life. There I revealed more of my intimacy. It was a very heartrending and difficult experience for me. That year, while I was writing the novel, I didn't exist for myself; it was perfectly dreadful. I put my entire being into play, all my preoccupations, my entire personal history, everything. Even though it is a novel set in the seventeenth century and all the characters are men, even though there are no women, there is more of my personal life there than in *Mejor desaparece*, the story of a young girl with her widowed father, or in *Antes*, in which the Ursuline sisters educate a girl. But there is much more of my personal life, of my intimacy, of my deepest secrets in *Son vacas, somos puercos*, although it is a story about men and homosexuals, a world in which there are no women. Everything has to become transformed inside of a book, everything changes its sign, everything is used differently. I, like Smeeks, the protagonist of *Son vacas, somos puercos*, felt that I had lost my body. I am the slave who lost his body, and I felt it while the novel was alive. I could remember each day during which I had lost my body since infancy. Why have I lost it? To what have I lost it? Why wasn't I retrieving the feminine world without prohibiting its existence? Everything changes signs in a book, entirely.

Are you working on something new?

Just last month, December 1993, *La Milagrosa* came out. La Milagrosa is a woman who has the ability to perform miracles, to obtain something impossible for those who seek her intercession. She heals the sick, fulfills the desires and wishes of others, and changes people's lives. She is a portrait of the Mexico City of today and the present political situation. The novel first deals with the character of La Milagrosa and then with a somewhat violent story of political intrigue and police persecution for political reasons.

Is the story fictitious or based on fact?

It is entirely fictitious. Everything in it is fiction, but everything could be real. There is a depiction of Mexico City as having an atmosphere that might be capable of believing in miracles and that, because of its political immaturity, might be able to become involved in an absurd situation like that of the novel. The work is a metaphor of the present political and social reality of Mexico City. The action takes place right now—there are references to October 1993 and January 1994. I believe it is a faithful, though metaphoric, depiction of the situation we are going through at this time. However, the book has the structure of a novel—there is a plot, a dead body at the beginning, details the reader has to follow in order to understand what is happening.

In addition, I have finished *Duerme*, scheduled for publication this year in Spain. You may recall that in *Son vacas, somos puercos* there is a female character on the ship, dressed as a man, who wants to participate in the adventures of the New World. Cheating a bit with the time sequence, I take this character and have her arrive in Mexico City in the sixteenth century. I wanted to portray the Mexico City of the end of that century, when it was taking shape as a mestizo city. She is a Frenchwoman, dressed as a French nobleman, dealing in contraband with the corrupt Spanish army. Without wanting to, she becomes involved in an intrigue with the criollos, who wish to use her to disguise one of their own as a Frenchman and allow him to escape. When changing her clothes, it becomes evident that the Frenchman is a woman, and the Indians think she is a kind of miraculous person who when dressed is a man and when naked is a woman. They fill her veins with the clean waters that filled the lakes of the valley of Mexico before the arrival of the Spaniards, thus making her immortal. They make her totally invincible as long as she stays in Mexico City; if she leaves the valley she won't die but will remain asleep, completely motionless. The Indians save her from death, dress her as an Indian, and then she begins to lead the life of an adventurer. Dressed as an Indian, a Spaniard, a warrior, a European, she traverses the colonial city and all its social classes. A poet takes her out of Mexico City because the court, having realized she replaced the criollo, is pursuing her. No longer in the valley of Mexico, she sleeps, having organized a revolt that forced the Spaniards out of Mexico. It is a completely transsexual novel, an adventure story that takes place in this very city.

I recall you once mentioned a work called Que viva. *Is it a novel?*

It is a short novel like *Antes* and *Mejor desaparece*, and I am not sure when it will be published. It is about a child, an eight-year-old boy in Mexico City, to whom something very strange happens. Everybody in the city except for him vanishes in something like an earthquake. One Tuesday, at 7:10 A.M., everyone else disappears. And it falls to him to inhabit this city alone, this monstrous city, this urban jungle, this colossal and strange city, and to inhabit it with the attitude of a child. He spends an endless amount of time plundering, burglarizing houses, breaking into cars, destroying everything, somewhat crazed because he is completely alone, even the bacteria have died. Nothing spoils, there

185   Carmen Boullosa

is always food. He can easily live like a prince—destroying, polluting, ruining—until many years later, and no one knows why, time returns to that very moment when everyone vanished. Suddenly it is 7:11 A.M. of that Tuesday when the novel began. All the houses have been invaded, like in the story of the three little bears, the city is in utter chaos, and the people don't understand what happened because a minute before nothing had. For them there has been no division in time, for the child there has. And that split in time in Mexico is what the novel is about.

Have you any other work in progress?

I have gone back to my novel about Teobert Maler. It is a story about an archeologist who, at the end of the last century and the beginning of this one, photographed a large part of the Mayan ruins of Yucatán and Campeche, the route of Usumacinta. Maler arrived in Mexico with Maximilian and Carlota, as a volunteer in the Austrian guard. He squandered his personal fortune on archeological explorations, taking pictures and drawing maps of the route of Usumacinta. Afterward, the Peabody Museum hired him to write some books on the work he had done. Unfortunately, all the material that he sends is used by the Peabody Museum and other archeologists to loot the Mayan ruins, because, when he retraces his steps, he realizes that the ruins have been emptied and destroyed. His passion for the Mayan ruins is such that he grows old and lives out the rest of his days in Mexico. I have finished the novel, but I always go back to it because I haven't found the voice I am looking for and the work has not yet turned out the way I want it. However, I am working on it again, and I am also writing essays.

Literary criticism?

No, not exactly. Lately I have been invited to give lectures, and, in fact, I am going to England for the forthcoming publication of *La Milagrosa* in London. I have been asked to speak about Mexican literature, to present a kind of personal overview. I have been working very hard on these lectures, but this has been very good for me in that I reread writers that I like and reexamine my passion for literature, my love for all that is literary, and the amazing complexity of the structure, soul, spirit, language of the Spanish books that fill our bookshelves. Although some essays have been published, I hope to collect them and the ones I am working on now and publish them in a book.

In Mexico there has been a generation of notable women writers before yours. Which ones do you admire and why?

I would love to give each one of them the gold, silver, and bronze medal because I like them equally. And they are Inés Arredondo, Elena Garro, and Josefina Vicens from that generation. I like Rosario Castellanos [1925–1974] very much, but she is of a previous generation. Inés Arredondo is a writer with some extraordinary short stories; her work is not very voluminous, but it is very powerful. And she is a writer one hundred percent feminine. I believe Elena Garro is two writers, not one, because *Los recuerdos del porvenir* [1963] and *La semana de colores* [1964] have a brightness and a joy that her later work lost completely, even though it didn't lose its vitality. I think that her vitality increased with her bitterness and disillusion. She is two writers—she is the one I have just described and the one of *Andamos huyendo Lola* [1980], *La casa junto al río* [1983], and *Testimonios sobre Mariana* [1981]. She is a writer who has always devoted herself to her work, who has no life other than her work, and she is much admired in Mexico. And Josefina Vicens, who, although she is a woman writer, is a man writer. She is not a feminine writer. She is a writer whose work could have been written by a man. *El libro vacío* [1958; *The Empty Book*, 1992] is a book with a male narrator, a very harsh masculine narrative voice that I admire a lot also.

Do you believe that the presence of this group has helped those women writers who followed them? What I mean is that there already was a tradition of literature written by women.

I wish it were so, but I am afraid not. It would make me feel enormously proud to consider myself part of the tradition of those three great, magnificent women writers. Also I should mention Amparo Dávila [1928], Guadalupe Dueñas [1920], Beatriz Espejo [1939]. I wish it were like that, but I'm afraid that this abundance of women writers of fiction is due more to the social need for a feminine voice than to a tradition that I wish we had preserved. It is a nonliterary phenomenon. No, it is an entirely different thing—the need to hear a feminine voice perhaps expressing values less literary than one should, which doesn't mean they are bad writers. I believe they would be better ones had they devoted themselves more to our literary tradition than to the social necessity, but then not so many would have appeared.

*When do you write and how do you relate your writing to your other
responsibilities—domestic, professional, family?*

When I was twenty, twenty-one, twenty-two, even until I was twenty-six, I thought that a writer couldn't have children or a family. Even in the first play that I was fortunate enough to participate in, called *Vacío* [Emptiness], the thesis of the work was precisely that a woman writer could not have children or a family. That was my premise, and I was absolutely sure that I would respect it all my life. And we used to discuss it a great deal during rehearsals; we rehearsed from twelve midnight to four in the morning because we all had other jobs.

But when I was twenty-six and a half or twenty-seven, I got up one morning and said, "Either I have a daughter or I'll die." I thought that I couldn't go on living if I didn't have a daughter. I sent the script, the one about not having children, that I had pre-written for myself, to hell; I met Mr. [Alejandro] Aura, an exceptionally generous man who has given me much life and much vitality; and I had a daughter with him, María. And my life changed. When María was born, I was panic-stricken because I thought that I wasn't going to write again, because I felt that my body had been seized, and since I write with my body (I don't know with what others write, but I literally write with my body), since I feel what I am writing with my body, I know that if my body is not in the writing the words are not alive and, consequently, my writing is no good. I went through a crisis of panic that I overcame by writing plays. When Juan was born, I was not panic-stricken again. If truth be told, my children have given me more time, more energy, more ability to write, because I feel stronger, more complete, although my schedule may be more difficult because of them. For ten years I worked in a theatre-bar, attending to its administration and putting on plays, work that was quite hard and that I can no longer do; my novels have left no room for that. I have a companion, friends. I write daily, because the work of a novelist if you don't write daily doesn't progress, it isn't any good. One needs five or six hours a day to write, because otherwise the novel doesn't move ahead. If only the days had more hours, but since they don't, I manage as only God knows how. But it gives me so much satisfaction and so much joy, and I feel that life truly is worthwhile when I write daily.

Do you think you have had any influence on younger writers?

I don't think I have had any. This business of literary influences is very strange. Authentic writers, writers who believe in literature as I do, what is it that shapes their work? Who knows? Not only other books, of course, but which ones? And to what degree? Which have greater influence? I can't recognize myself in any other author's text. In that sense I am not a model writer, I have nothing to envy. My work is all mine and doesn't resemble that of anyone else. I don't believe anyone wants to imitate it. It is sometimes disagreeable, caustic, even unpopular. I don't think it can be imitated. I am not one to create influences. I am a very strange writer, atypical, with an uncompromising literary position. One who loves literature doesn't look to imitate another writer, but searches for his own voice. I am not enviable except in that I work with devotion and loyalty for all that is literary. It saddens me to see that in young people the passion for literature is less intense than the passion for success and power or proximity to those in power. The world of literature is not separate, but it has its own life, its own light, its own meaning, its own authenticity. Only art is worthwhile, and its jewel is literature. I think that in the last moments of my life, when I look back to sum up, I will say, "I only had one life and I used it for the only thing that was worthwhile, for art." I think I made the right choice.

How would you summarize your contribution to
contemporary Mexican literature?

I love literature, particularly Mexican literature. It has extraordinary giants whom I worship, respect, and love. I don't know if I have contributed anything, if my books are worthy of being next to theirs. I don't know whether mine have yet found a place on the Mexican bookshelf. It fascinates me to dream that they are next to those of the writers I respect, but that is something the author can't say. I have absolute faith in my work. The meaning of my life is literature, and to it I have been devoting my passion, my imagination, my heart ever since I decided to be a writer some twenty-five years ago. I don't know whether I have only been a good reader, in that I have filled that bookshelf that I worship with my eyes and the passivity of a reader, or whether my books have had the privilege of occupying those shelves as living beings next to the books of the giants that I respect and love so much. That I cannot say. Time will be the judge. The years will pass, and if I am lucky I will grow old. Then we will know whether my work is forgotten and justifiably so, or whether it will be said that Carmen Boullosa really wrote books. She didn't just fill the pages with words, but she did what is worth giving one's life to.

Representative Selections

III

["III," from *Antes*]

Whenever I stayed over at my grandmother's house, I'd use her warmth to triumph over the darkness. We would sleep in the same bed, very close to one another, and I would smell her, hear her breathing, and think that the rhythm of her breathing was mine. I can't be sure now, but I think it was like that. I would take a rest from my dreams, from the confusion that brutally inhabited the world of my dreams whenever it could, and dream hers.

When I was with her I really slept. I would wake up after she did, with the light happily bathing my eyes; nothing had called to me during the night, nothing kept me awake, nothing said to me "Come." I was simply allowed to be there as I am now, but so distant from myself. The sounds hadn't managed to touch my shoulder.

At night, I was unable to invent a code to group the sounds that frightened me, but I was gathering them little by little, putting together a dictionary without definitions, an auditory lexicon. There must be a term for the thing I invented with the noises that chased me at night. But I couldn't explain them; I couldn't say "These are creaking closet doors," because, among other reasons, I was also afraid of the right-hand door of the closet, just because it was there, because it was near my right leg and I could feel it about to burst open, filled with the unknown. I didn't define the noises I'll enumerate because definitions wouldn't have helped me, wouldn't have calmed or reassured me at all. In fact, they would have added even more ingredients to the taste of my fear. How much more alarmed I would have been knowing how and where they came from!

There were sounds that chased me all the time, but they weren't the ones I feared most. Those I could hear when anyone still awake wandered past my bedroom. I didn't like them, but they were nice; they didn't let me sleep, they had the lasting quality of a certainty. They were the noises made by the wooden floor, by the insects smashing against the windows, ringing sounds like gold or copper sliding down the walls, small steps taken with cloth shoes, sweet and smooth steps. All of these were domestic, noble . . .

Then I would fall asleep, and the sounds that woke me up . . . the ones that woke me, I really had a holy fear of them, an indescribable fear, a fear without taste, a fear that was outside of me, that went beyond me. They were sounds perhaps fainter than the others but much more violent.

I've been remembering them for a while, trying to figure out which object they belonged to, but I can't. I know them; I'm very close to them, but I've never heard them again. I would have to search my house to find out where they came from, where, where, from what point in the house did they jump out to put me on guard, to make me understand that they were for me, that they were making their noise for me, moving back and forth in the darkness, groping here and there, bumping into one another without finding me.

I knew their blind hunt would be unsuccessful. When they came, even if they brushed against my neck or passed only a short distance from my feet, even if I heard them and they filled everything surrounding me, they never hit their target, the target that was my heart, before the darkness would devour it all.

Why was my heart the target? One can tell in two or three sentences how they chased me when I was only a helpless girl who waited for them without being able to get rid of them; one can say in a few words that all night without a break they kept me awake to trap me. It's easy to explain: "A very frightened girl suffers from nightly panic attacks because she hears them coming to her at night." "Just what is it that's coming? She was never asked and no one ever explained it to her."

I didn't know what to do about the persecution. When I was smaller, I would stay in bed or run to my parents' bed and they would let me protect myself with them. But Papa never let me sleep in their room because he thought my nighttime fears were just foolishness—that's the word he used to describe them. Some nights I managed to trick them, and I stayed asleep on a little rug at the foot of their bed, thinking that their closeness would provide protection, but when I was older, from about the age of nine, I stopped using the rug; if I didn't stay in bed to wait for the sounds to strike me, I would walk around the house trying to dodge them.

In time I learned to see them, but I never gave them names.

I don't want you to think that what I saw was what made the noise. The world of noises (cricket wings rubbing against each other, the dog's nightly walk on the lawn, a pigeon moving about, cars flying through the streets, rustling yucca leaves, curtains touched by mosquitos, perhaps objects looking for their place, or perhaps any one of those things), that's not what I *saw:* I wish I could have lived that story, the one about the explorer who could kill my nightly fears by exploring.

The dictionary of sounds was only a small part of the nonverbal world I invented or inhabited as a little girl. What filtered through the words was the world I shared with others: "Pass me the sugar, throw me the ball, I'm cold, I want to eat, I want more candy, I'm sleepy, I don't like the teacher, Gloria is my best friend, Anna Laura is the oldest girl in the class, how beautifully she walks, I don't want to go to Rosie's house, Tinina is a very good basketball player, I wish Papa would have pillow fights with us, Esther, I don't like it when you lock yourself up in your studio, my sisters have a different mother who isn't Esther, no one speaks about her in the house, their grandmother doesn't like me, sometimes they go to see her, I heard that Papa supports my sisters' grandmother, the poor things, Esther took us for haircuts and left us in the beauty parlor, the ladies were chatting about things I never hear at home, I'd like to have younger brothers, at school all the girls have younger brothers, my collection of foil chocolate wrappers is very small, my sisters' is very large, the gym uniform is ridiculous, my bicycle is red, the bricklayers who work at the corner sing all day long, Inés made us orange gelatin, I don't want to bring my lunch to school anymore, I want them to sign me up for the cafeteria . . ."

The nonverbal world was much more abundant, it had more inhabitants, situations, it was more sophisticated. A world without words corresponded to each word. Scissors, for example, what are scissors? Two knives that live together, opposing one another and in apparent harmony.

I'm going to tell you about the scissors. They were forbidden for all of us girls, an object that we shouldn't touch. We were allowed to use some junky old scissors: short, dull, and without points, hardly scissors at all.

That is, there were scissors and scissors. The real ones were adult weapons. They were good for sewing, for cutting fabric or hair. In the kitchen there were some dull, gray ones, big, thick, and heavy, so unlike any others that because of them one could say there were scissors, scissors, and scissors.

The first were the ones that Grandma used, that Mama used. To use them, you had to grow up. They were pale, shiny like the second ones (the girls' scissors), and they had—as if they were wrinkles—a mark of age, like the third ones.

The third ones lived in the kitchen. They had no owner, they had a purpose: to cut off the heads and feet of chickens, to cut up meat into small pieces for stew. Not only were we strictly forbidden to touch them, but I wouldn't even have wanted to: they disgusted me. Even though they were washed, they always looked dirty.

That night some different footsteps woke me up, sharper, light but dangerous. I heard them coming from far away, something was warning me that I had to stop them. I got out of bed and went toward them. In the dining room with the wooden floor something was dragging itself toward me. I wasn't afraid of it and went toward it. What was the turtle doing inside the house? They had brought it from Tabasco so that Grandma could make soup on Esther's birthday, keeping it on the terrace next to the kitchen so the dog wouldn't bite it and so it wouldn't bury itself, because we wouldn't be able to find and cook it if it were hidden in the earth.

What was it doing there? It was running around the dining room (we children know only too well that turtles do run), running toward me, its heavy load lighter because of fear. I'd been told not to go near it, that it could bite me, useless advice because there was no way to grab its head; bald and wrinkled, it hid it as soon as it sensed anyone approaching.

It ran toward me and touched me with its face when it reached the calves of my legs. I stooped down to it, and its eyes shone with panic; the only reason it didn't call my name or shout to me for help was because turtles can't speak. I picked it up and held it close to me, heavy as it was, and I still heard the steps, the dangerous footsteps that I had to stop at any cost.

I walked in the darkness with the turtle clutched to my chest like a helpless lover, as frightened as I was, and I spoke to it softly and said: "I am going to take care of you, don't worry." I stroked its shell and its head, which was resting on my shoulder; I patted its rough legs that were too short, and we stopped hearing the noise we were pursuing. Not another step. With assurance, feeling powerful, I took the turtle to the terrace next to the kitchen. I opened the door, put it on the floor, calm and I think exhausted after its long chase. I gave it a little water in a dish, closed the door, and went back to bed, surrounded by a pleasant silence.

No sooner had I put my head on the pillow when I sensed something strange and heard a mysterious breathing underneath it. I lifted it. Under the pillow of my bed were the grim kitchen scissors.

What were they doing there? I was afraid of them as children usually are, a sensation that I scarcely knew and which upset me so much I was hardly able to control myself. I picked them up with disgust, sensing their gross odor, debated with myself and ended up by taking them to the kitchen.

I don't know how I arrived at the decision, I don't know if the fear of a scolding convinced me (I imagined the scene on the following day: What were the scissors doing in my room?—a question that would not be asked in a nice way) or if it was the fear of the scissors. I took them and left them in their place, hanging from a nail on the kitchen wall. I was going back to my room to go to bed when I heard the sharp steps again.

When I understood, it was too late. I ran to the kitchen but there was nothing that could be done. The door to the terrace was open, the turtle was bleeding next to the guilty scissors, which were split in two, each half lying in a pool of blood on the floor. The turtle no longer had a head and was missing a leg.

Horrified, I returned to my bed and didn't cry because I was too scared. Who kept on opening and closing the door? Who had left the scissors under my pillow and why? As on other nights, the quick beating of my heart lulled me to sleep.

The following morning I ran to the kitchen to see what they had done with the turtle. I asked Inés, the cook, about the turtle and, as usual, she didn't answer me. She kept on squeezing orange juice for breakfast, as if no one had spoken to her: for her, we girls didn't exist.

I tried to open the door to the terrace, but as I expected, it was locked. Just then Inés said: "Leave the turtle alone, you've been told it bites."

I waited for Esther at the door of the bathroom. Why did she spend so much time taking baths? I went over the parts of her body, imagining which one she might be lathering, she took so long, but I ended up enumerating them all in my head before she opened the door. When she finally came out, wrapped in a towel, I asked her about the turtle.

"It must be there."

"But is it?" I asked her again.

"Why shouldn't it be there?" she answered me. "It has no way to escape."

I went back to the kitchen. The scissors, solemn and dark, hung in their place, while the cook turned her back on me. I vowed not to ask about the turtle again.

On Esther's birthday we did have turtle soup. As I stirred it with the spoon, I kept wondering from which turtle the soup had been made. I couldn't resist and, breaking the promise I had made to myself, I asked aloud.

"What turtle was used to make this soup?"

"River turtle," Grandma said to me.

"I know it's river turtle, but which turtle is it?"

A silence fell. They exchanged guilty looks.

"From one you never met," Esther said to me.

"And the one from the house?" I asked.

"I don't know how, but it got away," replied Esther.

"Why didn't you tell me?"

"You didn't ask."

"Yes, one day I did ask you."

"But it didn't escape that day, it went away later. One morning it just wasn't there. It just went away, who knows how? Maybe flying."

She laughed. And everyone at the table laughed, except me. I burst into tears. Without meaning to, I let my hair fall into the plate of soup, into that despicable plate of meat with bananas, into that green dish that up to that day I had been so excited about.

While Esther was saying to me, "What are you crying about? Calm down now, come on," my Grandma, who considered herself smarter, said, "She thinks we're eating her turtle, the one that disappeared."

Mary, Why Don't You?
(Impossible Dialogue in One Act)

["Propusieron a María" (Diálogo imposible en un acto),
from *Teatro herético*]

To JULIO CASTILLO

Important Note

No one can appropriate the authorship of the text you have in your hands, dear reader. *Mary, Why Don't You?* is the title I capriciously gave the transcription of the tapes, recorded with anthropological zeal, of the last conversation between Joseph and Mary, the night before she was lifted into the air.

Who taped it? Oh, reader, you will have to forgive me because whoever did it asked me to preserve his anonymity for several reasons, all of them easily understandable. First of all, because placing a tape recorder in a private home without the authorization of its occupants, as was the case, is punishable by law, and Joseph could readily, if he knew against whom, take legal action, something people in the public eye are so inclined to do.

Second, in order to escape the undoubtedly cruel punishment that his sect would impose on him, since to them was granted the revelation that Mary would consummate her assumption that night, a fact that neither Joseph nor Mary knew rationally, but a discerning reader will see that they sensed it, that they knew that their separation was imminent. If the sect of the perpetrator knew which one of them had put a tape recorder in the very home of Mary, they could punish the guilty party with something like hanging, but the worst part of it all is that he gave me—I who am irreverent, uninitiated, and even heretical—those tapes, although in all fairness to him, I have to tell you that he never imagined that I would publish them.

This anonymous hero (it seems to me that his scientific daring merits the title of hero) positioned two microphones for the taping: one at the foot of Mary's bed, the other at the foot of Joseph's bed. He started the taping, by remote control, at eleven o'clock at night (the time when the couple usually went to sleep), since the longest tape he could find was good for two hours of recording. He didn't imagine—according to what he told me—that he would manage to tape so much and such valuable material, but was only counting on the farewell between them, but the couple's sleepless night served to correct a fatal error in calculation: the recording is interrupted because the tape ran out just at the moment when Mary is lifted toward heaven, so that her last words, if there were any, as well as those or the reply of her companion, which is what aroused the curiosity of the anonymous man, were not recorded.

I did the transcription in the following way: I omitted background noises (except for the radio, when they "converse" with it) as well as anything I could surmise about their actions. I spared myself that. Since there were many pauses, I used them with the aim of simplifying their manipulation: I noted in them the numbers that the tape recorder allowed me to see through its openings and which perhaps refer to the number of feet on the tape or to some other measurement.

I will leave for the sociologists, linguists, anthropologists, and theologians the significances that can be inferred from this transcription.

MARY: I still remember what I felt when you fell asleep the first night we spent together. We had turned off the light, but I turned it on again because I was afraid.

JOSEPH: A while later I woke up and turned off the light, you were curled up, doubled over, on top of the blankets . . . breathing like a little girl.

MARY: If the minutes I spent with the light on and you asleep next to me were only a few, they were the longest minutes of my life . . . I felt everything was so strange . . . I didn't recognize you like that: in pajamas and asleep, you had nothing to do with the man who had taken me to lie in bed next to him . . . I felt like crying, going back home or getting dressed and waking you up or having supper again. The supper, yes, that's what I could have wished for . . .

JOSEPH: Everything, everything . . . You made me happy that night. I thought: at last she is mine, at last she is only mine, entirely mine . . .

MARY: I thought: was that it? From that night I expected a transformation, like when as a child I took communion for the first time; I expected to see myself changed into another woman, into someone who although she had my face was more, more . . . like when I took communion: I had so looked forward to it, I thought I was going to feel inside of me the miracle of having received it and when I still had the communion wafer in my mouth I seemed to see the miracle coming, but when nothing remained on my tongue, I thought, as I did the first night I spent with you, was that all?, was that it?

JOSEPH: All what?

MARY: What?

JOSEPH: Excuse me, I didn't hear what you said . . . I was distracted.

MARY: I didn't say anything. I was thinking about some things . . . just thinking . . . Perhaps I spoke out loud. Does it bother you? (*Transcriber's note: Here Mary turns on the radio.*)

JOSEPH: I don't even hear it.

MARY: Just for a little while.

RADIO: Don't feel concerned about those few extra pounds: you can put off your diet, since the new fashions will be more becoming than last season's styles.

JOSEPH: What is that? Change the station, some music, perhaps, even the news.

MARY: No, let me listen to her. That's the woman who talks about hairdos and things like that.

RADIO: So the light, soft colors will make any extra weight less noticeable. The skirts are amazing because of their narrow pleats all around.

JOSEPH: If one can't understand anything she says, why are we listening to her?

RADIO: For the woman who wants to follow fashion very closely: a youthful hat with a narrow brim in the same colors as the dress, a veil in a softer shade covering the neck, and bare to the waist.

MARY: Do you know what they told me? A husband would always force his wife to wear dresses cut very low in the back, and when he invited people to the house, after dinner he gave her a signal and she got up from the table and returned with the dress on backward: the low cut in the front and her back covered . . . This fashion is going to look terrific on her.

JOSEPH: Well yes, frontward and backward.

Both laugh.

(037)

MARY: What day is today?

JOSEPH: Is it Tuesday?

MARY: I think so.

JOSEPH: Was yesterday Monday?
MARY: I don't know.

(060)

JOSEPH: Listen to this, it's very funny.

"*Dear Friend:*

I take the liberty of writing to you and using the term 'dear' because for more than two years running I have been reading your column and I think your opinions exemplify innumerable attributes.

However, not only am I writing to you to praise you and to let you know that in me you have another admirer, but to consult you about the following problem: For two years, I have been living with a wonderful woman, if I were to describe her for her sexual qualities, (which mean a lot to this humble servant of yours, I don't know if you feel the same way), in spite of which it seems that our relationship as far as sex is concerned is decreasing slowly day by day, so that I can tell you that the better we get along in our daily life, and the more time we spend together, the worse we understand one another in bed. The more I respect her as a person, the less I desire her as a woman. Is what is happening to me normal? Is there some way to fight against this?"

Don't you think this is fantastic?
MARY: A gem. Surely they must have a writer making up . . .
JOSEPH: A woman writer.
MARY: Yes, a woman, concocting these letters . . . That one strikes me as impossible, it is an impossible story. Something like that could never happen to anyone.
JOSEPH: To no one. To no one. It is absolutely impossible from beginning to end.

Both laugh.

(083)

MARY: Would you do it with me some day? . . . Answer me, don't be like that. Would you do it? . . . Why not? . . . How does a man get close to a woman every night, how does he touch her between the sheets, what does he find in her hair, what do her lips taste like? . . . and he embraces her, he embraces her, he holds her tight until he almost crushes her . . .

JOSEPH: I embrace you every night, I love you every day.

MARY: But in my case those two things have nothing to do with one another. I want to know what it is like.

JOSEPH: I already explained everything you can understand.

MARY: How does he do it to her? How does he do it? The more I think about it, I don't know, I can't imagine it. No . . . Explain it to me so that I can understand; translate it for me . . . put it into whatever words are necessary so that I understand . . . What can you lose?

JOSEPH: You. I can lose you.

MARY: Oh! What do they do it with? I have touched you with everything and I am still chaste, innocent as a fresh flower: I touched you with my hands, with my hips, with my toes, I let you caress my ears, I brushed my lips over your eyelashes, without letting you go . . . I came to the conclusion that they don't do it with anything that I have. What am I missing?

JOSEPH: You aren't missing anything. You are too inquisitive to be perfect.

MARY: I am talking very seriously . . . With what? With what? Why don't I have that, that which I am missing to do what everyone, everyone, even those who say they don't do it, everyone, except me . . .

JOSEPH: It wouldn't make any difference to you, you wouldn't even notice it if you weren't idly thinking about something that has no solution, something you are never going to understand. Go do something else or change the subject.

MARY: What am I missing or what do I have too much of . . . Just tell me that. It hurts me here, in my heart, not to know.

(099)

MARY: Oh! How awful!

JOSEPH: What happened?

MARY: I was falling asleep . . . No, I fell asleep for a moment.

JOSEPH: And?

MARY: I had the strangest dream. Everything was happening at the seashore, in a forest that wasn't thick but shady, and the animal walking in it was kicking up damp earth with his legs.

JOSEPH: When I look at you, I think that . . . that you are for me . . . I don't know what I'm thinking. I don't know what I'm thinking.

MARY: I dreamt that this enormous bird, like a slow, fat duck that couldn't get off the ground no matter how hard he flapped his wings, was using his beak to kill the females with whom he had copulated; he was tearing them apart, he was pulling them to pieces . . .

JOSEPH: I don't know what I'm thinking when I look at you, but I feel as if a warm lake were bathing me inside, as if it were calming me, as if it were bringing me relief. I have never felt that, nothing like that. With you there isn't even the shadow of a storm, not the slightest harshness . . . And you removed the mirrors from my house; now there is no one to spy on me when I comb my hair.

MARY: The bird was killing them after having had them, after having played with them. All of them. Isn't that terrible? To kill the one you have only because you have had her.

JOSEPH: It's hard to believe.

MARY: To kill her because she was yours. That's impossible.

JOSEPH: It seems impossible to me.

Both laugh.

(112)

MARY: What day is today?

JOSEPH: Tuesday.

MARY: I know that already. What day, what date?

JOSEPH: The 24th.

MARY: Wasn't yesterday the 24th?

JOSEPH: I think so.

MARY: Then today isn't the 24th.

JOSEPH: I think it is.

MARY: But the day we saw Lupe was also the 24th. The dates don't repeat themselves.

JOSEPH: Sometimes not.

MARY: One day follows another.

JOSEPH: Sometimes yes. Not for us.

MARY: For everyone.

JOSEPH: For us every day will be the 24th.

MARY: Yesterday was the 24th.

JOSEPH: And any day that you may remember was the 24th. Yesterday,

today, and tomorrow, and the day after tomorrow and every day.
MARY: Forever?
JOSEPH: Until he comes and the life we have together is over.
MARY: Then today is the 24th.
JOSEPH: Yes, the 24th.

(135)

MARY: I keep thinking we are the perfect couple.
JOSEPH: Well, I wouldn't say quite perfect.
MARY: Yes. Perfect.
JOSEPH: We are happy.
MARY: Do you know why we're happy? Because, look, we don't have the demons that relationships usually have . . . jealousy, for example. What could you be jealous of me for, I who am absolutely pure?
JOSEPH: I don't know what jealousy is. I have never felt it in my own flesh. I chose you for myself because you were as pure in body as sifted flour, as . . . I don't know what to compare you with. You are mine like the teddy bears I used to get as birthday presents when I was a child.
MARY: I am completely yours because I have never been yours, isn't that so?
JOSEPH: I think so, I think we are the perfect couple.

(149)

JOSEPH: Would you like to be a widow? Not because you wish me harm, you understand, not that you want me to die, but just to be a widow.
MARY: What a question! Would you like to die? I mean, to get through the boredom of the weekend without feeling it.
JOSEPH: Oh! . . . And you're making fun of me.
MARY: Don't get annoyed. Are you serious?
JOSEPH: Yes.
MARY: Let's see. I don't know . . . I don't know.
JOSEPH: I think I would.
MARY: I think I would also.
JOSEPH: Why would you like to?
MARY: If you die, people will notice my virtue.
JOSEPH: That can be noticed from miles away.
MARY: Yes, but nobody recognizes how chaste I am. They imagine that you and I . . .

JOSEPH: What do you think! Nobody could doubt your immaculate flesh.

MARY: Yes. That's the normal thing.

JOSEPH: Nobody could imagine it with you, don't torment yourself.

MARY: People are evil, always looking for the fly in the ointment. Surely they think that because you and I are married, well that . . . you understand?

JOSEPH: Nobody imagines it, let there not be the slightest doubt about it. Not even I . . .

MARY: In any event, my virtue would be well known without you.

JOSEPH: That might be.

MARY: Why would you like to?

JOSEPH: It would give me great pleasure. And just because. Because of the absolute pleasure of being a widower.

MARY: How nice!

(192)

MARY: Would you like to be a widower?

JOSEPH: Of course not.

MARY: Not even a little bit?

JOSEPH: Not even a little bit. In the morning, in front of the mirror, when I'm shaving, what could I think of myself? . . . No woman could ever come to respect me as you do. There wouldn't be another one like you because there isn't any, there can't be . . . You are my little girl, my little sister . . . With you I can say that I know, I know . . . I know everything. I love you very much.

MARY: If I die, you could belong to all women at all times. Now, willy-nilly, to see another woman, you have to pretend with me, you have to lie to me.

JOSEPH: If I were to manage to have another woman, another one with whom to set up a home, the home would be a volcano threatened by the icy darkness of her shadow . . . I, for my part, wouldn't be like a brother but someone she could substitute me for, because if she knows desire she knows that I am not the only one who can and should be with her . . .

MARY: The night of desire.

JOSEPH: The one you and I will never, ever experience.

(203)

MARY: Are you sure that we don't know her?

JOSEPH: Who?

MARY: You know the one I mean, that one, the one who came out ahead of us there . . . I would bet that we have seen her . . . maybe at some dinner at your aunts' . . . or could she be one of your cousins? No, if she were one of your cousins you wouldn't have stared at her ass that way.

JOSEPH: For god's sake, what's the matter? What kind of language is that . . .

MARY: Oh, all right, her fanny . . . But since you didn't even see her face, it could be. It could have been your sister or your mother.

JOSEPH: Of course it wasn't one of my cousins, I wouldn't have stared at her like that; even if I hadn't seen her face, there is the mystical pull of one's blood: where there is one's blood or kinship, one shouldn't look.

MARY: Then I don't know from what, but we know her from something.

JOSEPH: Both of us know her and I am staring at her like that? No. Only if she is the cashier at the bank . . . Didn't you hear that noise?

MARY: The Gómez's daughter?

JOSEPH: Impossible. Remember the mystical pull of one's blood.

MARY: The mystical pull of one's blood.

JOSEPH: That is what is saving you; your divine blood joins us all.

MARY: It is what makes me different. I am like everyone's sister.

JOSEPH: Nothing ever takes hold of you.

MARY: Nothing touches me.

JOSEPH: You've never felt that your body was breaking up.

MARY: Never, nothing touches me. I don't know how they feel that. I don't know from where some women have I-don't-know-what flowing from their bodies, something that gives me the chills when I see it, when I feel it . . .

JOSEPH: You never . . .

MARY: Nothing like that.

(249)

MARY: When is he coming?

JOSEPH: I don't know.

MARY: Soon?

JOSEPH: I don't know.

MARY: Do you want him to come?

MARY: No . . . I don't know.

MARY: I know. I want him to come.

JOSEPH: But you won't see him. As soon as he comes, you will disappear from here.

MARY: And do you know where I'm going?

JOSEPH: To where I can't follow you. They haven't told you where?

MARY: No. They proposed three places to me: heaven, earth, and everywhere. Which do you think I picked?

JOSEPH: I don't know. And it makes no difference to me. When you go away, when the 25th comes, you will go away forever. On the 25th . . . I believe that by repeating the number, the number won't appear. 25. 25. 25. 25. 25 . . .

MARY: Don't repeat it! Don't repeat it! I hope it won't be true.

JOSEPH: 25. 25. 25!

MARY: When he comes, the inner sores that struggle to fester in all of us will emerge and he will make use of the pain to transform it into something else. I don't care about disappearing.

(258)

MARY: I know what you feel when you look at me. I know that you are filled with relief, with an unusual pleasure because when you relax, you know you are close to me more firmly than ever. I know, as if I had felt it myself, the pleasure, the delight, the serene joy of finding in my sweetness the strength of your foundation. It is enough for you to see me in order to know the certainty that I give you.

JOSEPH: And if I didn't have it? If I didn't have my woman with me? The city would go against me, it would first devour my eyes and I would never again see that which I find in you, in your face, in the movement of your neck; the city would go against me . . .

MARY: Because you have ascribed to me the attributes of the flower in the quality of the stem, you have given me the softness and the delicacy that we fantasize about in love and the firmness that we need on the ground in order to feel secure. Why do you see that in me?

JOSEPH: The city would devour my eyes and I would have to mingle among the multitudes to feel someone, I would have to use my hand blindly to feel an anonymous woman who is surely annoyed as she flees from my solitary and sad hand.

MARY: Even when you see a photograph of mine, your look seeks in the image all that you know how to create in me. You invent in me that wonder, that cave of pleasure, and you take it all out of your warm heart, because I am not yours, my love, I am not yours.

JOSEPH: I would have to fill my fantasy with solitary and painful images, with women who won't ever look at me . . .

MARY: I am not yours. If I am always in flight, how have you found your home in me, if the further I move away, the closer to you I am, and I see an animal running inside of me, running, running . . . I know that it will end up by his taking me with him, who knows where, I can't imagine where and I think: "I could avoid it if I were his, if I were his."

(269)

JOSEPH: We are only the dream of our savior, our son.

MARY: Savior, why?

JOSEPH: Because he is coming to redeem us from our fantasies.

MARY: If we are his fantasy . . .

JOSEPH: That's a notion of yours that has nothing to do with him.

MARY: It may be . . . But we are the father and mother who are only obligated to their son: there is nothing between us that brings us closer together than the announcement of his arrival.

JOSEPH: And our love? Or do you think that is a figment of the imagination?

MARY: Our love?

JOSEPH: When he arrives, he will, like a furious gust of wind, blow away everything that you and I think and feel about one another. He will be the truth.

MARY: He still isn't born or anything else . . . why did you think of him?

JOSEPH: I thought that in any event we have to get past the number 24. Two by two is going to be impossible. If we are three, we are an uneven number and then it is possible. You and I are two; you, he, and I, three. That's why I thought. To get past the 24th, to get past it.

(285)

JOSEPH: Would you do it with me some day?

MARY: What do you think! I can't.

JOSEPH: You haven't tried it.

MARY: One day I did try.

JOSEPH: Do you mean it?

MARY: With all my strength.

JOSEPH: If you wanted to you could.

MARY: I tried it already. Because one day I thought "perhaps, if I manage to fill myself with that, that which they enjoy with such pain (because I have spied on them, I have seen how they do it), if I were to allow myself to be possessed by that perhaps I would stop feeling the pull that I feel is closer with every moment and I would stop having that pain here, here." But I couldn't. Besides no.

JOSEPH: I want to do it with you.

MARY: No. I would disintegrate like soap in your hands. I would stop being what I am for you. It would be like emptying a glass in the sand and not having anything to fill it with. You wouldn't have anything with which to fill the glass of our love.

JOSEPH: But you would stay with me.

MARY: I would no longer be anything. It would be just the same if it were me or if anyone at all took my place.

JOSEPH: You would be with me forever.

MARY: Those are lies. No. Don't even talk to me about that. No.

(293)

JOSEPH: I think so, I think we are the perfect couple.

MARY: The perfect couple? Why?

JOSEPH: I never listen to you and you never listen to me. I don't hear what you tell me and I can speak freely to you because you don't hear anything I want to say. Oh yes, you hear very superficially, but I couldn't harm you with anything I say. It wouldn't upset you if, for example, I told you, "You are cold," "You aren't understanding," or "I can't talk to you." Any one of these statements would anger another woman.

MARY: I am not like another woman. Not at all like any other. No, I am not. And I listen to you and when you speak you say everything so that I don't understand, and when you come close to me, I feel, where is he? what can he be thinking of? of what? of what?

JOSEPH: I come close to you.

MARY: You come close to me to kiss me and I think, where are you? what do you feel? what can you be thinking of? of what?

(305)

JOSEPH: You would wake up at night because it bothered you to sleep with the window open. You would close it.

MARY: And you would wake up because you felt you were suffocating. You would open it; after a while the draft that came from the open window woke me, and I closed it, then you opened it . . .

JOSEPH: It was a pitched battle that sleep would win. That's why we didn't fight with one another.

MARY: With time it was the reverse.

JOSEPH: Now I can't tolerate the open window.

MARY: And I can't sleep with the window closed. I can't.

JOSEPH: And we could fight but laughter wins out.

MARY: I think: that is the wonderful part of marriage.

JOSEPH: It ends up by changing your soul.

MARY: By putting inside of you the other person's soul as if it were your own.

JOSEPH: I don't think it's quite like that, but it works like grafting: it produces the most beautiful and delicious fruits.

MARY: How nice! . . . Do you believe anything that we've said?

JOSEPH: That business of the window only seems to be a bad omen. Before, I wanted the doors open, now you, you want to go away, I know that you want to go away . . .

(323)

MARY (*singing*): Are you sleeping, are you sleeping, Brother John, Brother John?

JOSEPH: Singing now?

MARY: I don't want to any more, I don't want to any more, ding, dong, ding. Ding, dong, ding.

Peals of a bell and sacred music can be heard.

Curtain

Bibliography

Publications

El hilo olvida. Mexico City: La Máquina de Escribir, 1978.
La memoria vacía. Mexico City: Taller Martín Pescador, 1978.
Ingobernable. Mexico City: Col. Cuadernos de Poesía, UNAM, 1979.
Lealtad. Mexico City: Taller Martín Pescador, 1980.
Abierta. Mexico City: Col. Práctica del Vuelo, 1983.
Cocinar hombres. Mexico City: Taller Tres Sirenas, 1985.
Mejor desaparece. Mexico City: Océano, 1987.
Teatro herético. Puebla: Universidad Autónoma de Puebla, 1987.
Mi versión de los hechos. Mexico City: Cultura, 1988.
La salvaja. Mexico City: Taller Martín Pescador, 1988; Mexico City: Fondo de Cultura Económica, 1989.
Antes. Mexico City: Vuelta, 1989.
Papeles irresponsables. Mexico City: Universidad Autónoma Metropolitana, 1989.
Sangre. Mexico City: Taller Tres Sirenas, 1991.
Son vacas, somos puercos. Mexico City: Era, 1991.
Llanto. Novelas imposibles. Mexico City: Era, 1992.
El médico de los piratas. Madrid: Siruela, 1992.
Soledumbre. Mexico City: Universidad Autónoma Metropolitana, 1992.
Envenenada. Caracas: Pequeña Venecia, 1993.
La Milagrosa. Mexico City: Era, 1993.
Duerme. Madrid: Alfaguara, 1994.
Quizá. Caracas: Monte Avila Latinoamericana, 1994.

Translations

"Letter to the Wolf." Trans. Cynthia Steele. *New Writing from Mexico.* Special issue of *TriQuarterly* 85 (Fall 1992): 84–86.
"Storms of Torment." Trans. Suzanne Jill Levine. *New Writing from Mexico.* Special issue of *TriQuarterly* 85 (Fall 1992): 403–406.
"III," from *Before.* Trans. Gabriella de Beer. *Review: Latin American Literature and Arts* 48 (Spring 1994): 10–13.
The Miracle-Worker. Trans. Amanda Hopkinson. London: Jonathan Cape, 1994.

Angeles Mastretta

Angeles Mastretta ⁽¹⁹⁴⁹⁾

About the Author and Her Writing

Conversations with the Writer

Representative Selections

Aunt Clemencia Ortega ["Tía Clemencia Ortega,"
from *Mujeres de ojos grandes*]

Aunt Cristina Martínez ["Tía Cristina Martínez,"
from *Mujeres de ojos grandes*]

Memory and Precipice ["Memoria y acantilado,"
from *Puerto libre*]

Bibliography

About the Author and Her Writing

Angeles Mastretta is warm, delightful, uninhibited, a great conversationalist, and what might be described as hyperactive. Her eyes, her mind, and her person dart from one thing to the other as she juggles the many roles she plays. In speaking with her and reading her work, one is left with the impression of a woman equally committed to her family, to her profession, to the creation of memorable women characters, and to carving out a place for herself in Mexican literature. Her opinions of her own work leave room for interpretation; she is not convinced that hers are eternal truths. Mastretta laughs at herself with genuine delight and has an intuitive gift for humor. Both in speaking and writing, she uses her sense of humor and irony to connect with her listeners and readers, to transport them to the world she is creating, and to meet the characters she portrays. She does this with a prose style that is uncomplicated, sometimes colloquial, and always replete with descriptive words and phrases that dazzle, amuse, and capture the image projected. It is this prose style that endears her work to her readers.

Angeles Mastretta does not tell much about her early years except that she was born in Puebla and lived there for the first twenty years of her life. She speaks frequently of her father, who died when she was twenty-one years old, and evokes his image and memory in her writing. He was the son of an Italian consul who came to Puebla in 1910, and although he was born in Mexico, he left at age fourteen for Italy. He returned to Mexico some twenty years later and married her mother. She confesses to an absolute adoration of her father, who wrote for the newspapers of Puebla using an old green Olivetti typewriter. Writing was a game for him, and she believes that perhaps her father's experience as a writer is the reason she chose to be a writer. Entering the world of fiction was an evolving process that came out of her veneration of her father, her love of storytelling, and her late development as an avid reader of fiction. Certainly as a young girl, being a writer was not a profession she contemplated.

Mastretta left Puebla for Mexico City to study journalism and communications at the National University. After her father's death, she began working as a journalist to support herself. One of her first jobs was writing for the magazine *Siete*, published by the Ministry of Public Education, where she dealt with cultural issues and conducted interviews aimed at bringing the cultural world to people far removed from it. She also wrote a column, "Del absurdo cotidiano" (About Daily Absurdities), for the afternoon paper *Ovaciones;* directed the Museo del Chopo, a museum affiliated with the university; and did some television interviewing. In 1974 she was awarded a scholarship at the Centro Mexicano de Escritores (Mexican Writers' Center), where, among writers like Juan Rulfo (1918–1986), Salvador Elizondo (1932), and Francisco Monterde (1894–1985), she learned what pain and discipline writing entailed. In 1975, a collection of her poetry, *La pájara pinta* (Colorful Bird), was published. However, the novel she had in her head for some eight years remained there until an editor offered to pay her salary for six months so that she could give up her job and write her book. The six months became a year, and *Arráncame la vida* (*Mexican Bolero*, 1989) was published in 1985, winning the Mazatlán Prize for Literature for the best book of the year. Its immediate editorial success came as a surprise to Mastretta because it never occurred to her that she could earn enough from royalties to support herself. However, that success gave her the freedom to write *Mujeres de ojos grandes* (Big-Eyed Women; 1990), a collection of thirty-seven short stories about an extraordinary series of *tías* (aunts) at crucial times in their lives. In 1993, she published *Puerto libre* (Free Port), a collection of vignettes, impressions, stories, and sayings that reveal a more intimate side of the writer. In addition, Mastretta currently writes for the monthly magazine *Nexos* as well as occasional pieces for newspapers and other publications.

Arráncame la vida, to date Mastretta's first and only novel, has been a phenomenal publishing success in Mexico and the Spanish-speaking world, as well as in translation into numerous languages. It has attracted critical attention and catapulted its author onto the ever-growing stage occupied by women writers. What fascinates the casual reader and the literary critic alike is the question, what can this phenomenon be attributed to? The easy answer—the author set out to write a best-seller and the novel is no more than that—is not convincing and merits rejection. The key to Mastretta's success can be found in a combination of factors; in fact, there may be different keys for different readers.

Arráncame la vida, more closely translated as "Tear My Heart Out" or "Take All of Me," from the actual lyrics of a bolero, is a novel narrated by its protagonist, Catalina Ascencio. She tells her story from the time she met Andrés Ascencio, as an unsophisticated young girl in Puebla, to her marriage to him, and finally to her freedom from him upon his death. While the book is very much the story of Catalina— the naive young woman who, through a process of self-discovery and development, comes to have ideas of her own and the backbone to carry them out—it is simultaneously the story of the political career of General Andrés Ascencio—corrupt, cruel, and inhuman—and his manipulation of power. It takes us back to a time closer to the Mexican Revolution when political power was concentrated in the hands of a few strong men. No person or thing was permitted to stand in the way of those whose lives were dedicated to the wielding of power. Mendacity, duplicity, betrayal, murder, and cover-ups were the instruments employed to achieve one's ends. Into this world steps an innocent fourteen-year-old girl who, through her marriage to a politician, matures and develops into a young woman who plays multiple and, at times, contradictory roles. In the end, she manages to free herself to some degree from the patriarchal world that has repressed her and made her live according to the standards expected of a woman of her class and position. Consequently, the appeal of this novel is manifold. Catalina, as an emerging feminist, speaks to the women of our time, many of whom are struggling with the problems that beset her. Andrés, for those familiar with the history of Mexico, touches a raw nerve and, even for those less schooled in Mexican history, reveals the evil of a world of power and corruption. To this one must add Mastretta's skill in storytelling, her unencumbered style, her use of colloquial language, and her unabashed sense of humor. The novelist's humor, often expressed in terse descriptions or similes, makes reading her novel enjoyable and accounts in no small measure for its attractiveness.

Much speculation surrounds the novel, specifically about whether the fictional characters are based on real people. Mastretta is amused when she recounts how often she is approached by politicians and asked to identify her characters. With equal seriousness, she is accused of including untruths in her work, to which she counters categorically that she wrote a novel and not a history book. However, neither position precludes her having delved into Mexican history of the postrevolutionary years, specifically of the 1940s, to find a setting for her work and the model for Andrés Ascencio.

Mastretta, because of her training as a journalist, feels more comfortable writing about what could have happened, but insists that there is much more fiction than reality in her novel. She was attracted by the prospect of writing about power and about those who initiated and practiced the bad political habits from which Mexico suffers. She admits that there was a man in Puebla, Maximino Avila Camacho, often identified as Andrés Ascencio in the novel, about whom she was able to learn little from those who knew him. In portraying Ascencio, she tried to reconstruct vague childhood recollections but invented much more than she ever knew. Catalina Guzmán de Ascencio is a narrative voice that Mastretta invented, portrayed as a woman more like one of her own generation. She wanted her to struggle with her relationship to that kind of a man, to live her own life, feel her sexuality, to permit herself a love affair, to sing the songs of the period, and finally to feel happy as a widow. The other characters are also products of her imagination, as are the descriptions of the specific events, affairs, and murders.

Arráncame la vida, for all its freshness, smooth narration, earthy language, and memorable characters, is not entirely a new manifestation of the novel in Mexico. It does, indeed, form a bridge to the novel of the Mexican Revolution and is a strong reminder of it. Mastretta, like her predecessors and many of her contemporaries, uses her fiction to comment on the political and social realities of Mexico. General Andrés Ascencio, whether an invention or modeled on a real person, is the prototypical political boss: cruel and corrupt, false and hypocritical, scheming and manipulative. All his actions are taken in the name of the good of his country and his people, but in truth are only undertaken to further his own advancement and career. He too has to cope with the duplicity of those he trusts and, in the end, finds himself betrayed by another politician. Mastretta goes even further back in history to the early part of the century by having Catalina tell us the story of Andrés Ascencio's first wife, Eulalia, and their joint allegiance to Francisco I. Madero, Francisco Villa, and Emiliano Zapata. Although the story turns out to be a fabrication—in fact, Andrés was associated with the supporters of Victoriano Huerta, who betrayed Madero—it does evoke the history of the Revolution and connects the general to those turbulent years and to the fiction that emanated from those events.

Where Mastretta creates something entirely new is in Catalina's narrative voice that not only seeks to express itself but also to contradict for her readers Andrés's pious declarations in his official speeches. Although Andrés usually pooh-poohs her opinions, considering them worthless, Catalina does say what she thinks and points out his hypocrisy. Andrés, however, with his innate ability to manipulate, is a step ahead of her, and her attempts to live her life with a lover fail because he arranges to have the lover killed. Catalina is a woman in transition and she is sometimes contradictory. As is expected of her, she supports her politician husband, closing her eyes to his activities, playing the role of wife, mother, and hostess at dinner parties, and participating in his campaign tours. When, with time, she accepts the truth about Andrés, brought home to her by her lover, the conductor Carlos Vives, she begins to confront reality and herself with open eyes. She attempts to challenge the patriarchal system and take control of her life by opening a bank account, learning to drive, staying out late, and moving out of the bedroom. Yet she doesn't leave Andrés, probably for the same reasons that many abused women stay in such a relationship: fear and lack of economic security. Andrés's death—an ambiguous event, since we are not sure whether the black lemon tea he drank was deliberately supplied by Catalina, who knew of its noxious effects—and his funeral are the last acts of this drama. Catalina, who couldn't weep during her lover's funeral, now feigns grief and bursts into tears, but these are tears of joy at her anticipated freedom.

Mastretta's style that so delights her readers combines colloquial prose and lyrics of songs. Andrés's utterances are often earthy, whereas Catalina's are less so and tend toward humorous descriptions of herself, other women friends, and politicians. The novel has many depictions of customs that provide the local color of the period. Catalina's voice describes love affairs, official dinners, concert performances, family outings, and campaign stops using a wide-angle lens that captures each event in one close-up shot. The popular songs whose lyrics seem to connect different levels of the novel are another form of expression. For Andrés, the songs carry him back to more innocent times; for Catalina, they let her express what she can't say publicly, especially the pleasure she derives from her love affair. She sings with her lover Carlos as an emotional outlet, and at times loses herself in the songs sung by her chauffeur. All these factors make *Arráncame la vida* a novel with broad appeal. As Mastretta says, "I want to give my readers a plane ticket to another world," and she has done just that.

Mujeres de ojos grandes is a very different kind of book. It is composed of thirty-seven untitled chapters of unequal length, each dealing with a different *tía* (aunt). The women share a characteristic that Mastretta calls "anachronistic": they are ahead of their time and, like Catalina, do things that are more compatible with women of the 1980s or 1990s. These *tías*, each in her own right, are engaging, funny, serious, and above all, remarkable. Mastretta captures them at a critical point in their lives when a decision has to be made or an action taken. More often than not, the decision or action is unexpected or unusual and surprises not only the reader but the *tía* herself. Using her storytelling skill, the writer encapsulates the entire story in a few pages. In this work Mastretta presents a gallery of women who are probably the funniest, wittiest, and cleverest group ever gathered between the covers of a single book. They are young, old, middle-aged; some are pretty, others plain; some are single, others married; some live by the rules imposed by society, others are free spirits who follow their dreams and desires. They are women we know, women we would like to know, women we admire, women we might like to resemble. In short, they touch us all in some way, if only in making us laugh. By bringing them together, Mastretta has saved them from falling into oblivion.

Mastretta acknowledges that writing *Mujeres de ojos grandes* was a kind of exercise to prove to herself and others that she was a professional writer. She was disturbed by the impression in some quarters that she had produced "easy literature" because her novel was enjoyed by so many. This prompted her to search for a very different tone and style in her second work of fiction. People were beginning to think that she was her character Catalina Ascencio. However, Catalina's voice, as powerful as it was, was not Mastretta's voice, and it took a great deal of effort to detach herself from it. In addition, there is an autobiographical element that was the inspiration for the stories. When her baby daughter was gravely ill, Mastretta sat by her bedside telling her stories about extraordinary women, making them up, remembering, inventing, all with the aim of convincing her child that she was a link in a long chain of women that should not be broken. Subsequently, it occurred to Mastretta that she ought to write out these stories so that they wouldn't be lost.

Each of the thirty-seven women portrayed in *Mujeres de ojos grandes* finds herself in a different situation that prompts her to act in a certain way. Aunt Elena and her family were forced to give up their estate in Puebla to the rebels during the Revolution of 1910. Without protest, they handed over the deed to their property and went to live in Teziutlán. Their life continued almost as before. One afternoon, Elena saw her father drawing a diagram and realized it was a plan leading to an underground room at their ranch where her father had stored his wine collection. She sneaked into his carriage and, unbeknownst to him, accompanied him to the ranch. Once there she declared that she too loved port wine and helped him load the bottles into the carriage. No one believed her story, but she learned that even the most proper gentleman, such as her father, can have a screw loose.

Cristina Martínez, plain and with skinny legs, reached the age of twenty-one without a marriage proposal and with the certainty that she would remain an old maid. One day she returned from town saying that she had met a Spaniard in a jewelry store while trying on a diamond engagement ring. That afternoon a messenger arrived bearing the ring and an envelope containing a marriage proposal from Mr. Arqueros, the Spaniard. He explained that he was on the way to Veracruz to set sail for Spain and would like to marry her by proxy through the good offices of Emilio Suárez, one of Puebla's most sought-after bachelors. Six months later, after a church wedding with all the trappings except for the groom, Cristina left for Spain to join her husband. After a year of letters to her family from Spain, news arrived of the death of Mr. Arqueros, followed shortly thereafter by Cristina's arrival in Puebla as a black-veiled widow. Now she certainly wasn't an old maid and was happy to be back with her family. Gossip had it that Mr. Arqueros had never existed and that her inheritance came from contraband smuggled in her dowry. No one knows for sure, but Cristina and Emilio Suárez remained friends to the end of their days—an unacceptable relationship, since friendship between men and women is unpardonable.

In one of the shortest stories, Eloísa, a declared atheist, married a man of similar persuasion. They raised healthy and beautiful children without the benefit of religion. One daughter felt the need for divine help and came upon the Anglican Church. When she tried to convince her mother of the beauty of that faith, Eloísa responded, "If I haven't been able to believe in the true religion, what makes you think I am going to believe in a false one?" (*MOG*, 57).

Aunt Eugenia gave birth to her fifth child in a hospital because her midwife had died and the birth at home was a difficult one. However, her mistrust of hospitals and strange doctors, and her own idiosyncrasies during and after childbirth, caused her to become enraged and insult all the doctors and nurses until she reached the nursery, picked up her son, and after checking him for the proper number of fingers and toes as well as his eyes, nose, and navel, was satisfied when she felt the infant reach for her nipple. Meanwhile, her husband, who put up with his wife's bursts of temper, considered himself fortunate to be married to a woman who was beautiful, fascinating, and certain never to make his life dull. On a hospital visit he met the infamous physician Georgina Dávila, who had the arrogance and vanity to study medicine as if marriage weren't the most altruistic profession. She recited a litany of complaints about his wife, and without warning, he found himself falling in love with her. Georgina suddenly felt her body racked by desire. Three days later, Eugenia left the hospital with her newborn son and half a husband. Unable to control his life now split into two, her husband became unhappy and unable to make anyone else happy. When his heart gave out, Eugenia took him to the hospital because she knew that Georgina would be there. The two women embraced each other in anticipation of the man's death. For a week they both watched over and comforted him, assuring him that it was impossible not to love the other one. Years later, Eugenia, in remembering her long and close relationship with Georgina, says, "No one could have been better company. No one was unhappier than I, except for Georgina" (*MOG*, 72).

Then there is Aunt Magdalena, the beautiful wife in a warm and trusting marriage. One day her loving husband opens a letter addressed to her and written by a lover who states that he is breaking off their relationship. Although reading one another's mail was not a problem, the husband, shocked and hurt, seals the envelope and hides it. Then he pulls himself together and acts as if nothing had disturbed him. The following day he places the letter on the tray where all the correspondence is kept. Magdalena, upon reading the letter, first bursts into tears and then also pulls herself together. Later that day the husband joins his wife and their children, who are jumping rope, a game at which Magdalena is a champion performer. When she shouts, "I won, I won," her husband counters with, "Lucky in cards, unlucky in love" (*MOG*, 91). Magdalena, looking directly at him, says that she is lucky in everything unless he too wants to tell her that he doesn't love her anymore. He realizes that she knows he read the letter, and he stays with her.

Mariana, the perfect wife of a respected, handsome, and rich man, finds herself involved in an affair with a man from a neighboring town, Chipilo, where she goes weekly to buy cheese. She is consumed by guilt and convinced that if anyone were to find out she would be burned alive in the cathedral. One day, when returning in her car, she passes her husband's car on the road and waves. She feels so guilty that she decides to turn around and catch up to him in order to confess and ask his forgiveness. As she approaches, she sees the beautiful head of a woman resting on the front seat next to her husband. Her first reaction was relief, then grief, which changed to surprise, and finally to peace. For years the town gossiped about how Mariana put up with her husband's love affair. No one could understand how, even during that time of pain, she continued going to Chipilo every week to buy cheese.

Amanda Rodoreda was rumored to be the daughter of her father's best friend, Antonio Sánchez. The two men had lived and worked together so closely that Amanda's mother began to love Antonio as an extension of the love she felt for her husband. The morning after Antonio found out that Daniel Rodoreda's wife was pregnant, he left without a word. Amanda was born, and her mother died when she was ten years old. Another ten years went by, and as mysteriously as he had disappeared, Antonio reappeared and sought out his old friend. When Amanda was introduced to him she said, "Oh, you're the one whose daughter I'm supposed to be. What have you come back for? To marry me?" (*MOG*, 170). The father, upon hearing this, thought he was going out of his mind. But Amanda insisted and declared once and for all that she was Rodoreda's daughter, that her mother never went to bed with her father's best friend, and to prove it to all the wagging tongues, she wanted to marry Antonio Sánchez. A year later, they married in the cathedral, and the three of them spent the night at a ranch, dying of laughter and at peace.

Through Aunt Jose Rivadeneira's story, the next-to-the-last in the collection, Mastretta reveals her own moment of crisis and presents the premise for the stories in this collection. This *tía* gave birth to a daughter with eyes as big as two moons. Like all mothers, Jose thought her baby was the most beautiful child in the history of the world. At three weeks of age, the child fell gravely ill, and nothing the mother did to cure her had any effect. With a heavy heart and weeping uncontrollably, she took the baby to the hospital. Her husband, "sensible and prudent as men usually pretend they are" (*MOG*, 174), scolded her for her lack of good sense and hope and spoke of his faith in medical science. The half-hour daily visits to the intensive care unit were of no help, either to the mother or the child. However, sitting on a bench in the hospital corridor, Jose meditated about what she might tell her child to convince her that life was worth living. One morning, enlightened only by the ghosts she carried in her heart, she began to tell her daughter stories about the women who preceded her, what they were like, what grief they suffered, what joys they experienced, how they planted the seeds of the life she had to prolong. For days Jose remembered, imagined, and invented stories to tell her daughter until one afternoon the baby opened her eyes and looked at her eagerly and defiantly. Jose's husband thanked the physicians, who in turn thanked the advances of medical science. Only Jose knew that no science was as powerful as that hidden in the harsh and subtle discoveries of other big-eyed women.

Puerto libre is a collection of twenty-nine pieces, each independent of the other but linked by the nostalgic tone that Mastretta adopts. There are stories, memoirs, descriptive essays, sayings, and thoughts that cross her mind. In this book the writer is introspective, looking into herself to find out what makes her the way she is, what causes her doubts and uncertainties, where and from whom she learned to laugh and cry, what magnetic force keeps her in Mexico City when her heart is in Puebla. She ponders the passage of time and the fear of aging and death. She keeps alive the memory of her father because she needs him to keep from stumbling. Among others, topics touched upon include literature, love, advances made by women, New York and its taxi drivers. Some essays are poignant, moving, even sad; others are light, amusing, and clever. All are revealing of Angeles Mastretta, who describes herself as "un barco a la deriva" (a ship adrift). She calls her book *Puerto libre* (Free Port) as a tribute to those places that once fired the imagination with the unknown, the fantastic, and the outrageous.

The metaphor of the ship adrift appears in an essay, "Barcos a la deriva" (Ships Adrift), in which Mastretta goes back to her childhood in Puebla. With hindsight she realizes that the lifestyle of her family would be considered banal because of the time, effort, and conversation devoted to trivia. However, everyone has his or her madness and why should certain trivia be less significant than others? If she could be a ship she would like to be a sailing ship, quiet and aimless, pushed along by the wind. It was her destiny to be a woman, but spiritually she will always be a ship adrift.

"El manicomio del tiempo" (The Madhouse of Time) and "Don de tiempo" (Gift of Time) reveal the writer's reflections on the modern obsession with not wasting time, an obsession that carries with it the fear of the passage of time and of aging. The first piece was inspired by a saying embroidered on a piece of fabric by an inmate in an insane asylum in Puebla. Mastretta says that few voices bring her to sanity as that anonymous voice who embroidered "No arruines el presente lamentándote por el pasado ni preocupándote por el futuro" (Don't ruin the present by grieving over the past or worrying about the future; PL, 30). Mastretta interprets this to mean that one should reclaim the present and give time a dimension that our world has taken from it. We all live attuned to the clock, afraid to waste time. She points out that there is no time to be sick, to enjoy the company of one's friends, to talk more than five minutes on the telephone. This brings us to fear the passage of time and the inevitable aging process. One realizes that one is getting older when the pains of arthritis appear, when our friends begin to show a striking resemblance to their mothers, when a good-looking man is viewed as a prospective beau for one's daughter. Mastretta concludes that it is good to review the good things of the past and avoid self-pity. Age should be like a vacation, a period when one can do what one wants without feeling rushed or in a constant state of anguish about wasting time.

Sometimes, as in "Fe y quimeras" (Faith and Pipe Dreams), Mastretta shares with her readers her doubts and uncertainties. She senses that people have a need for leaders who embody eternal truths and pipe dreams, and whom they are ready to follow. However, as a writer she realizes that her craft consists of making the fantastic believable, reconstructing reality to make it more accessible and less ugly than it is. The writer does not aim to be a leader, thus leaving a void for politicians to fill. Mastretta cannot subscribe to this idea and feels more comfortable with people who can be trusted: those who have no pipe dreams nor answers to all problems, people who are capable of changing their minds, who have weaknesses, and who can admit their errors. Consequently, disenchanted and having lost faith in the absolutes, Mastretta believes in trivial things that neither politicians nor editorialists talk about. For example, she believes in her son Mateo's empty schoolbag as proof that he has no homework, in the smell of stationery stores, in credit cards, in carrot juice and dark chocolate, in fate. She doesn't believe that the PRI (Partido Revolucionario Institucional) always loses the elections or that it always wins them. She believes that she lives in Mexico City because she loves it and that Mexico is a country of survivors.

In "Mea Culpa," Mastretta also speaks of herself and what she considers her major defect—indecision—which derives from a more deep-seated defect—guilt. She believes that guilt is innate rather than learned and that there are two types: guilt of omission and guilt of commission. She then lists examples of each with explanations. "Culpa de plato" (clean-plate guilt) is that experience of not finishing one's plate and hearing one's father intone about all the starving children in war-torn countries. "Culpa de compra" (shopping guilt) is what she feels when she comes home from a shopping trip and asks herself why she bought purple shoes that don't go with anything, or salmon when no one eats fish except for her. "Culpa médica" (medical guilt) is what one experiences from failing to see the dentist every six months, not consulting the gynecologist twice a year, or not going to the eye specialist when going blind. "Culpa ecológica" (ecological guilt) is a very recent complex: What to do with the peels of fruits and vegetables? Why permit the garbage collector to mix the recyclables with the organic waste? "Culpa salarial" (salary guilt) is what the writer feels when charging a fee for his or her work. For some unknown reason, writers are expected to donate their services, whereas painters, musicians, doctors, and lawyers are free to charge.

Even when touching on the recent advances made by women in Mexican society in "La mujer es un misterio" (Woman Is a Mystery), Mastretta is beset by doubt. On the one hand, she realizes that, overall, women are no longer like the *soldaderas* (camp followers) who blindly and docilely accompanied their men and did their bidding. Perhaps because of the pace of these advances those who participated and witnessed them don't fully appreciate the extent of the changes in ideas and behavior. Many urban women have become self-sufficient, have entered professions that were once male bastions, exercise control of their bodies, and freely express their opinions. Rural women, to a lesser degree, are seeking their freedom from the patriarchal authority that governs their lives. Both groups are now marching to their own beat and waging their own battles without abandoning their men. However, Mastretta recognizes that despite all she sees and says, true equality for women is still a long way off. She recites examples that illustrate that the double standard and other inequalities are still in effect. A man involved in an extramarital affair is admired, whereas a woman in a similar situation is a whore; a fifty-year-old man who sleeps with an adolescent doesn't raise an eyebrow, whereas a woman of thirty-five who does so with a twenty-six-year-old man is repulsive. Why don't the husbands of women who hold high office devote themselves to social causes as volunteers? Why are most contraceptives oriented toward women when a man can make numerous women pregnant in a single week and a woman can only be pregnant once every ten months? And so Mastretta ends her essay disturbed by the contradictions she has pointed out and concludes that the mystery of women's identity has not yet been deciphered.

Mastretta's book of essays finishes with two intimate, nostalgic pieces that serve as a memorial to those important people who preceded her, who are connected to her in spirit, and who are her *cómplices* (accomplices or partners) in life. Although in "Muertos de todos nuestros días" (The Dead of All Our Days) and "Memoria y acantilado" (Memory and Precipice) her tone is more intimate and sentimental when she evokes those who are no longer alive but who still accompany her, one is reminded of her *Mujeres de ojos grandes*. Mastretta cannot let go of those who were important to her, whose passage through life left an indelible impression on her. They allow her to meet the day-to-day challenges, they make her laugh, they help her maintain her equilibrium as she walks on the edge of a cliff. There is her maternal grandfather, who appears in her dreams and makes her laugh; the writer Renato Leduc (1897–1986), whose voice and laughter fill her study; her friend Cinthia, the dancer, passes by with arms outstretched like wings; Manuel Buendía, the journalist, praises her for distancing herself from newspapers; Carlos Pereyra (1940–1988), the writer, scolds her for excessive use of the first person in her writing. But the person whose memory and image is evoked the most is her father, who died over twenty years earlier. He is her greatest *cómplice*. She is tormented by those who as adults are fortunate enough to have their fathers, comparing this state to "going through life under an enormous umbrella, like being able to walk on water, to finding the pot of gold at the end of the rainbow, like already having written the thirty novels I would like to write" (*PL*, 172). She thinks about him every day, sees him in other fathers, regrets all the things she never had a chance to tell him, talks to him, and lets him know about events that have taken place since his death. She is convinced that he is watching, and that certainty helps her walk on the edge of the precipice that surrounds her.

What has attracted attention in the literary world is that Angeles Mastretta, trained and known as a journalist, produced a first novel, *Arráncame la vida*, that became a best-seller. For her it was the culmination of a long-held desire to write fiction, which is now the primary focus of her career. Using her direct and humorous style, she has created memorable characters, both men and women, that have given her books broad appeal. More important, she has opened up avenues of debate and discussion about women's roles in society and their portrayal in literature. Catalina in *Arráncame la vida*, a traditional girl, assumes her role of wife, mother, and dutiful hostess in a nontraditional way. She questions the double standard, demythifies the sacred view of motherhood, and defies her dictatorial and hypocritical husband. And she gives us a new and different perspective on Mexico's political leaders of the postrevolutionary years, leaders who give lip-service to the ideals of the Revolution but betray it at every turn for their own interests.

The *tías* of *Mujeres de ojos grandes* are unforgettable and show Mastretta's talent for penetrating the female psyche. They are individuals she likes to call "anachronistic," ahead of their time, and Mastretta, portraying them with irony and humor, allows those fresh and nonsubmissive voices from a previous generation to be heard.

However, Angeles Mastretta is not just amusing her readers. She uses her style and characters to make them consider or reconsider serious issues of Mexican society and history: the violence, corruption, and hypocrisy of political leaders; the double standard society permits to govern behavior; loneliness; being single or different. Her next novel, *Mal de amores* (A Matter of Love), about a woman of the early part of the century with attitudes of her own generation, will be a challenge for Mastretta and put to the test her creative and narrative skills.

NOTE: Quotations or direct translations from Angeles Mastretta's works are cited using the following abbreviations: *MOG* (*Mujeres de ojos grandes*); *PL* (*Puerto libre*).

Conversations with the Writer

AUGUST 6, 1992; JANUARY 10, 1994

> *How and when did you begin to write?*

I don't remember exactly when I decided what I wanted to be and to what to devote my life. I was born and raised in Puebla and lived there until I was twenty. As a girl, I never said that I wanted to be a writer, but I worshiped my father, who died when I was very young. He wrote for several Puebla newspapers, and I can remember sitting on the floor watching his fingers peck away at an old green Olivetti. That's as close as I got to the written word as a child. I didn't become an avid reader until I was twenty, recognizing the beauty of literature very late. For my father, writing was a pleasure, a game, a way to lose himself in parodies and humor that he couldn't have allowed himself otherwise. Sometimes he wrote things not meant to be published—diaries, memoirs, reflections. Some of those texts were salvaged from the "shipwreck" of his desk after his death. Those papers and the green Olivetti were my only inheritance. Maybe that's why I chose to be a writer, but also because I like to tell stories.

> *When and how did you begin to publish?*

I began publishing in newspapers when I came to Mexico City, and I made my living from journalism until I was twenty-nine. I conducted interviews and wrote articles and columns about different subjects. One day, an editor who was setting up a publishing company approached me and asked me to work with him in seeking out new writers. I told him that I didn't want to do that, that I wanted someone to find me, since I had been wanting to write a book for a long time. He asked me what I earned and offered to pay my salary for six months in exchange for the book. I gave up my newspaper work and my job at a museum, but after six months, I hadn't finished my novel. It took me another six months, and after publishing the book, I began to think about what I would do next and what sort of work I would have to look for, since, obviously, I didn't think I could live off the book alone. In Mexico an edition is a printing of 3,000 copies, and if you publish two editions—some 6,000 copies—then you've done very well. When the book came out, it was very successful in Mexico as well as in other countries, and that allowed me to devote myself to writing another book.

227 Angeles Mastretta

*As part of your literary training, what writers did you read
and which ones influenced your prose?*

I used to be able to answer that question with great ease. It was enough
for me to enumerate my likings. However, now it is more difficult for
me because I suppose we are influenced by everything we have read,
even by what we didn't like. Clarín [1852–1901], [Benito] Pérez Galdós
[1843–1920], [Count Leo] Tolstoy [1828–1910], [Honoré de] Balzac
[1799–1850], Virginia Woolf [1882–1941], Karen Blixen [1885–1962],
Jane Austen [1775–1817] are writers that we all read and that certainly
are important. [Carlos] Fuentes [1928], [Gabriel] García Márquez
[1928], [Jaime] Sabines [1925], [Julio] Cortázar [1914–1984] are some
of the more recent voices. But saying that one writes [like] or wants to
write [like] or is influenced by them is saying a lot and very little.

I believe that asking a writer that question is like asking people,
"Who has influenced the way you speak?" They wouldn't know what
to answer because they are surrounded by voices. Sometimes they repeat something they just happened to hear, and other times they express something in a new way for the first time. The same thing happens
with writers. We are affected by everything we have read and suddenly
we come upon a voice as if it had gone out to look for us, when in reality we have been searching for it ever since we were first attracted by
words, ever since we discovered the passion they arouse in us.

I could tell you that the music of some writers affects me as much as
the hum produced by my relatives when they talk about something that
excites them, or the strange melody that my friends create when they
talk about their love affairs. The problem lies in what emerges from
that medley when I let it pass through my ears, when I attempt to organize it in my words, and when I set out to write literature. Therein is
the difficulty, the adventure, the struggle, and, sometimes—rarely—
the pleasure.

Do you prefer European, Latin American, or North American writers?

I prefer good writers. My favorite writer is usually the one I am reading at the moment. I don't read my nonfavorite writers. I abandon
those who don't arouse my curiosity, the ones who put me to sleep,
those who tell me something I don't want to know. I want literature to seduce and move me before it appeals to my reason and my obligations.

What is your opinion of the women writers of your generation?

I believe there are excellent writers in my generation. But I think that we have to transcend the fashion of being women. A while ago an editor was saying to me, "Why do you want to transcend that fashion if, because of it, you also sell books? It is a marketing phenomenon. You can't say that you don't want to write for women or that you don't want to write like a woman." No, I don't mean that I don't want to write for women, nor do I mean that I don't want to write like a woman. What I mean is that I want to write for women and also for men, and that I want to write like a woman but also like a writer, and I want to be considered a writer and not specifically or exclusively a woman writer. I want to write so that when they speak of Mexican literature in general I will be included in it, and not only when they speak of Mexican literature written by women. Because that is like belonging to the minor leagues or being like one of those delightful people who instead of playing the piano now write, or instead of doing beautiful embroidery now write because computers are in style. And then, isn't it nice that they write and transcribe their telephone conversations? No, that's not what it is all about. It is a matter of hard work. That [attitude], for me and other women writers, of course, has become a challenge and sometimes an obstacle.

You say that there are many excellent women writers in your generation, but you don't specify any names.

I don't want to go into detail. I believe that we women writers have to begin by being generous and accepting of others. We are all very recent, we have just begun writing, none of us has thirty books. Each of us has published two, three, or four books. What I think is that we women writers are testing ourselves and hearing ourselves for the first time. What is true is that for the first time so many of us women are writing simultaneously. Maybe we'll be able to form an opinion in ten years.

Do you believe there is a Mexican literature "written by women?"

Yes, you can say that there is a group of women writing, but there is also a group of men writing, and it doesn't occur to anyone to ask if there is a Mexican literature "written by men." This gets one to thinking once again, are we going to achieve our share of acceptance in society? Yes, there is a literature that we women are writing, but I believe what we ought to be thinking and planning is to form part of the literature that we writers are producing.

What you are saying is that the women who are writing are part of today's writers and do not form a separate group.

That is what I would wish. I would wish that would happen, but it is not happening. I think that in the minds of people we do constitute a separate group.

And by "people" you mean the critics?

I think it's both the critics and the reading public. This is becoming more and more exhausting, because how often can you attend a conference about literature "written by women?" Please, don't let them organize another conference on that subject. They are going to drive all of us women crazy, with everyone talking about literature "written by women." Can't we talk about something else?

Yes, it is a very popular topic.

Someone was telling me, "Look, you are discouraging your public. There are many women who read you lovingly because you are saying what women want to say, because you represent women." What a bore. Although I wouldn't have the nerve to do what Karen Blixen did and sign with a man's name, sometimes I think she was right.

To what do you attribute the success of Arráncame la vida—*to its theme, its style, or to the fact that its author is a woman?*

That's a very difficult question. I suppose there are those people who can say why or analyze why, but for me it's very hard because it is something that I experienced as if it were magic. I didn't write the book thinking it was going to be a success. I wrote it because I wanted to, but not deliberately so that it would be a best-seller. This is one of the things I have been accused of, and I find it very amusing.

Nobody can set out to write a best-seller.

Of course not, but in Mexico we still have the theory that there is "difficult literature" and "easy literature." According to this theory, I created "easy literature." The fact that *Arráncame la vida* is a book that people like inevitably makes it "easy literature." It has been very difficult to get the idea across that behind the person who wrote the book there is a writer. I even believe that's what led me, to some extent, to write *Mujeres de ojos grandes* in a tone and style so very different from *Arráncame la vida*, not because I had to prove to anyone that I was a writer but that I had to prove it to myself. I knew that I didn't have the voice of Catalina Ascencio, that I couldn't narrate another book with that voice, because it was a voice invented for that novel, and of course, many people who criticized it and perhaps many of those who liked it believed that I was Catalina Ascencio, they believed that I spoke like that.

It took a great deal for me to detach myself from the voice of Catalina because it was very powerful, and I had used it for so long, but I knew that it was not my voice. That's why it took me longer to write *Mujeres de ojos grandes*. Now, if I were to set out to write obscure books, I could. I don't feel like writing obscure books. I want to give my readers a plane ticket to another world. I want them to get to that world and feel it deeply and have it be accessible to them without the need to do more than what a reader has to do, which is to become attached to your book.

But I think that the success of *Arráncame la vida* can be attributed to many things. To the fact that I'm a woman? I and other women who are writing at this time are fortunate to be writing in an age in which there are many women eager to read stories specifically about women. Often I am asked, "Why do you write about women?" And I reply with another question, "Do you ask a man why he writes about men? Why do you offend me with that question?" I write about women because I am a woman, but I also create male characters. *Arráncame la vida* is a book with a story about politics and, therefore, it has attracted men as well. It is the story of a woman, but it is also the story of power and of a man who wields it, and of the men and women who suffer because of it.

Going back to the theme of Arráncame la vida, *is it based on the political and social situation of Mexico, or is it completely fictitious?*

I think that it is a combination of the two. Everything that one transforms into fantasy or that one puts into a book is, after all, a work of the imagination. Everything that one grasps from the real world to put into an imaginary world ends up becoming false. Of course I made use of things taken from reality for this book. Like other writers, I have to be certain that what I'm writing could have happened. Therefore, in *Arráncame la vida* I resorted to real characters and situations that would help me weave the fiction that my novel became. It appealed to me to tell about power, to imagine the emotions and the thoughts of people who decided the fate of others. During the thirties and forties of this century, Mexico as we know it today was taking shape. Many of the ways of conducting politics, of sensing and creating problems, as well as the authoritarianism and the lack of justice that govern our country today originated at that time. I was attracted to the idea of looking inside of those who initiated the bad political habits from which we still suffer.

I don't know at what point reality becomes fiction in *Arráncame la vida*. I do know that in this book there is much more fiction than reality. When I tried to learn about the history of the man who would be identified with General Ascencio, those who knew the most about his life and peculiarities spoke the least about him. So I resorted to my recollections. As a little girl, hiding behind an armchair or under a table, I heard the horror stories they told about him. By that time he had been dead for more than ten years, but he was still a vivid and frightening topic of conversation. My relatives tremblingly spoke about things that I'll never be sure were true. I reconstructed what I remembered, but I made up much more than I knew.

In the case of the woman who narrates the novel I was even more radical; I invented her entirely. When I had to decide who would be the narrative voice of the book, a woman more like the women of today than of that time presented herself, and without deliberately wanting to do it, I had the women of my generation struggle with that phenomenon of a man, allow themselves a scandalous passion, sing the music that accompanied their mothers, distort with their belligerent and eager voices a world that perhaps wasn't entirely the way Catalina tells it, but was one that filled her with passion, as it did me, even more than the world she came from. In Puebla, where I was brought up, there was a political boss like Andrés Ascencio. That man was never married to a woman like my narrator. I invented that woman. The girl-friends, the lover, the fact that the political boss kills the lover—I invented all of that. None of it is true, and it has been very difficult for many people in Mexico to accept this. At the beginning, you have no idea how, for example, the modern politicians said, "Listen, be nice, make me a list of the people who appear there, who's who." And I said, "I can't make you that list because nobody is anybody." And they didn't believe me. "No, no, I saw that so-and-so is really there." "But no," I said "that's not him." And that was also a problem among the older people who said, "There are many untruths in what you put in the book." But I never actually said that I was going to write a history book, it says novel. Of course there are things taken from Mexican reality.

The women in Arráncame la vida, *do they symbolize the women of today or those of earlier decades?*

I believe that in a certain way many of the women in *Arráncame la vida* are anachronistic. By anachronistic I mean they are ahead of their time. They are women closer to us than to those of the thirties and forties. I think so, but I am not very sure. What I am sure of is that in those years there were women who thought and lived the way we do. Those women are our predecessors, and today we can say those kinds of things, and that is very clear in *Mujeres de ojos grandes*. In those days, of course, they could live that way, and there were many who did. What happened was that if they did, they didn't announce it for all to hear, but I'm sure there were women who thought that way.

Do you consider yourself a representative of women's liberation?

I don't want to take on more responsibilities than I can handle. I do think that my characters are women in search of their liberation, but they are not proponents of feminism. My intention was to use the curiosity of a nonconformist woman in order to tell of a world that aroused my curiosity and, when faced with it, I couldn't help but show myself to be a nonconformist. The behavior of my characters is contradictory and does not conform to any thesis. They discovered that there was no reason for things to be the way they were, that it was possible to try to live them in another way.

Is there a relationship between your journalism and your literary creativity?

Yes, I think there is a close connection between my journalism and my literary work. In fact, my background has sometimes had an excessive influence on me because I really trained to be a journalist. What happens to me is that I have to start from things that occurred in order to believe the story that has already taken off. And that is related to my background in journalism. Just like a hairdresser who has to grasp your hair with clips in order to cut it, everyone needs his tools and everyone searches for them. I believe the imagination, of course, is the first great tool and simultaneously one's words. And afterward, every writer has to find a handle to hold on to.

How would you classify Puerto libre?

Puerto libre is a book of reflections that tells me many things about myself. The themes that I deal with in this book are ones I have become very attached to in recent years. It is a book of literary essays not about literature. They are my travels through life, through my emotions, through my intimate world, my ambitions, my dreams, my desires, my yearnings. It is a book in which I reveal more of myself than in the others. In the others I am creating fiction and, of course, I put myself in my books like any other author. But the texts of *Puerto libre* are written from within me; they are about me.

Do you think there is a feminine way of writing that is different from a masculine way of writing?

I am not sure how to answer. I could say yes, that there is an exclusively feminine discourse, that only we women can speak of our passions, our boredom, our doubts, but then what would you say about Emma Bovary or Anna Karenina? Aren't they perfectly drawn female characters? Haven't they been read and worshiped by women for years?

And the descriptions of interiors? One could say that the way Virginia Woolf or Isak Dinesen [Karen Blixen] or Agatha Christie [1890–1976] or Jane Austen describes a house, a tea set, or bed linens is exclusively feminine; however, Balzac's linens and dining rooms are clear images in the memory of any reader. Sometimes I think that only a woman can speak of a recollection related to smells and tastes with precision, but then why is [Marcel] Proust's madeleine so famous?

Love—literature's favorite theme—but also forbidden or impossible passions, laughter, absolute will, power, hate, and war are themes chosen equally by men and women. And they can be treated with the same literary skill by either of the sexes. The works that move the world—those that captivate it to the point of becoming part of our collective memory—are those that are well written, not those written by men or by women.

Are there any autobiographical elements in your narrative work?

Yes, of course, but I am not any of my characters. For example, I had a very close relationship with my father. My image of him is fabled, mythical, and so are the fathers in my books. Catalina Ascencio has a wonderful father whom she loves deeply. And in *Mujeres de ojos grandes*, where perhaps the lovers and the husbands aren't as loving as one might wish, the fathers are always marvelous. That is autobiographical. Maybe what I am narrating is my longing for my father, my nostalgia for him, and also my tastes in food and clothes. The things that are in my books haven't happened to me. I haven't had a general for a husband, or a lover who is a conductor of an orchestra or a violinist or a pianist or a Spaniard, as have the women of *Mujeres de ojos grandes*. It all crisscrosses. I believe that the stories and the novels of every writer are interlaced with his or her autobiography.

Are you working on something new?

A novel, but you already know that plans are always the fantasies of writers. Novels are made from fantasies, and when you finish them, they never are the same as when you talked about them. That's why I'm very fearful of talking about what I'm doing, because I think that if I talk about it too much I am going to stop doing it. Every writer has myths and rituals when it comes to what he's writing.

I am inventing a woman who will inevitably live in Puebla. I don't know why, but I always end up requiring that my characters live, at least for a while, in Puebla. This is about a woman who had already gone to live in Mexico City in 1900, but I couldn't accept her early childhood outside of Puebla. I need the stimulus of that nostalgia so that a story can go through my head. My character is a woman who has the attitudes of the 1970s in 1910, something quite possible because the period of the Revolution from 1910 to 1940 was rather permissive. It produced change, was prosperous and very vital. During that time people who were different or strange were accepted, and their irreverent behavior was not considered deserving of punishment. Those years turned things around in such a way that a woman who didn't marry, for example, didn't have to be an embittered old maid. She could be a woman with various passions, with a public and private personal life governed neither by local institutions nor by social norms, but rather by what she decided to do with her life.

My new character inherits a pharmacy, which gives her certain freedom, because women without money have no freedom. She is capable of supporting herself; of enjoying her profession, not as a clerk in a pharmacy but as a healer; and of being madly in love with a man who is eccentric, an adventurer who comes and goes and returns to her as he would to his house, but he doesn't live with her. This perhaps sounds very odd.

At this moment some of the characters have escaped from me, and others have developed for no particular reason, for example, the parents of the woman. In addition, there are many things that are difficult because they occur in another time. If you create a pharmacist you have to know what drugs he used, what illnesses were known, and how they were treated. You have to learn a lot, starting from where shirts and dresses were sold to what the sweets were like and even the clothing that was worn. I consulted everything from newspapers and journals to histories of the Porfirian period and found that, although the political history of the Revolution is well documented, little has been written about the way people lived.

My protagonist is going to become a physician of the type that is in vogue now. She is going to be a doctor who works with intuitions more than with certainties, a doctor more given to homeopathy, to self-knowledge, to relaxation and exercise, to all those things that are in fashion. She will be a forerunner of all that and will be somewhat alone in her aim. At the same time, she will be a woman who is very capable of combining different medical treatments and theories and resolving whatever problems come up.

Will she be single or married?

I am struggling with that right now. I created her as an exceptionally educated woman, not an educated woman like my grandmother or so many other grandmothers. She is not brought up in a very religious, conservative family with ideas more typical of the nineteenth century than the twentieth, just the opposite. She is brought up by parents very obsessed with modernity, with the new century, with the possibility that things can be different in the twentieth century. They are dreamers of the twentieth century, they have enormous faith in it, and they bring up the girl in that faith and certainty. For example, they believe there is no reason why she can't have affairs with men, that she doesn't have to marry in order to fall in love with someone. That is how she is brought up, and afterward she is not going to know what to do. I think she will have in her mind and in her expectations a world that is better than the one she will encounter. I think the boyfriend will end up becoming an extraordinary character, very strong. Their relationship, having begun as children, is one that inevitably binds them together. However, it is a relationship that I will have to tone down, among other reasons because of *El amor en los tiempos del cólera* [1985; *Love in the Time of Cholera*, 1988], because if I create a story with a very long love relationship I have to do it knowing that there is a novel like García Márquez's. It is something one can't overlook. So this has to be a more tempered love, more continuous. The love in *El amor en los tiempos del cólera* is idealized, one that occurs at the very beginning and is not recovered until the end. That passion is one that survives precisely because it was never expressed, it was never realized. No, the passion I am creating will be just the opposite. It is going to be a passion that survives, but survives the worst there is, which is habit. I want my characters to grow old feeling for one another the same thrill they felt when young, but they will grow old together.

It is in my head, but I don't know how it is going to turn out. Surely it will be very different from what I have said. Books in progress are like lovers: they are what one likes to talk about most, but should talk about least.

Do you have any other ideas for novels?

I have very many, but they are useless because I haven't worked them out. Every morning something goes through my head and I say, "Oh, I've got to write a novel about that." If not every morning, at least once a week I say, "What a story! I've got to use that story in a novel." But those ideas don't count. I think I am certain that the novel after this one will occur in the eighties or nineties. From so much moving around in the past I am nostalgic for the present.

In Mexico there have been several generations of notable women writers before yours. Which ones do you admire and why?

To begin with, I admire Nellie Campobello [1909–?]. Do you know who she is?

Of course I do. I wrote about her years ago.

I'm glad that you know who she is because you have no idea how shocking it is when someone comes along and asks you, "Who is the person who wrote this?" and then has no idea who Nellie Campobello is. We should learn to recover the past. Not only that, but we should go back and read those women writers and make others do so as well. You can't imagine how many readers there are who haven't read Nellie Campobello, and I'll tell you why. Simply because women weren't in fashion at that time. Why isn't Nellie mentioned among the great writers of Mexican literature? Fortunately, she appears among the novelists of the Mexican Revolution, but sometimes not even there. Nellie Campobello is known as a graceful dancer who also wanted to relate what happened to her mother and what she witnessed as a little girl. That reputation is unjust. Here we had a great writer who perhaps didn't write many more books because she had no money, because she had to live and, of course, because she had conflicting vocations. In those days nobody guided you. Being a writer was the worst thing that could happen to you. You didn't earn a cent, nobody paid you any mind, and you wrote just to amuse yourself. Maybe that's why Nellie Campobello wasn't a very prolific writer. But what she did write is marvelous and enlightening. She is a woman who, in the period of the Revolution, thought as she did, saw what she saw, and was capable of describing the horror with perfection. If there is anyone who has truly made me experience the worst of the Mexican Revolution, it is Nellie Campobello and Martín Luis Guzmán [1887–1976]. But Nellie had an extraordinary ability to relate the crimes, the horror, the intolerance, the injustice, and the hunger from the perspective of a young girl.

Other writers?

Other writers? Elena Garro [1920], whose *Los recuerdos del porvenir* is sufficient to consider her an exceptional writer. Rosario Castellanos [1925–1974], in whose poetry we women continue to see ourselves, whose urgent and desperate voice still makes fun of itself, reminding us who began all of this. And I don't have to mention Sor Juana [Inés de la Cruz; 1648–1695], a genius who dazzles us all.

Elena Poniatowska [1933]? María Luisa Mendoza [1938]?

I admire them and rediscover them every day. I don't like to speak of them as predecessors because they are my respected and eloquent contemporaries. I would say the same for Julieta Campos [1932] and Luisa Josefina Hernández [1928]. Just think about it. In time, all of them and all of us who began publishing five, ten, or twenty years later will be viewed as part of the same generation. What difference does it make who wrote the first book? What will make the difference is who wrote the best books, and that debate, fortunately, we will not witness.

Do you believe that the presence of different groups of women writers has helped those who followed?

In what way does the presence of some help the others? I believe in many ways. In the same way that the presence of some men writers helps us. Everything helps, everything that we hear from others, what others discover and reconcile, even what others despise and leave out.

When do you write and how do you relate your writing to your other responsibilities—domestic, professional, family?

I would love to wake up at eight in the morning, with my head clear and my emotions in place, and be able to sit at my computer without anyone interrupting me, without anyone asking me what to prepare for lunch, without my daughter asking me to fix her ponytail, without my son asking me to listen to his second version of Batman. But I have to listen. I have many domestic complications and personal matters that are disruptive. I really believe that my being a woman, my feminine upbringing, and what is considered feminine behavior makes me put off my profession. I think that if I were a man I could close the door and come out of my study to have breakfast, lunch, and dinner, to give my children two pats on the head, and continue completely involved in whatever occurs to me, in my words or in whatever wants to go through my head. And that doesn't happen to me.

I write whenever I can. During those months of the year when my children go to school, I try to work when they're not at home. But I don't start at eight in the morning, because I have a husband, and I have breakfast with him and we talk. Then it is usually from ten to two or three. But my time is always full of stops and interruptions because I am constantly being asked to do things that I accept. Not only domestic things, but to give a lecture or to write an article because someone begs you, "Please write something for me about the Mexican rebozo [shawl] for a foreign publication." "But I'm not interested in the Mexican rebozo." And one ends up saying, "Well, since I agreed," and then I write something I never wanted to write. Other things come along that I accept because sometimes I can't concentrate, or in some cases because of the negative feminine quality that can't say no. What I should say is, "Point number one, I don't want to do it; point number two, I cannot do it because I have too many other things to do." That is very difficult for me.

Do you think you have had any influence on younger writers?

Yes, I think I have had some influence on younger writers and also on those who began to write late and have been readers of my books. Don't ask me to give examples because I can't. The truth is that I live almost as isolated as María Luisa Puga [1944]. Perhaps because of my children I live a very self-centered life. I don't go to the university, I don't teach. Although it may sound vain, it is more out of laziness that I don't read cultural supplements. I read many, many books and talk about literature with my friends. And I am not very crazy about those meetings about women writers and literature. I try as hard as possible not to get involved in them. It is inevitable that there is a division between men and women. But in literature, for some reason that I can't fathom, it is more pronounced. Why, for example, aren't there conferences for women physicians, or women economists, or women bookkeepers, or women architects? If any, they are probably very rare. Each one is a profession, and the women are professionals like anyone else. The same goes for women dentists. Women dentists don't get together to say there is a special feminine dentistry. Why do we take this into our heads? And it is not just we women writers, it is also the fault of the critics, of the university professors, who are the ones who organize conferences about women. I don't like to work a great deal on the topic of women writers. I confess that because I am a woman perhaps I write with greater facility about women, but maybe it is because I am myself. After all, there are many men who write with enormous facility about women or whose great works are about women—[Gustave] Flaubert [1821–1880], for example.

I think what is happening in Mexico is nothing new. There have always been women writers, but in recent years there has been a notable increase in their number.

Yes, something like a population explosion. And not only more women writers with respect to those who came before, but there are more women writers than men, more successful women writers than men, and more readers of books written by women than by men. I am not making this up, that is what the publishers will tell you. At this rate, those who will have to begin organizing conferences about men will be the men, because they are going to feel mortified.

Representative Selections

Aunt Clemencia Ortega

["Tía Clemencia Ortega," from *Mujeres de ojos grandes*]

Clemencia Ortega's boyfriend didn't realize what a jar of madness and passions he was opening up that evening. He reached for it as if it were marmalade and opened it, but from then on, for his entire life, his carefree comings and goings in his English suit or with his jai-alai racquet were infused with that perfume, that awful concoction, that poison.

Aunt Clemencia was pretty, but underneath her dark curls she had ideas, and that eventually turned out to be a problem for him. Because for the short term it had been her ideas, not just her passing fancies, that had brought her without any problem to the secret bed she shared with her boyfriend.

In those days, not only did properly brought up girls from Puebla not go to bed with their boyfriends, it didn't even occur to the boyfriends to suggest the possibility. It was Aunt Clemencia who unhooked her bra when, after much petting, she felt her nipples become as pointy as two tops. She was the one who put her hands into his trousers, reaching for the place where men keep the mascot they take everywhere, the animal they lend you when they feel like it and then take away, indifferent and calm, as if it had never known us. It was she who, without being forced, brought her hands near his throbbing prick, she who wanted to see it, she who was groping for it.

And so her boyfriend never felt the shame of those who take advantage, or the obligation of those who make promises. They made love in the pantry while everyone's attention was focused on Aunt Clemencia's cousin, who that morning had put on her bridal gown to get married as is God's will. The pantry was dark and silent when the banquet ended. It smelled of spices and nutmeg, of chocolate from Oaxaca and chile peppers, of vanilla and olives, and of cake and codfish. The music heard in the distance was interrupted by shouts for the newlyweds to kiss, for the bouquet to be thrown to some poor ugly girl, for the in-laws to dance. To Aunt Clemencia it seemed that there couldn't have been a better place in the world for what she had chosen to do that afternoon. They made love without making promises, without turning themselves inside out, without the weighty responsibility of knowing that they were being watched. They were what you would call happy, for a while.

"You have oregano in your hair," her mother said to her when she saw her dancing by near the table where she and Clemencia's father had been sitting for five and a half hours.

"It must be the bouquet that fell on my head."

"I didn't see the bouquet hit you," said the mother. "I didn't even see you when they threw it. I was calling you."

"A different bouquet hit me," Clemencia replied with the shamelessness of a mischievous little girl.

Her mother was used to answers of that kind. Although they sounded completely silly to her, she attributed them to the mental disorder that stayed with her daughter after the fever accompanying a severe case of measles. She also knew that in those cases it was better not to ask any more questions so as to avoid getting caught up in a mess. She restricted herself to reflecting on the fact that oregano was an exquisite herb that had not received its full measure of justice in the kitchen.

"It hasn't occurred to anyone to use it in desserts," she said aloud, as if to finish her thought.

"How nicely Clemencia dances," said the woman seated next to her, whereupon they began to chat.

When the boyfriend to whom Aunt Clemencia had given herself in the pantry wanted to marry her, she replied that that was impossible. And she said it with such seriousness that he thought she was offended because instead of asking her earlier he had spent a year enjoying clandestine fragrances, during which time he built up his bakery business to a chain of six that sold bread and sweet rolls and two more that sold cakes and gelatin desserts.

But it wasn't for that reason that Aunt Clemencia refused, but for all the reasons that she had never had time or need to explain to him.

"I thought that you had understood a long time ago," she told him.

"Understood what?"

"That my plans didn't include getting married, not even to you."

"I don't understand you," said the boyfriend, who was an ordinary man. "Do you want to be a whore all your life?"

When Aunt Clemencia heard that, she regretted in a second all the hours, afternoons, and evenings that she had given that ingrate. She didn't even have the strength to feel offended.

"Go away," she told him. "Go before I charge you the fortune you owe me."

He got scared and left.

Shortly thereafter he married the daughter of some Asturians, baptized six children, and allowed his memories to fade with time, letting them become moldy just like water that becomes stagnant around the sides of a fountain. He became a fierce cigar smoker, a regular afternoon drinker, an insomniac who didn't know what to do with the early morning hours, an insatiable seeker of business opportunities. He spoke little, had a couple of friends with whom he went to the shooting range on Saturday afternoons and in whom he could never confide anything more intimate than the childish rage that consumed him when he missed more than two pigeons. He was bored.

One Tuesday morning, nineteen years after the boy from Puebla had lost the perfume and the lips of Aunt Clemencia, a man from Yucatán appeared and offered to sell him the best-stocked grocery store in town. They went to look at it. They entered through the back storeroom, an enormous room filled with seeds, sacks of flour and sugar, grains, chocolate, fragrant herbs, chiles, and other products for kitchen pantries.

All of a sudden, feeling his entire body in turmoil, the man took out his checkbook to buy the store without even having seen it all, paid the Yucatecan the first asking price, and ran out to the house with the three courtyards where Aunt Clemencia still lived. When they told her a gentlemen was asking for her at the door, she ran down the steps that led to the patio full of flowers and birds.

He saw her approach and wanted to kiss the ground on which that goddess of harmony that the thirty-nine-year-old Clemencia had become was treading. He saw her come close and would have liked to disappear, thinking how ugly and worn-out he looked. Clemencia noted his embarrassment, she felt bad about his potbelly and nearly bald head, about the bags that were beginning to show under his eyes, about the look of boredom that he would have liked to erase from his face.

"We have gotten old," she said to him, including herself in that disastrous state so as to relieve him of his anxiety.

"Don't be kind to me. I have been an idiot and it shows everywhere on me."

"I didn't love you because you were smart," said Aunt Clemencia with a smile.

"But you stopped loving me because I was an idiot," he said.

"I have never stopped loving you," said Aunt Clemencia. "I don't like to squander things, least of all my feelings."

"Clemencia," said the man, trembling with emotion. "After me you've had a dozen boyfriends."

"I still love them all," said Aunt Clemencia, untying the apron she was wearing over her dress.

"What?" said the poor man.

"With every flutter of my heart," answered Aunt Clemencia, coming close to her ex-boyfriend until she could feel him trembling like she knew he would be.

"Come on," she said later, taking him by the hand to go out into the street. At that point he stopped trembling and hurriedly took her to the store he had just bought.

"Turn off the light," she told him after they entered the storeroom and the smell of oregano enveloped her head. He stretched out his arm behind him, and in the ensuing darkness made up for the twenty years of absence whose weight was lifted from his body.

Two hours later, combing the oregano out of Aunt Clemencia's dark curls, he asked her again:

"Marry me."

Aunt Clemencia kissed him slowly and got dressed quickly.

"Where are you going?" he asked her when he saw her going toward the door waving good-bye to him.

"Tomorrow morning at this time," said Aunt Clemencia, looking at her watch.

"But you do love me," he said.

"Yes," replied Aunt Clemencia.

"More than any of the others?" he asked.

"Just the same," she said.

"You're a . . . ," he began to say when Aunt Clemencia stopped him.

"Careful with what you say because I'll charge you, and your thirty bakeries won't be enough to cover it."

Then she opened the door and left without another word.

The next morning Aunt Clemencia received at her house the deeds for thirty bakeries and one grocery store. They came in an envelope with a card that read: "You are a stubborn woman."

Aunt Cristina Martínez

["Tía Cristina Martínez," from *Mujeres de ojos grandes*]

Aunt Cristina Martínez wasn't pretty, but there was something about her skinny legs and her brusque voice that made her interesting. Unfortunately, the men of Puebla weren't looking to marry interesting women, and Aunt Cristina reached the age of twenty without anyone having proposed even a proper courtship. By the time she was twenty-one, her four sisters were married for better or worse, and she spent the entire day with the humiliation of remaining behind as a spinster. Before long, her nieces and nephews would call her an old maid, and she wasn't sure she could endure that blow. It was after that birthday, which ended with her mother's tears when she blew out the candles on the cake, that Mr. Arqueros appeared on the horizon.

One morning Cristina returned from downtown, where she had gone to buy some mother-of-pearl buttons and a yard of lace, reporting that she had met a well-bred Spaniard in the La Princesa jewelry store. The diamonds in the window had made her go in to ask how much an engagement ring that was her life's dream cost. When they told her the price it seemed reasonable to her, and she bemoaned the fact that she wasn't a man so that she could buy it at that very moment with the aim of putting it on her finger some day.

"They can have the ring before the bride, they can even choose a bride that will go with the ring. We, on the other hand, just have to wait. There are those who wait their entire lives, and those who are burdened forever with a ring they dislike, isn't that so?" she asked her mother during lunch.

"Don't quarrel with men any longer, Cristina," said her mother. "Who is going to look after you when I die?"

"I am, Mama, don't worry. I am going to look out for myself."

In the afternoon, a messenger from the jewelry store appeared with the ring that Aunt Cristina had tried on, stretching out her hand to admire it from all angles while saying a lot of things similar to those she had repeated to her mother in the dining room. He also brought a sealed envelope with Cristina's first and last name on it.

Mr. Arqueros was sending both things with his affection, his respects, and his regret at not bringing them himself because his ship was leaving for Veracruz the next day and he was traveling part of that day and all night to arrive on time. The message proposed marriage to her: "Your ideas about life, about men and women, your delightful voice and the carefree way you walk dazzled me. I will not return to Mexico for several years, but I suggest that you join me in Spain. My friend Emilio Suárez will introduce himself to your parents shortly. I place in him my trust and in you my hope."

Emilio Suárez was the man of Cristina's adolescent dreams. He was twelve years older than she and was still a bachelor when she was twenty-one. He was as rich as the forest in the rainy season and as unfriendly as the woods in January. All the girls in the city had chased after him, and the luckier ones only came away with the prize of an ice cream in the town square. However, he appeared at Cristina's house to ask, in the name of his friend, for her hand in marriage by proxy in which he would gladly act as the representative.

Cristina's mother refused to believe that she had only seen the Spaniard once, and as soon as Suárez disappeared with the answer that they were going to think about it, she accused her of having acted like a slut. But her daughter's look of amazement was such that she ended up by asking for her forgiveness and for permission from heaven, where her husband was, to commit the foolishness of marrying her off to a foreigner.

When Aunt Cristina recovered from the anguish typical of surprises, she looked at her ring and began to cry for her sisters, her mother, her girlfriends, her neighborhood, the cathedral, the town square, the volcanoes, the sky, the mole sauce, the stuffed tortillas, the national anthem, the highway to Mexico, Cholula, Cuetzalán, her father's aromatic bones, the stews, the spicy chocolates, the music, the smell of tortillas, the San Francisco River, her friend Elena's ranch and her Uncle Abelardo's fields, for the moon in October and in March, for the sun in February, for her defiant spinsterhood, for Emilio Suárez who in his entire life of looking at her had never heard her voice or noticed how the devil she walked.

The following day she went out to the street with the news and her ring shining on her finger. Six months later she married Mr. Arqueros in front of a priest, a notary, and Suárez's eyes. There was a mass, a banquet, a dance, and farewells. All with the same enthusiasm as if the groom were on this side of the ocean. They say that there hadn't been a more radiant bride in a long time.

Two days later Cristina left from Veracruz heading for the port where Mr. Arqueros, with all his gentlemanliness, would pick her up and take her to live with his aunts in Valladolid.

It was from there that she sent her first letter telling them all that she missed them and how happy she was. She didn't use up much space describing the landscape crowded with little houses and farmland, but she sent her mother a recipe for meat prepared with red wine that was the regional dish, and her sisters two poems by a Mr. García Lorca that had turned her inside out. Her husband proved to be a cautious and hard-working man, who was always laughing about his wife's way of speaking Spanish and her stories of ghosts, her blushing every time she heard the word "damn," and her terror because there everybody said to hell with god for no reason at all and swore invoking the Lord's name without any respect.

The letters came and went for a year before the one in which Aunt Cristina informed her family of the unexpected death of Mr. Arqueros. It was a brief letter that seemed to be emotionless. "That's how bad she must feel," said her sister, the second one, who was aware of her sentimental whims and her wild passions. All of them were saddened by her grief and expecting that as soon as she recovered from the shock that she would write to them with greater clarity about her future. That's what they were talking about one Sunday after lunch when they saw her walk into the living room.

She brought gifts for everyone, and her nieces and nephews didn't let her go until she finished distributing them. Her legs had gotten heavier and she was wearing very high heels, black like her stockings, skirt, blouse, jacket, hat, and veil that she hadn't had time to lift from her face. When she finished the distribution she pulled it off together with her hat and smiled.

"Well, I'm back," she said.

As of that time she was the widow of Arqueros. She wasn't burdened by the hardships of being an old maid, and she frightened off any others with her out-of-tune piano and her ardent voice. You didn't even have to ask her to go to the piano to accompany a song. She had in her repertoire all kinds of waltzes, polkas, ballads, arias, and pasodobles. She wrote the lyrics for some preludes of Chopin and she sang them evoking love affairs no one ever knew about. At the end of her concert she allowed everyone to applaud her, and after getting up from the little bench to take a deep bow, she stretched out her arms, showed her ring, and then, pointing to herself with her aging and beautiful hands, said convincingly: "And I'll be buried in Puebla."

The gossips say that Mr. Arqueros never existed. That Emilio Suárez told the only lie of his life, having been convinced by who knows what

247 Angeles Mastretta

trick of Aunt Cristina. And that the money she called her inheritance, she had gotten from the contraband she smuggled in the suitcases with her trousseau.

Who knows. What is certain is that Emilio Suárez and Cristina Martínez were friends until the end of their days. Something no one ever forgave them for, because friendship between men and women is an unpardonable sin.

Memory and Precipice

["Memoria y acantilado," from *Puerto libre*]

Is Father's Day in June or July? Those who invented the date ought to know. When my father died twenty-two years ago, Father's Day didn't exist, and since his death, I celebrate Father's Day every day. I don't buy him gifts, but I talk to his slight smile and to the continuous questioning look in his expression in the portrait where I look for him.

I wonder whether there will come a time when orphaned girls stop looking for their fathers. Because everyone is ready to feel sorry for a child, an adolescent, even a young woman who has lost her father, but a fortyish woman with her orphanhood on her back is more pathetic than touching. I don't want you to think that I don't know, or to think that knowing has done me any good either. All of me, with my desires and memories, turns to the grief of being an orphan as to water.

Sometimes I go along the street singing a song or playing a game with my children to find images in the clouds, and suddenly there they are, as in a dream that they don't enjoy sufficiently, a father and his daughter talking about nothing, a daughter and her father winking at the future when they part, a father who takes his daughter out to eat, a daughter caressing the back of her father's neck, a father who is alive like a real treasure, a father and a daughter who don't understand what a luxury it is to have one another and don't have nightmares about the abyss of losing one another.

Then the most unseemly envy torments me, envy provoked by those who have a father and who gamble away or openly waste the pleasure of having one.

Having a father as an adult must be like strolling through life under an enormous umbrella, like being able to walk on water, like finding the pot of gold at the end of the rainbow, like already having written the thirty novels that I would like to write.

I don't know, but for some time now I have been imagining that having my children's grandfather back would be like existing in a different way and grabbing hold of my existence in the securest way possible.

Perhaps the grief would be less intense and the loss easier to accept if I had finished doing all the things that daughters should do with their fathers, or more specifically, if I had at least been able to begin to say the things that my clumsy adolescent tongue didn't even get around to thinking.

I always have at hand, for my own ears or for whoever wants to listen to me, one long list of things that I didn't say and another of things that I didn't do for my father. Usually I keep them to myself, but sometimes they come out at the most inopportune times and I burden people who look at me as if they never wanted to see me again, or I burden those who are suffering even greater grief and for that very reason have pity on me.

The time before last that I went to the eye doctor, after finishing his routine examination, the good man had the daring idea of asking me about my general health, aside from my eyes.

"Well, look," I said to him, "an hour ago when I left my house, just after closing the door, I had the distinct feeling that my father, who died twenty years earlier, had just died a minute before. Otherwise, I'm okay."

The doctor had seen me twice before that visit and up to that point considered himself my eye doctor, not my psychotherapist. At any rate, he put his hand on my shoulder and said:

"I'm glad that otherwise you're okay."

I didn't go back to see him for about a year and a half. Our next meeting could have been routine; however, when he saw me in the waiting room he cut short my wait, had me go into his office, and sat down next to me in one of the armchairs for the patients.

"Do you remember my wife?" he asked. "The lady who helped me run the office?"

"Of course," I answered him, remembering the warmth of that slender and attractive woman.

"She died suddenly," he said to me sadly, as if he were questioning it.

"You poor thing," I said, putting my arms around him. "Otherwise, how are you?"

Then we looked at one another like two old friends, and since that time we have been friends.

That's what happens to me suddenly. A while ago, in an Italian restaurant, while three musicians were ruining the song "Torna a Surriento," I spilled my grief over the spaghetti, and I still haven't recovered from the embarrassment I made my listeners suffer. Today I find myself with this free port open to the ship of my recollections, and I don't think I can keep them quiet. However, we are all fortunate that I can warn you in time and whoever doesn't want to see how I unload my cargo is free to go elsewhere, without our having to offer each other excuses.

So I will continue: of all the things that I didn't say when I still could, now I regret most not having said the following:

- Papa, it doesn't matter that you aren't rich.
- Papa, now I have understood why you aren't rich.
- Papa, tell me about the war and about the other things that grieve you.
- Papa, in a little while you won't have to support us. Don't be foolish enough to die, because the rest will be the best part. The life remaining will be a reward.
- Papa, you yourself are a reward, and I know how lucky I am to have you.

I could go on, but it wouldn't be fair to put things on this list I didn't say because I didn't know them or because they hadn't happened to me. We relatives end up knowing a lot more about those who lived close to us when we can no longer talk about it with them. Furthermore, one of the first ways of establishing some kind of conversation with our dead is to search for them in the past that we didn't know about them. Another way is to retrace the steps that were theirs and that we didn't share. From those two searches I have gotten thousands of questions, admonitions, and pieces of information. I will tell you only some of those with which I have wasted my time pursuing the eyes of the unrelenting portrait that all his children and, of course, our mother, have a copy of some place in our homes:

Papa, I now know the hills of Piamonte. I went with Veronica. We visited the house your grandfather left you when he thought that you would be the only one of his children to stay and live in Italy. We found out from the buyers that you had told them you were selling it in order to buy yourself a house in Mexico, the country where you were born and where ultimately you would live the rest of your days. Don't think that we wondered out loud why you didn't buy the house in Mexico. Both of us knew why, and we talked about it that evening: you used it to replace the money they lent you when you had the idea of importing the FIAT line to Puebla and your investor friends wanted profits the first year.

We also ate in the restaurant where they still make the raviolis that according to Aunt Angelina were your favorite. They are a delight.

Papa, the Italians have become prosperous, and Rome is one of the most expensive cities in the world.

The virgin of the Duomo, the Piazza Fontana, and the Avenida Italia are once again beautiful and stately, they are no longer a heap of charred ruins. Don't worry any more.

The Fonda de "Michelé," where you stood in line so often for your portion of boiled cabbage and sticky rice, has become an elegant restaurant in the middle of Olmetto Street.

On the Piazza Ludovica, where you used to take the bus that lurched along until it got to Stradella, there is a boutique selling women's clothing where a dress costs more than a Volkswagen.

How did the voyage of the Liberty Ship that took you from Naples to New York end? Did they imprison the Cuban who escaped from the captain in Gibraltar? Did you find out what the count of Montebello, a cousin of the king of Italy—according to you—was doing packed in that same "can of sardines" that saved you from starvation? Why was it that you only wrote for a week in your diary about your return home? Was it that as soon as you stopped seeing the Mediterranean and plunged into the present that it was no longer worthwhile recording?

Aunt Angelina, your cousin, showed us a letter that you sent your Italian relatives in 1969, twenty-four years after having left them. Why, if you loved them as much as your letter says, did it take you more than twenty years to write to them?

Would you have been able to leave after living with us for twenty years and not ever write?

Did you know that the woman who was your girlfriend during the war became an alcoholic? You had already died when a letter of hers arrived, which your daughter Veronica read and lost. She laughs at me when I complain to her about it.

Why didn't you ever explain in detail how much and in what way the Puebla of our childhood bored you?

You know what? I still miss our evenings sitting in front of the TV, predicting the endings of the Mexican films and being afraid that at midnight they would cut off the transmission before the melodrama ended. I can't watch Pardavé without crying.

You wouldn't believe it, but in Mexico we now have sweet grapes and they import chianti and San Pellegrino mineral water, as if the entire middle class had been born in Italy.

The film The Godfather *now has three parts. It would have fascinated you.*

I live with a man who makes noises at night like the ones you used to make and in the afternoon is a wonderful conversationalist. In the morning he is almost always in a hurry. The two of you would get along well. He also has a distrust of the ocean.

I have two children. One has your smile but doesn't yell "God damn" because he didn't hear it from you, but when he argues it seems like he was born in the middle of a trattoria. *The other one has eyes like a bird and always wants to talk to me when I am writing. I think the two are like gods and, in case you wondered, I adore them to distraction.*

My mother built a house that looks out on the volcanoes on the land she inherited as the firstborn and for which she fought so hard. It's a pity that you didn't stay to share that silence.

You're right, I should never have gotten into that mess. But the fact is that the mess got into me.

These are some of the things I have spoken to him about, without getting any response except one, perhaps made up: the more or less frequent sensation that someone is watching me and almost always becomes my accomplice. I note in my mother a complete lack of confidence in such an interpretation, but it helps me walk along the edge of the eternal precipice that surrounds us.

Bibliography

Publications

La pájara pinta. Mexico City: Altiplano, 1975.
Arráncame la vida. Mexico City: Océano, 1985; subsequent eds., Mexico City: Cal y Arena.
Mujeres de ojos grandes. Mexico City: Cal y Arena, 1990.
Puerto libre. Mexico City: Cal y Arena, 1993.
Mal de amores. Mexico City: Alfaguara, 1996.

Translations

Mexican Bolero. Trans. Ann Wright. London: Viking, 1989.
"Aunt Concha Esparza." Trans. Amy Schildhouse. *New Writing from Mexico*. Special issue of *TriQuarterly* 85 (Fall 1992): 30–32.
"Aunt Jose." Trans. Amy Schildhouse. *New Writing from Mexico*. Special issue of *TriQuarterly* 85 (Fall 1992): 28–29.
"Aunt Leonor." Trans. Amy Schildhouse. *New Writing from Mexico*. Special issue of *TriQuarterly* 85 (Fall 1992): 24–27.
"Aunt Natalia Esparza." Trans. Amy Schildhouse. *New Writing from Mexico*. Special issue of *TriQuarterly* 85 (Fall 1992): 21–23.
"Aunt Clemencia Ortega." Trans. Gabriella de Beer. *Review: Latin American Literature and Arts* 48 (Spring 1994): 18–20.
"White Lies." Trans. John Incledon. *Pyramids of Glass: Short Fiction from Modern Mexico*, 12–16. San Antonio: Corona, 1994.

Conclusion

The five writers considered here, individually and together, provide much to reflect on and also raise some questions. Is it important to view them as women writers or will they be absorbed into Mexican literature as authors who came into their own in the last decades of the twentieth century? Have they made unique contributions to Mexican letters? Are they in the mainstream of contemporary Mexican literature? How will their work be judged by the critics in thirty years? Since María Luisa Puga, Silvia Molina, Brianda Domecq, Carmen Boullosa, and Angeles Mastretta are actively writing at this very time, one expects that their work is evolving, thus allowing us only provisional answers and judgments.

As for being considered women writers, if the present trend continues, women writers in Mexico will be in the majority and the need to identify them by gender will disappear. They themselves, although feminists, are not overly concerned with being labeled women writers and submit that society and the literary world has not discriminated against them because they are women. Their goal and desire is to be taken as serious writers and, as Angeles Mastretta enunciated so clearly, to be included in Mexican literature. All are willing to accept the premise that women bring to literature their own perspective, based on their physiology and their unique experiences. For Silvia Molina it is very possible that a feminine point of view be appropriated by men, just as a masculine point of view can be appropriated by women. Whereas for Brianda Domecq women narrate from a marginal perspective, for Carmen Boullosa writers have no gender, although she does believe there is a feminine way of perceiving reality. One senses from all five writers what María Luisa Puga pointed out: today's writers want to go beyond the issues of feminism, write about those things that preoccupy or fascinate them, and take their places as serious practitioners of the craft.

To their professions as writers, Puga, Molina, Domecq, Boullosa, and Mastretta each brings a different background and preparation. Some started writing as children, others much later; some studied literature and writing formally at the university or in literary workshops, others are wholly or partially self-taught. All are avid readers, and their knowledge of Mexican and other literatures is vast. Although devoted to their craft, they participate in numerous activities that take them away from their writing but in many senses complement and nourish it. María Luisa Puga coordinates and teaches writing workshops for children and adults, work that is consequential in raising the literacy level and in instilling a love for language and reading. Silvia Molina runs a publishing company that publishes books for children, an exceptionally important undertaking in our society where children are drawn to television or comics. Her books are attractive, well written by her and other established writers (Puga and Boullosa, among others), and aim to make reading a pleasure rather than a chore. Brianda Domecq participates in symposia and other professional meetings and writes for cultural supplements to promote the corpus of literature written by women. Carmen Boullosa has made literature her life, and everything she does is designed to make it as meaningful for others as it is for her. She does poetry readings, lectures in Mexico and abroad, has directed plays, and has published books in her own press. Angeles Mastretta writes for the monthly magazine *Nexos* and is called upon for television and other personal appearances.

In the last analysis, it is the work of each writer that has brought her to the attention of the reading public and will determine the place she will occupy in the history of Mexican literature. María Luisa Puga brings to her writing her background as a self-made, self-taught woman. Her search for space in which to be herself and from which to view the world has led her to many places. She has lived for a time in Mexico City, traveled for ten years in Europe and Africa, returned to Mexico City, and now has established herself in Zirahuén, Michoacán. Each place has allowed her to observe human relationships and given her the insight with which to penetrate the psyche of the characters she creates. Often, although not exclusively, she creates complex and engrossing women—Nyambura of *Las posibilidades del odio*, Susana of *Pánico o peligro*, Antonia of *Antonia*, Vero of *La viuda*—who struggle against the current of conformity and manage to live as they choose and not as others would have them live. Puga's ability to capture a moment, sometimes absurd, unexpected, or inexplicable, is well demonstrated in her short fiction. Her reflections on the act of writing manifest themselves throughout her work in her self-conscious narrative techniques. She is at times part of her work and establishes a relationship between herself, the reader, and her fictional world. Whether her work is set in Mexico City, Zirahuén, Acapulco, Nairobi, London, or Rome, this writer captures the pace of the particular city through her story, her prose, and her penetrating insight into ordinary people, making her work memorable.

Silvia Molina's work reflects her belief that writing is a game with a complex set of rules. She plays at inventing herself and tantalizes the reader with the quandary of whether she is any one of her women protagonists. The nameless young woman of *La mañana debe seguir gris*, who breaks away from her family and tradition by having an affair in London with a poet, and Dorotea of *La familia vino del norte*, who researches her family's secret and in doing so achieves her own identity and independence, have some experiences in common with their author, but they are not Molina. Her use of history—a growing presence in contemporary Mexican literature—is interesting in that sometimes it appears to lend authenticity to a work and at other times to offer a different or contradictory view of the official rendition. *La familia vino del norte*, which focuses on the postrevolutionary period, is another link to the novel of the Mexican Revolution, once again attesting to its viability. In this novel, as in *Imagen de Héctor* in which she pieces together the image of a father she never knew, Molina puts to rest myths and creates her own reality. As a writer of short stories, Molina captures the pain and problems that ordinary people face in their familial and societal relationships. Her "game" is one that readers enjoy because of her simple, elegant, and unadorned prose, which she hones deliberately so that all one's attention is centered on her story.

Brianda Domecq, bicultural and bilingual, is possessed by a sense of urgency to write about women and to promote women's writing. In her fiction and essays, she demonstrates her keen understanding of history and literature as she takes on the subject of women and the myths that surround them and portrays their struggle to free themselves from a patriarchal and repressive society. Her recreation of Teresa Urrea in *La insólita historia de la Santa de Cabora*, a combination of imagination and historical research, is a masterful humanization of an almost mythical figure. Domecq succeeds in showing Teresa's fight to claim her identity and achieve her empowerment and freedom to live on her own terms. In appropriating Mexican history and using the past to understand the present, Domecq, too, is in the main current of contemporary Mexican fiction. Her ability to combine a wonderful sense of humor, tinged with malice, with an extraordinary use of language to express her ideas in her essays or to portray herself and others in her fiction make her work thought-provoking and often arresting.

Carmen Boullosa's imagination, like her person, is in constant motion, creating complex works of fiction. Her novels have traversed the strange and difficult world of childhood to those set in colonial times and to others in contemporary Mexico City. All are intricate works that challenge the reader with a mixture of reality and fantasy, contradictions, historical and fictional characters, movement in time, and other narrative techniques. Underneath Boullosa's writing one senses that her texts are probings into her deepest concerns—the conflictive reality of family relationships in *Mejor desaparece*, the painful world of childhood in *Antes*, the source of some of the world's problems in *Son vacas, somos puercos*, the political situation in Mexico prior to the 1994 presidential elections in *La Milagrosa*. She is a very intense writer whose prose requires close and careful reading. Boullosa's sense of humor manifests itself in nearly all her works in amusing scenes that can stand alone as vignettes. Already very prolific, this writer promises to keep challenging her readers as she works at her craft.

Angeles Mastretta's work has aroused extraordinary interest among both general readers and serious students of literature. Her best-selling *Arráncame la vida* draws a chilling portrait of the postrevolutionary years in Mexico by rewriting the history of a period that the official version would rather hide. Set in Puebla and narrated by Catalina, this fictional work allows us to view the politics and society of the time from a very different perspective. Catalina describes the self-interest of her husband, whose duplicity betrayed the very ideals of the Revolution he claimed to support, and through her evolution from an innocent young girl to a defiant woman demythifies the traditional views of wife and mother. The *tías* of *Mujeres de ojos grandes* are a delightful collection of women—clever, creative, ahead of their time. Mastretta pays them homage and gives them a voice that in their generation was silenced. This writer's popularity can be attributed to many factors, among them her ability to express something serious in a fresh and easily accessible way and her creation of characters whose humanity touches the readers or tantalizes them into trying to identify them. Mastretta struggles to make her writing appealing and enjoyable and to give her readers a ticket to another world. In doing so, she has hit a responsive chord among a wide and growing readership.

These five writers have already proven the seriousness with which they view their profession. Writing is not a pastime but a painful calling that has transformed and shaped their lives. The writing of each one is becoming known, and recent translations have further promoted interest in their work. One anticipates with curiosity the books in progress. Puga's *Inventar ciudades,* an outgrowth of her move from the big city to an isolated small town, will deal with the restructuring of one's daily life. Molina's yet untitled novel about a man in the process of a divorce, who receives anonymous letters from a woman, seems like a modern love affair with game-playing. Domecq is working on a novel that will use her dreams as a framework for a story tracing several generations of women from the mid-nineteenth through the twentieth century, beginning in the United States and ending in Mexico. She is particularly concerned with the effect of feminist movements on the women's characters and on their relationships. Carmen Boullosa's *Que viva,* about a lone child-survivor of an earthquake, and her novel concerning an archeologist enamored of the Mayan ruins, reflect the writer's interest in Mexico's present and past. Angeles Mastretta is working on *Mal de amores,* a novel whose female protagonist from Puebla is brought up by very modern parents, allowing her a love affair without marriage. This woman, with attitudes of the 1970s in 1910, will study to be a physician but practice nontraditional medicine.

Each of these works in progress is an outgrowth of the writer's already published novels and unquestionably will appropriate some of their techniques. We as readers will most likely be called upon to piece together events rather than follow them consecutively, to enter the world of fiction with the novelist as she addresses or informs us about her writing, and to go back in time to earlier centuries, or maybe only to the earlier part of the twentieth century, as she searches in the past for the origins of the present or for hidden clues to our existence as human beings. All this will make María Luisa Puga, Silvia Molina, Brianda Domecq, Carmen Boullosa, and Angeles Mastretta writers worth watching and reading.

Further Readings

On Mexican Literature and Women's Writing

Agosín, Marjorie, ed. *A Dream of Light and Shadow: Portraits of Latin American Women Writers*. Albuquerque: University of New Mexico Press, 1995.

Bassnet, Susan, ed. *Knives and Angels: Women Writers in Latin America*. London: Zed Books, 1990.

Bowen, David, and Juan A. Ascencio, eds. *Pyramids of Glass: Short Fiction from Modern Mexico*. San Antonio: Corona, 1994.

Bradu, Fabienne. *Señas particulares, escritora: Ensayos sobre escritoras mexicanas del siglo XX*. Mexico City: Fondo de Cultura Económica, 1987.

Brushwood, John S. *La novela mexicana (1967–1982)*. Mexico City: Grijalbo, 1984.

Castillo, Debra A. *Talking Back: Toward a Latin American Feminist Literary Criticism*. Ithaca: Cornell University Press, 1992.

Castro-Klarén, Sara, Silvia Molloy, and Beatriz Sarlo, eds. *Women's Writing in Latin America*. Boulder: Westview Press, 1991.

Cluff, Russell M. "El nuevo cuento mexicano (1950–1990): Antecedentes, características y tendencias." In *Perfiles: Ensayos sobre literatura mexicana reciente*, ed. Federico Patán, 47–88. Boulder: Society of Spanish and Spanish-American Studies, 1992.

Cortés, Eladio, ed. *Dictionary of Mexican Literature*. Westport, Conn.: Greenwood Press, 1992.

de Beer, Gabriella. "Mexican Women Writers of Today." *Review: Latin American Literature and Arts* 48 (Spring 1994): 6–9.

———. "Escritoras mexicanas de hoy." *Nexos* 17, no. 199 (July 1994): 69–75.

Duncan, J. Ann. *Voices, Visions, and a New Reality: Mexican Fiction Since 1970*. Pittsburgh: University of Pittsburgh Press, 1986.

Foster, David William. *Mexican Literature: A Bibliography of Secondary Sources*. 2d ed. Metuchen, N.J.: Scarecrow Press, 1992.

———, ed. *Mexican Literature: A History*. Austin: University of Texas Press, 1994.

Fox-Lockert, Lucía. *Women Novelists in Spain and Spanish America*. Metuchen, N.J.: Scarecrow Press, 1979.

Franco, Jean. *Plotting Women: Gender and Representation in Mexico*. New York: Columbia University Press, 1989.

———. *Las conspiradoras: La representación de la mujer en México*. Mexico City: El Colegio de México/Fondo de Cultura Económica, 1994.

García, Kay S. *Broken Bars: New Perspectives from Mexican Women Writers*. Albuquerque: University of New Mexico Press, 1994.

García Pinto, Magdalena. *Women Writers of Latin America: Intimate Histories*. Trans. Trudy Balch and Magdalena García Pinto. Austin: University of Texas Press, 1991.

González, Alfonso. *Euphoria and Crisis: Essays on the Contemporary Mexican Novel*. Fredericton, N.B.: York Press, 1990.

Kaminsky, Amy. *Reading the Body Politic: Feminist Criticism and Latin American Women Writers*. Minneapolis: University of Minnesota Press, 1992.

Langford, Walter M. *The Mexican Novel Comes of Age*. Notre Dame: University of Notre Dame Press, 1971.

Lara, Josefina, ed. *Diccionario bio-bibliográfico de escritores contemporáneos de México*. Mexico City: Instituto Nacional de Bellas Artes, 1988.

Leal, Luis. "Female Archetypes in Mexican Literature." In *Women in Hispanic Literature: Icons and Fallen Idols*, ed. Beth Miller, 227–242. Berkeley: University of California Press, 1983.

López González, Aralia. "Quebrantos, búsquedas y azares de una pasión nacional (Dos décadas de narrativa mexicana: 1970–1980)." *Revista Iberoamericana* 59, nos. 164–165 (July–December 1993): 659–685.

Magnarelli, Sharon. *The Lost Rib: Female Characters in the Spanish-American Novel*. Lewisburg, Pa.: Bucknell University Press, 1985.

Marting, Diane E., ed. *Spanish American Women Writers: A Bio-Bibliographical Source Book*. Westport, Conn.: Greenwood Press, 1990.

Miller, Beth. *Mujeres en la literatura*. Mexico City: Fleischer, 1978.

————, ed. *Women in Hispanic Literature: Icons and Fallen Idols*. Berkeley: University of California Press, 1983.

Miller, Beth, and Alfonso González. *26 Autoras del México actual*. Mexico City: B. Costa-Amic, 1978.

Patán, Federico. *Contrapuntos*. Mexico City: UNAM, 1989.

————. "Recent Mexican Fiction." In *The Novel in the Americas*, ed. Raymond Leslie Williams, 91–100. Niwot, Col.: University Press of Colorado, 1992.

————, ed. *Perfiles: Ensayos sobre literatura mexicana reciente*. Boulder: Society of Spanish and Spanish-American Studies, 1992.

Peden, Margaret Sayers. *Out of the Volcano: Portraits of Contemporary Mexican Artists*. Washington, D.C.: Smithsonian Institution Press, 1991.

————, ed. *The Latin American Short Story*. Boston: Twayne, 1983.

Peña, Margarita. "Literatura femenina en México en la antesala del año 2000. Antecedentes: Siglos XIX y XX." *Revista Iberoamericana* 55, nos. 148–149 (July–December 1989): 761–769.

Robles, Martha. *La sombra fugitiva: Escritoras en la cultura nacional*. 2 vols. Mexico City: Diana, 1989.

Schaefer, Claudia. *Textured Lives: Women, Art, and Representation in Modern Mexico*. Tucson: University of Arizona Press, 1992.

Sefchovich, Sara. *México: País de ideas, país de novelas*. Mexico City: Grijalbo, 1987.

————, ed. *Mujeres en espejo: Narradoras latinoamericanas, siglo XX*. 2 vols. Mexico City: Folios, 1983–1985.

Silva-Velázquez, Caridad L., and Nora Erro-Orthman. *Puerta abierta: La nueva escritora latinoamericana*. Mexico City: Joaquín Mortiz, 1986.

Steele, Cynthia. *Politics, Gender, and the Mexican Novel, 1968–1988: Beyond the Pyramid.* Austin: University of Texas Press, 1992.

Teichmann, Reinhard. *De la Onda en adelante: Conversaciones con 21 novelistas mexicanos.* Mexico City: Posada, 1987.

Trejo Fuentes, Ignacio. "Dos décadas de narrativa mexicana." In *Perfiles: Ensayos sobre literatura mexicana reciente,* ed. Federico Patán, 101–111. Boulder: Society of Spanish and Spanish-American Studies, 1992.

———. "New Directions in the Mexican Narrative." *Manoa: A Pacific Journal of International Writing* 4, no. 2 (Fall 1992): 34–37.

Valis, Noel, and Carol Maier, eds. *In the Feminine Mode: Essays on Hispanic Women Writers.* Lewisburg, Pa.: Bucknell University Press, 1990.

On the Works of María Luisa Puga

Acevedo-Leal, Anabella. "El reconocimiento de la realidad a través de la alteridad en *Las posibilidades del odio.*" *Monographic Review/Revista Monográfica* 8 (1992): 223–228.

Anderson, Danny J. "Cultural Conversation and Constructions of Reality: Mexican Narrative and Literary Theories After 1968." *Siglo XX/20th Century* 8, nos. 1–2 (1990–1991): 11–30.

Bradu, Fabienne. "María Luisa Puga." In *Señas particulares, escritora: Ensayos sobre escritoras mexicanas del siglo XX,* 118–135. Mexico City: Fondo de Cultura Económica, 1987.

Castañón, Adolfo. "María Luisa Puga: Posibilidades de lo severo." In *Arbitrario de la literatura mexicana,* 446–453. Mexico City: Vuelta, 1993.

Castillo, Debra A. "Writing in the Margins: Rosario Castellanos and María Luisa Puga." In *Talking Back: Toward a Latin American Feminist Literary Criticism,* 216–259. Ithaca: Cornell University Press, 1992.

Duncan, J. Ann. "Further Innovations, 1970–1982: Huerta, Puga, Azuela, Samperio, Ruiz, Campbell, Hiriart." In *Voices, Visions, and a New Reality: Mexican Fiction Since 1970,* 195–217. Pittsburgh: University of Pittsburgh Press, 1986.

González, Alfonso. "María Luisa Puga: Self-Realization and a New Consciousness." In *Euphoria and Crisis: Essays on the Contemporary Mexican Novel,* 36–43. Fredericton, N.B.: York Press, 1990.

López González, Aralia. "Dos tendencias en la evolución de la narrativa contemporánea de escritoras mexicanas." In *Mujer y literatura mexicana y chicana: Culturas en contacto,* 21–24. Vol. 2. Ed. Aralia López González, Amelia Malagamba, and Elena Urrutia. Mexico City: El Colegio de México/El Colegio de la Frontera Norte, 1990.

Patán, Federico. Review of *La forma del silencio.* In *Los territorios nuevos: Notas sobre la narrativa mexicana,* 274–277. Mexico City: UNAM, 1992.

———. Review of *Pánico o peligro.* In *Los territorios nuevos: Notas sobre la narrativa mexicana,* 272–274. Mexico City: UNAM, 1992.

Pfeiffer, Erna. "María Luisa Puga." In *Entrevistas: Diez escritoras mexicanas desde bastidores*, 123–135. Frankfurt am Main: Vervuert Verlag, 1992.

Reckley, Alice. "The Historical Referent as Metaphor." *Hispania* 71, no. 3 (September 1988): 713–716.

Rodríguez Hernández, Raúl. "María Luisa Puga: Aspectos de una nueva sensibilidad de narrar." In *La escritora hispánica*, ed. Nora Erro-Orthman and Juan Cruz Mendizábal, 152–158. Miami: Universal, 1990.

Salceda, Verónica. "La historia, dentro de la creación literaria de acuerdo a María Luisa Puga." *Dactylus* 10 (1990): 54–60.

Valdés, María Elena de. "Crítica feminista de la identidad en *Inmóvil sol secreto*." *Journal of Hispanic Research* 1 (1992–1993): 239–248.

On the Works of Silvia Molina

Bolívar, María Dolores. "*Ascensión Tun* en la tradición del discurso de la mujer en América Latina." *Nuevo Texto Crítico* 2, no. 4 (1989): 137–143.

García, Kay S. "History and Herstory: Silvia Molina's *La familia vino del norte* and *Imagen de Héctor*." In *Broken Bars: New Perspectives from Mexican Women Writers*, 131–155. Albuquerque: University of New Mexico Press, 1994.

———. "Silvia Molina: Interview." In *Broken Bars: New Perspectives from Mexican Women Writers*, 113–129. Albuquerque: University of New Mexico Press, 1994.

———. "Silvia Molina: Introduction." In *Broken Bars: New Perspectives from Mexican Women Writers*, 107–112. Albuquerque: University of New Mexico Press, 1994.

Teichmann, Reinhard. "Identidad e historia en Silvia Molina." In *Mujer y literatura mexicana y chicana: Culturas en contacto*, 121–125. Vol. 2. Ed. Aralia López González, Amelia Malagamba, and Elena Urrutia. Mexico City: El Colegio de México/El Colegio de la Frontera Norte, 1990.

Torres, Vicente Francisco. "Silvia Molina: Entre la historia y la novela." In *Esta narrativa mexicana: Ensayos y entrevistas*, 147–158. Mexico City: Universidad Autónoma Metropolitana, 1991.

On the Works of Brianda Domecq

Brushwood, John S. Review of *La insólita historia de la Santa de Cabora*. *Chasqui: Revista de Literatura Latinoamericana* 20, no. 2 (November 1991): 148–150.

———. "Aspects of the Supernatural in Recent Mexican Fiction." In *Perfiles: Ensayos sobre literatura mexicana reciente*, ed. Federico Patán, 127–139. Boulder: Society of Spanish and Spanish-American Studies, 1992.

García, Kay S. "Brianda Domecq: Interview." In *Broken Bars: New Perspectives from Mexican Women Writers*, 165–185. Albuquerque: University of New Mexico Press, 1994.

———. "Brianda Domecq: Introduction." In *Broken Bars: New Perspectives from Mexican Women Writers*, 157–164. Albuquerque: University of New Mexico Press, 1994.

———. "Magic and Play in Brianda Domecq's *La insólita historia de la Santa de Cabora* and *Once días...y algo más*. In *Broken Bars: New Perspectives from Mexican Women Writers*, 187–203. Albuquerque: University of New Mexico Press, 1994.

González, Mirta A. "Mastretta, Domecq y Sefchovich: La mujer y la literatura mexicana." *Siempre!* (La Cultura en México), June 17, 1992, 2–4.

López González, Aralia. "La huella de lo reprimido: Fisuras y suturas." *Signos: Anuario de Humanidades* 5, no. 1 (1991): 239–248.

Patán, Federico. Review of *Bestiario doméstico*. In *Los nuevos territorios: Notas sobre la narrativa mexicana*, 101–103. Mexico City: UNAM, 1992.

On the Works of Carmen Boullosa

Ortega, Julio. "Fabulaciones de Carmen Boullosa." In *Arte de innovar*, 327–339. Mexico City: Ediciones del Equilibrista/UNAM, 1994.

Patán, Federico. Review of *Antes*. In *Los nuevos teritorios: Notas sobre la narrativa mexicana*, 58–61. Mexico City: UNAM, 1992.

———. Review of *Mejor desaparece*. In *Los nuevos territorios: Notas sobre la narrativa mexicana*, 56–58. Mexico City: UNAM, 1992.

Pfeiffer, Erna. "Carmen Boullosa." In *Entrevistas: Diez escritoras mexicanas desde bastidores*, 25–46. Frankfurt am Main: Vervuert Verlag, 1992.

———. "Procuro pulir mi 'feminidad' asalvajándola." In *Exiliadas, emigrantes, viajeras: Encuentros con diez escritoras latinoamericanas*, 35–52. Frankfurt am Main/Madrid: Vervuert Verlag/Iberoamericana, 1995.

On the Works of Angeles Mastretta

Anderson, Danny J. "Displacement: Strategies of Transformation in *Arráncame la vida*, by Angeles Mastretta." *Journal of the Midwest Modern Language Association* 21, no. 1 (Spring 1988): 15–27.

Bailey, Kay E. "El uso de silencios en *Arráncame la vida* por Angeles Mastretta." *Confluencia: Revista Hispánica de Cultura y Literatura* 7, no. 1 (Fall 1991): 135–142.

de Beer, Gabriella. "Entre la aventura y el litigio: Una entrevista con Angeles Mastretta." *Nexos* 16, no. 184 (April 1993): 33–39.

———. "Interview with Angeles Mastretta." *Review: Latin American Literature and Arts* 48 (Spring 1994): 14–17.

Fornet, Jorge. "*Arráncame la vida* en la encrucijada." *Casa de las Américas* 30, no. 178 (January–February 1990): 119–124.

García, Kay S. "Angeles Mastretta: Interview." In *Broken Bars: New Perspectives from Mexican Women Writers*, 71–87. Albuquerque: University of New Mexico Press, 1994.

————. "Angeles Mastretta: Introduction." In *Broken Bars: New Perspectives from Mexican Women Writers*, 63–70. Albuquerque: University of New Mexico Press, 1994.

————. "Fidelity, Credibility and Duplicity in Angeles Mastretta's *Mexican Bolero*." In *Broken Bars: New Perspectives from Mexican Women Writers*, 89–105. Albuquerque: University of New Mexico Press, 1994.

Gerendas, Judit. "Hacia una problematización de la escritura femenina." *Escritura: Revista de Teoría y Crítica Literarias* 16, nos. 31–32 (1991): 91–101.

Gold, Janet N. "*Arráncame la vida*: Textual Complicity and the Boundaries of Rebellion." *Chasqui: Revista de Literatura Latinoamericana* 17, no. 2 (November 1988): 35–40.

Gomis, Anamari. "Ella encarnaba boleros." Review of *Arráncame la vida*. *Nexos* 8, no. 91 (July 1985): 52.

González, Mirta A. "Mastretta, Domecq y Sefchovich: La mujer y la literatura mexicana." *Siempre!* (La Cultura en México), June 17, 1992, 2–4.

Llarena, Alicia. "*Arráncame la vida* de Angeles Mastretta: El universo desde la intimidad." *Revista Iberoamericana* 58, no. 159 (April–June 1992): 465–475.

López González, Aralia. "Dos tendencias en la evolución de la narrativa contemporánea de escritoras mexicanas." In *Mujer y literatura mexicana y chicana: Culturas en contacto*, 21–24. Vol. 2. Ed. Aralia López González, Amelia Malagamba, and Elena Urrutia. Mexico City: El Colegio de México/El Colegio de la Frontera Norte, 1990.

McMurray, George. "Two Mexican Feminist Writers." *Hispania* 73, no. 4 (December 1990): 1035–1036.

Peden, Margaret Sayers. "Angeles Mastretta." In *Out of the Volcano: Portraits of Contemporary Mexican Artists*, 87–91. Washington, D.C.: Smithsonian Institution Press, 1991.

Pfeiffer, Erna. "Angeles Mastretta." In *Entrevistas: Diez escritoras mexicanas desde bastidores*, 113–122. Frankfurt am Main: Vervuert Verlag, 1992.

Robles, Martha. "Angeles Mastretta." In *La sombra fugitiva: Escritoras en la cultura nacional*, 317–324. Vol. 2. Mexico City: Diana, 1989.

Rosa, María Eugenia de la, ed. "Angeles Mastretta." In *Protagonistas del cambio: Mujeres mexicanas de éxito*, 259–273. Mexico City: Planeta, 1994.

Schaefer, Claudia. "Popular Music as the Nexus of History, Memory, and Desire in Angeles Mastretta's *Arráncame la vida*." In *Textured Lives: Women, Art, and Representation in Modern Mexico*, 88–110. Tucson: University of Arizona Press, 1992.

Teichmann, Reinhard. "Angeles Mastretta." In *De la Onda en adelante: Conversaciones con 21 novelistas mexicanos*, 505–522. Mexico City: Posada, 1987.